Photograph: courtesy of Andrew Godber

Since 1987 Adrienne Brady has lived overseas in Singapore, Brunei, Libya and the Middle East taking opportunities to explore ancient and lost worlds. Her adventures in Asia – including encounters with sea pirates and the Tamil Tigers – are surpassed by those experienced while travelling throughout Libya: arrest, interrogation and finally deportation as a CIA suspect which bring these travels to an end are recorded in her memoir *Kiss The Hand You Cannot Sever*. Resident in the Emirates from 1996-2006 her travel features were published in *Friday Magazine (Gulf News)*, *Khaleej Times* and *Property World Middle East*. Accounts of her more recent explorations – throughout Oman and into the heart of Africa – form the backbone of this memoir.

Adrienne Brady is also a prize winning poet.
She lives in Dorset.

Also by Adrienne Brady

Non-fiction
Kiss The Hand You Cannot Sever
Melrose Books

Poetry Anthologies – contributions
Quintet – Staple, UK

From Then ... Til Now
Poetry Press – USA

Basic English Series, Poetry 2
Go and Open the Door, Poetry 3
Macmillan Education
- UK and Australia

let me be - a junior anthology of poetry
Macmillan, Swaziland

Summer Comes Barefoot Now
Editor – EPB, Singapore

Magazines – contributions include
The Spectator
Poetry Review

Success as an international prize winning poet led to an entry in the
International Who's Who in Poetry and Poets' Encyclopaedia

Way South
Of
Wahiba Sands
Travels With Wadiman

To the memory of my beloved Wadiman
Richard Wilson Chapman

Adrienne Brady

Way South
Of
Wahiba Sands
Travels With Wadiman

Austin Macauley
PUBLISHERS LTD.

Copyright © Adrienne Brady 2013

The right of Adrienne Brady to be identified as author of this work has been asserted by her in accordance with section 77 and 78 of the Copyright, Designs and Patents Act 1988.

Photograph Selections, Adrienne Brady and Richard Chapman
© Adrienne Brady 2013

Illustrations © Jasmine E. Brady 2013

All rights reserved. No part of this publication may be reproduced, stored in a retrieval system, or transmitted in any form or by any means, electronic, mechanical, photocopying, recording, or otherwise, without the prior permission of the publishers.

Any person who commits any unauthorized act in relation to this publication may be liable to criminal prosecution and civil claims for damages.

A CIP catalogue record for this title is available from the British Library.

ISBN 9781849633499

www.austinmacauley.com

First Published (2013)
Austin Macauley Publishers Ltd.
25 Canada Square
Canary Wharf
London
E14 5LB

Printed and bound in Great Britain

Acknowledgements

The journeys recorded in this book, throughout Oman and into Africa, interwoven with episodes from our lives in the Emirates and finally Devon, highlight the dramatic changes taking place in the lives of local people, changes that were in progress, before our very eyes.

I remain indebted to the people we met on our travels, especially the gentle and welcoming people of Oman; their kindness to strangers never failed, whether it was the need to be towed out of deep sand, pointed or guided in the right direction across featureless, interminable gravel plains, or the welcome we always received when arriving unannounced on the doorstep of an isolated village.

From our more recent, guided travels in Africa with the travel company Explore, special thanks to Dario – lead driver-cum-guide – for a safe expedition through the Ethiopian Rift Valley into the Lower Omo region. I remain grateful to Mark Thompson, from 'Hidden Gambia'. Armed with a supply of river boats and 4x4s, Mark made exploring remote reaches of the Gambia River and its surrounds possible, and so memorable.

Special thanks to: Andy McTiernan and Julie Bell – management, editing and marketing team of *Property World Middle East*, a Dubai-based international magazine, and the editing teams of *Khaleej Times* and *Friday Magazine* (*Gulf News*), for such splendid presentations of the travel features and photographs that now form the basis of this memoir; my granddaughter, Jasmine Elizabeth, for her evocative title page images; Father Michael Wheaton, for casting an incisive eye over some of the religious sections, plus drawing attention to and providing details of footsteps linking Devon with our travels in Ethiopia – and, by no means least, for being my Angel of the Lord; Rodger Witt, friend and Editorial Consultant, for insightful comments and suggestions.

Sincere thanks to Joan Bekker – Richard's sister and closest sibling – for her friendship and for sharing her recollections of growing up with Richard in Southern Rhodesia; friends and colleagues of Richard, especially Captain Dave MacKenzie – his regular sailing companion in The Gulf – and his wife Hilary, for their undiminished love and support. Last, but by no means least, heartfelt thanks to three generations of my family, especially my daughters, Catriona, Fiona and Justine, for so much support in every possible way.

Finally my gratitude to Annette Longman and Robert Brookes, and the editorial, production and promotion team of Austin Macauley for bringing *Way South of Wahiba Sands* to fruition; especial thanks to Vinh Tran, the production coordinator, for his patience and advice.

In some instances, the names of people we travelled with or encountered have been changed to protect identities.

Transcription of place names: to resolve the wide divergence of English transcriptions of place names in the countries visited – spellings vary considerably locally, in books and on maps – I have endeavoured to select the most straightforward and to remain consistent.

Extracts reproduced by kind permission of the following:

Zelda Pinto, Motivate Publishing, Dubai
Extracts from *Oman, An Arabian Album* by Ronald Codrai
Travelling the Sands by Andrew Taylor

Mohana Prabhakar, Apex Publishing, Oman
Extract from *Oman Today* by Sean Mooney

Nick Chator, Robert Hale Ltd
Extracts from *Warlords of Oman* by P.S. Allfree

Jon Gifford, Oleander Press
Extract from *Travels in Oman: Arabia Past and Present* by Philip Ward

Tana Lapage, Safari Experts
Extracts from *An Expedition to Southern Ethiopia* by Tim Lapage

Lyn Hughes, Wanderlust travel magazine, 2005
Extract from *Ethiopia* by Tony Wheeler

Barnaby Rogerson, Eland Publishing Ltd.
Extracts from *Travels into the Interior of Africa* by Mungo Park

David Marsden, Chimpchatter
Extract from *The Forest Dwellers* by Stella Brewer

Helen Brocklehurst, AA Publishing
Extract from *Cyprus, Spiral Guide* by George McDonald

Kelsey Ford, New Directions Publishing, USA
Extracts from *The Poems of Dylan Thomas* by Dylan Thomas

Maps: UAE and Oman, Motivate Publishing, Dubai
 – adjustments, thanks to Asha Zhang
 The Okavango Delta © Gametrackers, Botswana

I have drawn upon a wide variety of sources, both during my time in the Emirates and since. Opinions and errors are mine. I am especially indebted to the writings of those authors mentioned in the Bibliography. Every effort has been made to contact the copyright holders of all quoted material. Late responses and inadvertent omissions will be rectified in future editions.

*Life is eternal and love is immortal
and death is only an horizon
and an horizon is nothing save the limit of our sight.*

William Penn (1644-1718)

United Arab Emirates and the Sultanate of Oman

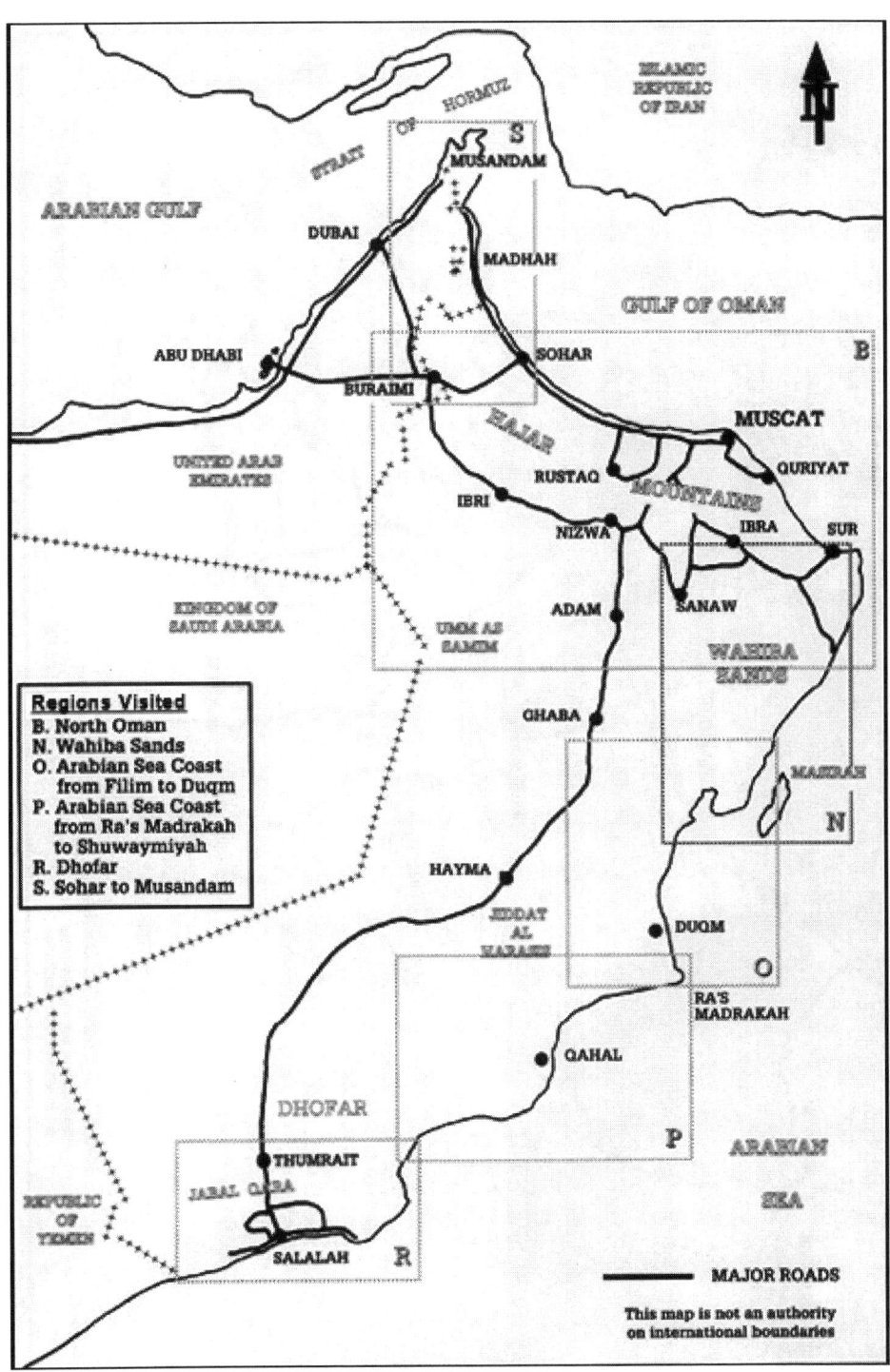

CONTENTS

Acknowledgements xi

Towards the Horizon 1

The United Arab Emirates 3

Oman 11

The Jebel Akhdar 12

The Western Hajar 23

The Eastern Hajar 33

The Saiq Plateau 43

South of Wahiba Sands 48

Musandam 59

African Connections 104

Addicted to the Okavango 137

In Transit 149

Ethiopia 157

The Gambia 195

Cyprus 225

Reaching the Horizon 240

Afterword 243

Bibliography 244

Towards the Horizon

1841 – A wagon train, travelling from Port Elizabeth to Grahamstown in South Africa, is attacked by a local tribe. All the passengers are believed dead. Then, the sound of crying: the sole survivor – a baby boy – is uncovered from amidst the wreckage, taken in by a local chaplain and brought up in his household: a household that was to become that of the first Bishop of Grahamstown. This is the story told of the remarkable start in life of Thomas Richard Proudfoot, the great maternal grandfather of my partner and travel companion, Richard Chapman.

I cannot claim such a dramatic beginning for my near ancestors; nevertheless, my parents had the pioneering spirit and spent a good part of their lives in Egypt, India and Burma before settling in Surrey to bring up the family. What Richard and I inherited and shared was a spirit of exploration. From our first meetings at Abu Dhabi Sailing Club in the summer of 1996, we became soulmates: our love of the sea, the wilderness and exploring natural and lost worlds bound us together.

When not working – Richard, at Abu Dhabi International Airport, and me, at the desert-based Cambridge High School – we did what most expats in the Emirates did: head for the beach, the sea, the bar. Some months after we met, Richard was the owner of *Sunset Song*, a 25' Jaguar sailing yacht, and a remarkable and reliable Ssangyong Musso - 4x4 - both were to become second homes. Visitors expecting a five star Emirati lifestyle were in for a surprise; instead, they were introduced to our life at sea, dodging Arabian dhows, sailing up the Gulf to get an offshore view of the Burj Al Arab, sailing down the Gulf to circle the Palm and, for the more stalwart, sailing round the emerging Arabian World.

Trips overland meant countless hours trundling through mountain and desert *wadis* – dried up riverbeds used for off-roading – earning Richard the title of Wadiman, a title he adopted. The unspoilt natural beauty of Oman was right on our doorstep. We set out to explore this remarkable country, its landscape and history – the latter so divisive that mountainous regions kept some of the greatest explorers and travellers at bay into the mid-twentieth century, including William Thesiger and Ronald Codrai.

Growing up in Zimbabwe meant that travel through untamed lands was second nature to Richard. Before long, we were heading back to his homeland to hire a Land Cruiser camper and making a month long solo trip through the deserts and inland deltas of Namibia and Botswana. Further plans to follow mountain and rift valley trails through the heartlands of Ethiopia and to explore the reaches of the mighty River Gambia took shape.

As our journey continued, there was a sense that it was being shaped on two counts: firstly, by the interweaving of previous footprints – explorers, inhabitants, rulers and invaders – linking past and present, as well as the countries we visited; secondly, that of life itself as a journey moving towards a final horizon. In April 2008, we made a long intended trip to Cyprus. A week after our return, Richard was diagnosed with bladder cancer. Six months later, the cancer was out of control: the horizon that had once receded into the distance was unexpectedly rushing towards us.

Writing about our shared journey in this life, has undoubtedly kept the pain of Richard's absence alive. Increasingly, the sense of loss is accompanied by an awareness of his spiritual presence, especially outside – under the pine tree in the garden of my house in Poole, a place we came to when 'on leave', sundowner in hand, listening to the robin's heartstopping song; walking on neighbouring heathland, his image before me, binoculars trained on movements in a nearby tree; watching yachts bowl into Poole Harbour as the dying sun turns sea and sky blood red… at these moments especially, I feel that he is close.

The United Arab Emirates

The origin of existence is movement. Immobility can have no part in it, for if existence was immobile it would return to its source, which is the Void. That is why the voyaging never stops, in this world or in the hereafter.

Ibn-al-Arabi, *The Book of Revelations on the Effects of Voyaging*
(12th century Arab philosopher)

Homeland of Gazelles

Intent on reaching the fast lane on my right, an Arab in a black Mercedes suddenly pulled out in front of me. To avoid a collision, all I could do was brake and swerve. Instead of roaring into the distance, he stayed alongside and kept pace with me. I knew he was there, but unnerved and angry, I kept my eyes on the busy road ahead. Finally I looked across, and we exchanged glances. He raised his hand and inclined his head in a gesture of apology. When I gave in and acknowledged his gesture, he touched his forehead in a gentle salute before taking off like a jet on the runway.

That evening, while watching the news in Richard's Sharjah-based flat, the camera zoomed in on an Arab attending the opening of yet another enterprise in Dubai.
'It's him,' I called to Richard. 'It's the guy who cut me up on the motorway.'
The image of his distinctive lean and angular face and neatly cut dark beard brought back the memory of the incident.
'That,' declared Richard, 'That is Sheikh Mohammed. None other than the Crown Prince of Dubai.'
We agreed that although guilty of reckless driving, the Sheikh had clearly been late for an important appointment and his determined, apologetic gesture more than made up for it.

To go back to the beginning – at least as far as recorded history of the current ruling family is concerned – takes us to a day in 1761 when Sheikh Dhiyab bin Isa, leader of the Bani Yas Tribe, set out from Liwa Oasis on a hunting expedition. Part of the group followed a fleeing gazelle across desert and coastal dunes, and then through low-lying shallow water onto an island. The hunters failed to capture their prey, but to their astonishment, they discovered a spring of fresh water. When the Sheikh was told, he decreed that the island should be known as *Abu Dhabi*, the Father or Homeland of Gazelles.
Members of the Bani Yas Tribe, antecedents of the current rulers of Abu Dhabi and Dubai, set up home on this island and continued to enjoy their Bedouin lifestyle of hunting, fishing and pearling. A century or so later, a gathering of the more adventurous members of the Al Bu Falasah section of the Bani Yas, led by Ubaid bin Said and Maktoum bin Buti, formed a splinter group, abandoned Abu Dhabi and settled round a creek in neighbouring Dubai, setting up a harbour based trading centre in pearls from the creek and copper from Oman. Then, in the 1930s, when the Japanese production of cultured pearls ruined the market for natural pearls, a miracle occurred – to be precise, the discovery of oil. The decade that saw the demise in the trade of the natural pearl was the same decade that witnessed the first oil-strike on the island of Bahrain.
That was just the beginning. The ensuing 1970s oil boom transformed the lives of Bedouin tribes living in their *barasti* (palm-leaf) settlements, on the islands and coastal plains of the lower Gulf. The Homeland of Gazelles was destined to become the fast developing modern city it remains to this day.

Abu Dhabi, Dubai, Sharjah
1996 -1998

In the final decades of the twentieth century, the outgoing leaders of the Bani Yas, who had settled in Dubai, continued to take the lead in the development front. Dubai was growing at a fast pace on land and at sea. Dredging to build islands in the shape of palm trees and, the more ambitious, in the shape of the world, to accommodate mansions for celebrities and millionaires, was taking its toll on the quality of sailing and fishing. Sluggish currents and a build-up of sewage were just two of the more obvious side effects.

By the turn of the century, easy catches of king fish or barracuda for barbecue suppers were rapidly declining, while reports of the disappearance of dugong and other endangered species natural to this region steadily increased.

Changes on land included a network of roads to accommodate the development of high-rise towers, shopping centres, hotels, business and trading centres proliferating across the previous sandscape of rolling dunes. The dual carriageway, with its central reservation of palm trees, linking Sharjah to Dubai and Abu Dhabi, that had greeted us in the mid-1990s, was replaced by a floodlit six-lane motorway. But even that failed to cater adequately for the increase in traffic. What with congestion and an eclectic mix of drivers, from wealthy Arabs to less wealthy immigrants, and a flexible approach to the rules of the road, driving was becoming increasingly stressful and hazardous.

In the long run, it was the ability of the original Bedouin tribes to accept and adapt to the sudden development throughout the region in a matter of decades, instead of the centuries taken by other nations in times past, as well as an open-minded attitude towards the ever growing international expatriate community, that made the Emirates a safe, fascinating and challenging place to live in and explore.

For the most part, the expatriate population, on fixed, or relatively short-term, renewable contracts, remained insulated from the local populations and the high-rise world developing around them. They lived in air-conditioned accommodation, drove air-conditioned cars to air-conditioned workplaces, schools or clubs and, at the end of each month, collected worthwhile tax-free salaries.

Not all the workforce lived within this comfort zone. The immigrant labour force – largely from India, Pakistan and Bangladesh – lived on compounds or in camps with basic facilities, worked long hours in killer temperatures for minimum wages in order to send the remittance to families at home. It is upon the shoulders of these construction workers that the foundations and development of the rapidly growing Emirates skyline relied and continued to rely.

Neither did each individual Emirate develop at the same pace. This became evident when Richard was transferred from Abu Dhabi to Sharjah in 1997; it was not unlike stepping back in time. In the 1950s, Sharjah was considered the most important coastal settlement of the then Trucial States. The headstart was initiated in 1932 when Imperial Airways – the forerunners of British Airways – constructed an airfield and used the airport as a stopover en route to India. Then, in the 1940s, when the fort and airfield were taken over by a garrison of the RAF, Sharjah became the first Emirate with an international airport.

It has long been overtaken by Abu Dhabi and neighbouring Dubai, so much so, that in the late 1990s, Sharjah was lagging behind its rivals in all aspects of development, including accommodation for expatriate residents. No matter how eminent or senior, airport employees were housed in an ancient and dilapidated block of concrete flats. As the recently appointed Manager of Air Traffic Engineering at Sharjah International Airport, this was Richard's new home.

It boasted few comforts but with some amusement, residents compared their lot to that of their predecessors of less than half a century earlier. That Sharjah's premier reputation, built on the presence of the airport, was at odds with the quality of the accommodation on offer was made clear by the author Philip Allfree. In his 1954 appraisal, he describes the Royal Air Force headquarters as:

… something of a slum …a compound of low tin-roofed huts, each with a clanking air-conditioner which looked and sounded like a traction-engine.

– *Warlords of Oman*

By comparison, Richard's ageing apartment – the place we retired to after a day's sailing – was verging on upmarket, especially when we converted the concrete balcony into a mini-jungle and attracted a pair of bulbuls which honoured us by nesting there.

Dubai Offshore Sailing Club (DOSC) – home to *Sunset Song,* Richard's Jaguar sailing yacht – was as informal and friendly socially as it was for sailing. It all began in June 1974, when a group of friends, led by Colonel Guy Temple of the Dubai Defence Force, was granted an enclave of land alongside a dhow fishing harbour in Umm Suqeim by HH Sheikh Rashid bin Saeed al Maktoum, the Ruler of Dubai.

Limited facilities at the club meant and continued to mean that its appeal was to those with a genuine love of the sea and sailing. By the time we arrived in the 1990s, modernisation included walk-on moorings, air-conditioned facilities at the clubhouse for full English breakfast before sailing, and tables and chairs under palm trees – complete with harbour and sea views – for sundowners after sailing. Who could ask for anything more?

A longstanding memory of a sailing, and after-sailing experience highlights just one of the characteristics that made Richard such an invaluable travelling companion – he was completely unfazed by unexpected or untimely events. Tall, wide-shouldered with forget-me-not blue eyes and an easy dimpled smile, he was self-possessed and endowed with a positive attitude to life and its pitfalls. His measured and calm assurance was reflected in his movements. I never saw Richard run. His idea of speed was to lengthen his stride and increase his pace to a fast stroll.

On one occasion, after a leisurely cruise along the coastline, we were on our way back to the clubhouse when, wind-filled sails at full tilt, a succession of racing dhows descended upon us. We were at the turning point for their race before they headed back up the Gulf to the finishing line. Various less polite versions of 'Get out of the way!' in Arabic and English rained upon us. The skipper, who was doing his best to oblige and keep *Sunset Song* away from the dhows on one side and the rocky shore on the other, had been left shorthanded by his crew. Negligent of her sailing duties, she was standing on the prow, camera in hand, getting shots of dhows and their magnificent curvaceous sails silhouetted against the setting sun.

Safely back at DOSC, we put *Sunset Song* to rest, ordered sundowners and food and sat under a date palm, overlooking the moorings and harbour. Since our table was positioned near the walkway, it was inevitable that returning fellow sailors would stop to chat; some joined us and invariably bought rounds of drinks. Sometime later, when I got to my feet to pay a visit to the ladies' room, I discovered what it is to be virtually 'legless'. Then, as I gingerly made my way back towards the table, overcome by a great rush of nausea, I emptied the contents of my stomach under a conveniently positioned palm tree before collapsing onto a nearby bench.

Eventually concerned by the length of my absence, Richard located my prostrate form, helped me to my feet and guided me to the Ssangyong-Musso. While on the highway en route to his apartment, in response to sudden demands to relieve my still-churning stomach, he navigated several emergency stops. On arrival, all attempts to assist me from the Musso failed; then, to his veiled amusement, he discovered that I was attached to the seat by a tangle of fishing line and hooks that must have been left on the bench I had collapsed onto.

While sailing provided opportunities to visit and camp overnight on unspoilt coastal islands, it also drew our attention to the wisdom of not straying beyond certain boundaries. On one occasion Bill Dibb, a fellow expat sailing friend and owner of a Drascombe Lugger, invited Richard and me to join him for an afternoon sail off the coast of Abu Dhabi. We were cruising towards what appeared to be a previously unexplored, idyllic island – the perfect place for a spot of beachcombing and a swim – when, in the shade of a shoreline palm tree, we saw a man pointing a large gun at us. As Bill instructed his crew to get ready to 'go about', I distinctly remember him saying, 'Don't worry if we get arrested. I have contacts.' Uncertain of the effectiveness of the contacts of a British doctor of microbiology, I did worry. Bill and Richard would be together. I would be alone. Women under arrest are separated from men, and a solitary Emirati-style jail experience was not on my list of 'must do' before I left Dubai.

On land, a favourite place to escape to was the Aviation Club, owned by Dubai Duty Free. In addition to housing the Dubai Tennis Stadium, graced by some of the world's top players as a warm-up venue before the season proper, its attractions include a temperature-controlled outside pool complete with a swim-to bar, surrounded by reclining sun beds and shaded by palm trees. There were the further pleasures of two restaurant-cum-bar complexes, Century Village and Irish Village, with menus and music to suit every taste; these were surpassed by The Cellar – a contemporary and relaxed restaurant, offering quality food and wine list, with equally impressive décor: its stained glass windows added a touch of a medieval guildhall. As a handy retreat from the glitzy five star evolving world of Dubai, it was invaluable.

On the other hand, an alternative and equally popular place to take visitors for an evening out was Rosie's, a Chinese restaurant in Sharjah, celebrated more for character than class. To this day, Sharjah remains the only 'dry' Emirate. Close affiliations with Saudi Arabia have seen to that. European visitors known to the staff would be warmly welcomed and escorted to a screened corner table. To accompany the food, pots of 'red tea' were on offer. Sipped from porcelain teacups, the brew had the unmistakeable texture and taste of red wine.

But Rosie's had more on offer than red tea. On one occasion, a guest had a surprise encounter with a scantily clad Chinese girl, who disappeared as quickly as she had appeared from a mysterious second doorway to the ladies' loo. Investigations revealed a stairway leading to an upper floor, where one can only guess what favours might have been available.

It was when we joined the Abu Dhabi Natural History Group that forays into surrounding desert and mountainous terrain took place, preparing the way for independent travels. The off-road route to the east coast resort of Fujairah from the most northern Emirate, Ras al Khaimah, across the jagged peaks of the Western Hajar Range, through Wadi Bih and Wadi Khab Shamsi, added to the pleasure of a weekend away from the ever-growing congestion in the Gulf Emirates. The route not only tested off-road driving skills – the frequency of encountering lose fallen boulders from flash flooding, sudden changes in direction and increases in gradient through narrow precipitous gorges saw to that – while its passage through some of the highest peaks and mountain plateaus of the Arabian Peninsula provided breath-taking and unforgettable views.

From a historical perspective, Fujairah's coastal position was pivotal. Forts and burial grounds, some dating back to the fourth millennium BC, hold many secrets of the past. On one occasion when camping over a weekend, we set up our tent next to a tumble of rocks on an otherwise empty beach. The following morning, we were surprised and somewhat unnerved to discover that we had slept alongside a burial ground.

This part of the northern coastline – an area of arrivals and departures – is littered with ancient burial grounds. In Dibba, a 30 metre long tomb from the Iron Age has been discovered in an Islamic graveyard. Further discoveries included skeletons, fragments of pottery, metal arrowheads and other artefacts dating back to at least 1,000 BC, as well as Hellenistic pieces of pottery and smaller round tombs. However, the most startling find was that of a vast graveyard where close to ten thousand people are buried. Said to be the site of an ancient battle fought in AD 633, it marked the last stand of local people against Islam and the final stage of the Muslim conquest of the Arabian Peninsula.

Once famed in the ancient world as a great city, Dibba's praises were sung by the poet Abu Bakr in the Caliph's court in Baghdad. The poem told of an ancient city with riches beyond compare. Along with Fujairah, Dibba was destined to become a five star resort.

Further expeditions included trips through wadis to various oases, including *Liwa* – The Wide Valley, on the edge of *Rub al Khali* – The Empty Quarter, once a life saving caravan stopover for traders and travellers from Oman and Saudi Arabia.

Another favourite route through the unspoilt dunes and rock formations of Wadi Al Faya, culminates in *Jebel Maleihah* – Fossil Rock. This aptly named, dramatic limestone outcrop, resembling the shape and form of a gigantic prehistoric creature rising from surrounding dunes of sands, became a favourite picnic spot and place to hunt for fossils that never failed to delight visitors.

There were times when longer, uncharted off-road expeditions proved to be more of a challenge than expected. It was when my daughter Justine and her husband, Andrew, spent a day trundling through desert wadis and a night in Richard's aged and previously untested 'four man' tent that Andrew christened Richard 'Wadiman'. The tent was so confined and overheated from the sunbaked sand beneath that Justine spent the greater part of the night – chancing encounters with scorpions, snakes or fearsome spiders – sitting in a canvas chair under the stars.

Finally, strange nearby scuffles and cries drove her back to share the tent's safety and discomforts, which now included a chorus of heavy breathing and snores. Recompense was achieved the following morning when, after trundling through more wadis, we came upon an oasis with pools of water deep enough for a cooling off swim. However, there was another treat in store. The way home took us through rolling dunes. Bogged down in deep sand, we had to be rescued, and were towed to safety by some kindly locals.

On another occasion, on our way to explore Liwa Oasis, we headed into the foothills of some dramatic dunes for a coffee break. Seduced by the untouched wind sculpted dunes, I set off on a photo-shoot. Trudging through deep sand – not unlike trudging through deep snow but in mind-bending temperatures – made me begin to question my sanity. Then my intention of reaching the summit was interrupted by the appearance of a 4x4 that came growling towards me and lurched to a standstill alongside.

'Get in!' was the unceremonious greeting from the Arab at the wheel. Unsure of his intention, I was relieved to see that Richard and the Musso were still within sight.

'Thank you,' I responded nervously, pointing in the direction of the Musso, 'but I'm okay.'

With that, my accoster accomplished a roundabout turn and took off in a swathe of sand.

It was unexpected discoveries that provided the greatest pleasure and best photo opportunities – whether an 'out of the blue' oasis; the sudden appearance of a camel racing party across a desert plain; a hand-carved door still standing at the entrance to a house in a deserted village; sand-falls sliding and cascading like water over precipitous rock formations; a deserted graveyard marked with anonymous small triangular shards of rock; a weaver bird's nest in an isolated quiver tree or the silhouettes of ghaf trees, cropped by camels striding across dunes at sunset.

Meanwhile, our horizon had shifted over the border into Oman. Until 1970, when Sultan Said bin Taimur was deposed and Sultan Qaboos took power, Oman was not just unknown to the outside world but 'still almost as closed and little known as Tibet'.[1] Even, in the late 1990s, tourism as such was in its early stages, and largely restricted to day trips to selected sites from emerging hotels in Muscat and Nizwa. Our interest was further heightened from reading Philip Allfree's *Warlords of Oman*. On contract to the Sultan of Oman's Armed Forces from 1957 to 1962, his forthright, humorous and colourful accounts of experiences training and leading local men – some from a Bedouin tribe with a long history of desert piracy – in attempts to take control of Oman's mountainous interior – added a certain frisson to our planned expeditions. A visit to Oman was high on the agenda.

---

[1] John Bullock, *The Gulf*

Oman

The impetus that drove Thesiger and the travellers before him into the desert – the search for something timeless within themselves – has survived. And once the engine is turned off and the car is hidden in the shadows, perhaps even the modern traveller can detect the faintest scent of what the explorers felt in the liquid blackness of a desert night.

Andrew Taylor, *Travelling the Sands*

The Jebel Akhdar

The Liquid Blackness of Desert Nights,
October 1998

We weren't going into the desert but we were going into the mountains that border the desert, share their great barren wonder and keep them at bay. We hoped to find the same sense of liquid blackness, experienced by past explorers in the remoteness of nights in the great canyons that sever Oman's Jebel Akhdar; the highest mountains of the Hajar Range, they extend in a great 500 mile arc along the coast, dominating the landscape. Travelling in the Ssangyong-Musso – packed with a 'two man' tent, a cool-box of supplies, bottles of frozen water, cameras and our 'off-road bible'[2] – we were escaping from the noise, pollution and congestion of Thesiger's growing 'Arabian Nightmare' for an encounter with the wilderness.

Inland explorations through the Emirates to Fujairah on the east coast had familiarised us with the start of our journey from Dubai, through the Western Hajar to the eastern border post into Oman. From a distance, the outlines of these mountains have the magnetic appeal that all mountains have for me, intensified when their shadows are first glimpsed across infinite stretches of featureless desert plains: they tug on the spirit as they tug on the eyes. Close up however, although they have both grandeur of size and drama of form, their barren slopes of loose scree resemble vast slag heaps. Ironically, this is just what they are: slag heaps of lava, surrounding a magnificent eroded limestone chain, thrust from the ocean's floor and running parallel to the Gulf of Oman.

Khor Kalba, a tidal creek at the southernmost tip of the Emirates eastern coastline, is the site of one of the oldest mangrove forests in Arabia. Its closeness to the border with Oman made it an ideal place to stop for a picnic lunch. In the shade of a ghaf tree among a tangle of roots and dried mud-flats at the water's edge, we fill granary rolls with slices of cheese and tomato and pour coffee from a flask. Within seconds, and out of nowhere, we are bombarded by a whirling mass of flies.

When Richard's remedy of making rapid wrist-flicking circles with the hand before attempting to thrust morsels of food into the mouth fails to disengage the determined invaders, we dive into the car. The untimely attack reminds us that nature is less than perfect. Although it was the end of October, temperatures in the high thirties and oppressive humidity were persisting. Waiting for winter in the Middle East is like waiting for spring in Europe. It never comes, but when it does it is 'very heaven'.

---

[2] Heiner Klein and Rebecca Brickson, *Off-Road in Oman*

'Serves as a bird-hide,' Richard announced, stretching for his binoculars. Sure enough, from our air-conditioned capsule and with the aid of his binoculars, we were able to watch white collared kingfishers operating from a nearby tree, and the stop and start movements of waders with matchstick legs on the mud-flats, as well as occasional fish leaping to avoid unseen prey, or to catch a meal of their own.

The plan was to enter Oman through the Khatmat Malaha border post and follow the first stage of a largely circular course that begins heading south along the coastal plain between the Hajar Mountains and the Gulf of Oman, before turning inland through the Sumail Gap. This gap or wadi – formed when an ancient river carved the only natural passage between the Western and Eastern Hajar Range – would take us west, to where the foothills of the Western Hajar border the vast plains and dunes of The Empty Quarter, before marking the inland route north, back towards the Emirates. On the map, it looked as if it had been planned by someone throwing a lasso around the mountains. It was the detours off this route, where the frayed edges of the lasso penetrate the great canyons, that we were keen to explore.

The first stage of the journey south, across some two hundred kilometres of flat coastal plain, distanced from both mountains and sea, brought to mind Philip Allfree's description of the way of life in an isolated landscape of date-palm groves, interspersed with a succession of barasti settlements of some forty years ago:

> ... draped with fishing nets they perched precariously on dunes of sand lining the salt flats of the coastal plain; at regular 50 mile intervals there was a town with a market and mosque and a mud castle in which sat the Sultan's Governor dispensing justice and collecting bribes.
>
> *– Warlords of Oman*

Now the drained and cultivated Batinah coast – marked by areas of intense greenhouse cultivation and plantations of date palms and bananas – is furnished with a smooth tar road. We were enjoying the sense of space and noticeable lack of congestion and aggression on the roads, increasingly prevalent in the Emirates. Finally, after travelling for some eight hours, the turn off for our first staging post – the ancient capital of Rustaq – was before us.

Dwarfed by striding pylons, we flew along the straight black tarmac road, chasing a succession of mirages that lured us inland across the wide gravel plain towards the ancient settlement. Once an important trading centre, guarding routes into the mountains, it was known for a glorious, if bloody, past. All of a sudden, we sensed that our adventures were about to begin. A fleeting outline of Al Hazm castle appeared and disappeared as shadows of mountains, that had remained little more than a dream on the horizon for the past hours, rushed towards us. Not one row but row upon row, changing from grey to brown to dusky purple. Then modern Rustaq, spread along the foothills, glowed luminescent white in late afternoon sunlight. As we circled the development, tantalising glimpses of the magnificent restored fort and honey coloured walls of the old settlement had to be just glimpses, with the promise of a return visit.

We were looking for the entrance to Wadi Bani Awf, a wadi that would lead us to our first camping spot for the night.

Veering south-east along a wide floodplain under an impeccably blue late evening sky, between rows of tilted mountains alive with deepening shadows, it was possible to imagine the grinding of plates and the giant upheaval that pushed this mountain chain lopsidedly, inch by inch, from the ocean floor. Like a mighty stallion of the gods, the most dramatic reared before us from a jumble of peaks. Silhouetted against the fading sky, it presented one magnificent steeply sloping flank, reaching some 2,000 metres. From the knife-edge, the other side fell away in a series of gargantuan steps. Then at last, in growing darkness, propped in a tumble of rocks at the roadside, a sign took shape in our searching headlights.

'Bani Awf,' I called.

Turning the Musso at right angles, tyres crunching over pebbles, Richard headed across the stony plain towards a black slit in the mountain's wall. At the start of the narrow canyon, the floor of pebbles increased in size and depth, becoming increasingly unstable. We slipped and rolled and rumbled across the lose surface. Hanging like petrified curtains, rock sides changed to polished buttresses with huge womb-like pockets of loose scree, then to vertical walls of sedimentary layers of sand decorated with small stones.

It was as if, like a diminished Alice in Wonderland, we were passing through a perfectly sliced and parted segment of currant cake. In places where the canyon walls were further apart, patches of reeds, grasses and shallow pools marked the course of a streambed. Glowing like candles, dusky blooms of pink oleander lined our route. Massive boulders, resembling the craniums of Titans tossed to the wadi floor, drew our eyes up the dark sides to the pale stream of sky and left us wondering if they had been swept downstream in winter floods when water gushed from saturated rock walls, or if they came hurtling down from overhead.

Suddenly, a row of date palms appeared and behind them several more growing on small terraces, cut into the side of the hill and supported by walls of stones. A rough cement-like channel about a foot high, following the top of the highest wall, carried water to the palms and to a small settlement perched on a ledge above the wadi floor.

The *aflaj* system of channelling water – trapped in the upper levels of a mountain to irrigate terraced crops – is a tradition so old that an Omani legend attributes its origin to Solomon, son of David, who visited Oman on his magic carpet and caused his *djinns* (spirits) to construct ten thousand water channels in ten days. However, it was during the period of Persian control that many of the finest underground *aflaj* systems, similar to the *qanat* in Persia, were constructed. A group of women and children gathered round a watering place smiled and waved to us as we rumbled by.

Our progress through the canyon was marked by further settlements among narrow terraces of date palms, wherever the sides of the canyon allowed. Then, just as our off-road bible promised, at approximately ten kilometres from the start, the rock walls opened out and we found ourselves following the meandering bed of a stream. To one side, a great bowl had been carved out of the wall of rock and the wadi floor stretched from side to side for 100 metres. We made for a huge ghaf tree, standing guard near a tumble of rocks on the far, dry and more sheltered side.

The ticking of the cooling engine was matched by the hum of insects busy in the great leafy canopy of our tree. Huge and hornet-like, marked by red and yellow bands and with pollen sacks, distinct as chimney sweepers' brushes on their dangling legs, they hovered around us like disorientated mini helicopters. Suddenly, the sound of voices echoed from a distant wadi. Then the crunching of wheels over stones echoed too, until a pick-up truck appeared. Catching up with its sound, it towed it into the shadows. While Richard cleared a patch of the sharpest flint-like stones, I struggled with the collapsible spines of our tent wishing, not for the first time, that it was one of the instant pop-up varieties.

Richard's African wilderness upbringing meant that he shared none of my fears of deadly animal and insect life, but he did nurse his own fears of attack by unfriendly tribes. In spite of my protests, and in spite of it being the late twentieth century, I knew that these fears were not entirely unfounded. Every European adventurer's account of travels in Arabia describe the constant fear of attack by warring armed tribes and, in some instances, by those natives paid to guide them. Others didn't survive to tell their tales.

Even the intrepid Thesiger, after his travels to the western side of Oman's Hajar Mountains, confirms one or two narrow escapes from tribal elements intent on reacting to the intrusion of a foreigner. Ronald Codrai tells the story of the amusement he caused by hiring well-known bandits as his guides in the late 1940s. He came to no harm, and furthermore tells us that the infamous Sheikh of the Bani Riyam tribe – dubbed 'Lord of the Green Mountain', because his tribe's habitat included the 9,800 foot-high *Jebel Shams*, Mountain of the Sun – invited him to accompany him back to his mountain home: an offer he regretted that he was unable to accept.

In more recent times, in his account of his 1991 search for the lost city of Ubar in the desert region of southern Oman, Sir Ranulf Fiennes encountered local tribesmen, who were less than friendly, and armed with Kalashnikovs that had replaced traditional weapons. Throughout the world, mountains have become the retreat of rebels, notorious for fighting to keep their independence and freedom, and to protect their territory. Oman was no exception.

As Richard built a small fire inside a circle of stones and our surroundings drained into darkness, we watched the half-moon and Mars grow brighter. Then, slowly at first, more stars appeared until with a sudden silent rush, the lake of sky was throbbing with jewelled lights.

Morning revealed the ancient beauty of our tree. It looked older than time. From its root–bowl, the gnarled trunk was cleft in two; from each base separate horny arms twisted and stretched in opposite directions for several metres, before turning skywards in a magnificent gesture of supplication. Its vast crown of leaves thrummed with insect life. The deeply ingrained bark of a horizontal trunk, decorated with artistic whorls and flourishes, provided convenient, if not comfortable seating and shelf space.

Hot water for morning tea was soon boiling on our new Hail single gas burner: a discovery that deserves every possible marketing cliché. As we made and sipped our brew, the outlines of two women appeared. Wearing heavy turbans and clad in brightly coloured sarong-type garments, they were making their way across the wadi. Their well-rounded figures and the huge turbans wrapped round and piled on their heads, raised questions about their origins. Were they descendants from Africans, brought to Oman when Omani rule extended from Zanzibar to parts of Persia and Pakistan?

Then, as if a light had been switched on, sunlight flooded the canyon and the women and their history were gone. At the same time, birdsong was replaced by the demented shrieking of cicadas. Heat was up and it was time to be on the move.

We followed the track for a further four kilometres to the end of the wadi, where it disintegrated and split. Assuming that the just distinguishable tyre marks, forking roughly in opposite directions, represented the T-junction in our guide book, we took the right-hand branch. If we were on the correct track, it should lead us to the village of Bilad Sayt – the fortified mountain village claimed for the Saudi-backed Imam in 1957. Climbing steadily on a sandy trail that skirted the side of a mountain, we were now part of the outer landscape.

A sense of relief at being released from the awesome and, in retrospect, oppressive feeling in the depths of the canyon swept through me. Before us, lopsided peaks tumbled into the distance. At other times, our view was blocked by the intimidating walls of our immediate terrain, and then, as the sides fell away, the panorama opened up, offering a constantly changing kaleidoscope of jagged slopes, deep chasms and occasional glimpses of settlements growing out of the hillside. Although I dreamed of seeing the elegant form of an oryx standing on a rocky ledge as we turned each corner, I had to be content with the occasional goat nimbly picking its way over rocks.

One minute we were climbing, and the next we found ourselves racing downhill. On one switchback corner, in order to avoid an old man kneeling on his prayer mat in the middle of the track, or hurtling over the precipitous edge if we attempted to swerve round him, Richard had to pull in sharply to the mountain wall. We juddered to a halt, the bumper resting on the rock face. Undoubtedly, it was one of our nine lives saved. The old man, too, must have had heavenly thoughts. Scrambling to his feet, he gestured in a flapping movement over his heart before lifting his mat to let us pass.

'*Shukran.* Thank you,' Richard called. 'Sorry to frighten you,' he added, hoping the old man would understand.

As we left, his bent figure – prayer mat rolled under his arm – was hurrying along the track. In the distance, a plantation of date palms pinpointed a settlement near the wadi bottom.

'Snake Gorge,' Richard enlightened me. 'Mostly harmless,' he continued, as a comforting afterthought. 'Even venomous ones disappear and stay hidden when they sense an intruder. They strike only when surprised.'

I wasn't convinced. I'd done my homework. Oman was home to a good number of venomous snakes, specimens with hinged front fangs competed for ferocity with those with fixed fangs. My list of those best avoided included the venomous hood-necked cobra, a sluggish puff adder and the side-winding horned viper. The latter's reputation for striking and biting like lightning placed it at the top of the list. With these less than comforting thoughts in mind, we followed a downhill trail, rumbled over the streambed marking the bottom of Snake Gorge, and made a deft switchback turn to begin the steep ascent up a narrow track gouged out of the mountain wall.

On my side, the vertical slope dropped into a deep gorge. Now, the reality of the edge we had so recently avoided confronted us. As if it would protect us from falling, I was inching towards Richard and attempting, unsuccessfully, not to imagine the sensation. Would we drop like a boulder to the bottom and explode into fragments of pain and metal, terror and bone, or bounce off the rock walls, spin like a coin and land James Bond-style, brushing the dust from our clothes? As nervous as I was, the compulsion to look was irresistible. On the opposite side, impressive splits in the rock face twisted and gaped, measureless caverns opened into darkness, and great horizontal chasms tore apart in tortuous shapes. It was little wonder that it took the SAS to finally remove the Lord of the Green Mountain from his impregnable stronghold.

Since the start of our excursion, there had been a noticeable absence, not only of wildlife that has been hunted to extinction, but of birds of prey. This was the landscape of kestrels and falcons wheeling against imperious blue sky, flying their shadows over rugged peaks. The skies were empty, but it was encouraging to know that positive movements are underway in Oman to protect, preserve and reintroduce native wildlife.

Finally, a signpost for Hat confirmed that we were on the right course. After a few hundred metres, a group of palm and ghaf trees and a worn pathway over rocks, leading towards a narrow gorge, fitted the off-road description of a trail to Bilad Sayt. With the Musso snug in the shade of a group of palm trees, we gathered our swimming gear and a snack lunch, and started to climb the polished trail towards the sound of running water. The increasing gradient of the zigzag route ended abruptly before a fall of water cascading into a pool from a ledge some five metres overhead. Behind the sparkling curtain, a jungle of ferns and tufted grass sprouted from the rock face.

While we were standing, recovering from the climb and taking in the beauty of this unexpected Eden, from out of nowhere, the figure of an elderly man appeared and was beckoning us forward. Dressed in a white *dishdasha* – long loose collarless, shirt – with a turban bandaged on his head, he silently led us beneath the falling water. On the far side, we followed in his footsteps along a polished trail that wound uphill towards the entrance to a narrow gorge, directly over the falls. I arrived breathless, just in time to see the outline of our guide glide into darkness and then dissolve in the frame of bright sunlight at its far end. The white of the robe, the fluid movements, the silence – it was as if a biblical Angel of the Lord had been sent to act as our guide.

'Let's follow,' Richard said, leading the way into the dank tunnel. At the far end, another uphill slippery climb took us to a small sunlit plateau. Our ethereal guide was nowhere to be seen, but we had arrived at the perfect lookout platform. Framed by the sheer cliffs of Jebel Akhdar, growing from and melting into the hillside, was the settlement we were searching for. The rectangular stone and mud-walled houses of Bilad Sayt overlooked cultivated terraces that blended into a background of late summer rusts, bronze and gold.

The peaceful and idyllic setting gave no hint of an eventful past. Strongly fortified and surrounded by walls and towers, this mountain stronghold was claimed by Talib, brother of the imam, who was supported by King Saud. In the summer of 1957, Talib ran up his standard at Bilad Sayt and proclaimed the restoration of the Imamate for his brother, Ghalib bin Ali. This claim of power, supported by Suleiman, Lord of the Green Mountain, was an act of defiance that was to lead to war against Said bin Taimur, the ruling sultan.

In retrospect, it did not seem inappropriate to see the imam's followers as forerunners of today's Islamic insurgents; as well as many on-land targets, they used time-bombs to blow up ships and aircraft. Just weeks previously, I had the ghostly experience of diving on the wreck of the Dara – a British Indian Steam Company Liner – in the Gulf. In April 1961, the Dara was blown up off the coast near Dubai, caught fire and sank, with the loss of several hundred lives. Like current-tugged pennants we descended, hand below hand, down a rope leading to the anchor line and encrusted tomb. Memories of intense cold, a shroud of nets, heavy with accumulated drift, hanging like ragged curtains, and emotionless gaping fish, stay with me.

En route from the Indian continent, the liner was taking expatriate passengers to Dubai and then Muscat. It is believed that the bomb, set by Saudi-backed Omani terrorists, was timed to go off in Muscat, but bad weather in the Gulf caused a delay of several days. The result of the explosion was the greatest loss of life at sea in peacetime since the Titanic. The major difference between these saboteurs and those of the late twentieth century appeared to be that martyrdom rarely occurred, and when it did, it was more by accident than design. One thing is certain – if the Sultan's forces had not been successful in taking control over the mountainous interior, we would not be exploring it.

By the time we reached the bottom of the gorge, hot, dishevelled and thankful for suppressed guerrilla warfare, we were more than ready to cool off in the pool beneath the waterfall. Using fingers and toes we tested the temperature – so cold that even I admitted it was painful.

'Sheer punishment!' Richard announced. Obdurate and perched like a heron on a rock, he watched my masochistic entry.

'But so is the heat!' I claimed, before the cold took my breath away.

The numbing effect was instant. Minutes later, I clambered out to join Richard on the rocky platform. Anaesthetised from the neck down, I felt strangely elated. The sense of euphoria continued well into the thawing out process, which followed during our picnic lunch.

Since the track we had followed to view Bilad Sayt ended abruptly at the footpath to the falls, we prepared to retrace our route. Viewing the scenery from the opposite direction was just as spectacular: a majestic pink mountain that appeared and disappeared between neighbouring sand coloured and grey peaks, added a further dimension as we wound our way round and up and down. Released from the canyon, we headed left along the side of the wide flood plain towards Rustaq. From time to time the track narrowed through rock walls and then widened into great open bowls. Daylight revealed what darkness had hidden. On the final approach to Rustaq, sizeable settlements, guarded by impressive forts, took shape. Although varying in size, the forts followed a recognisable design of high crenellated walls with rounded cannon-deflecting towers at each corner.

In the 1957 struggle for power, resident tribes from these mountain villages, won over by bribes from Saudi Arabia, supported the imam and his brother Talib against the sultan. Heavily armed and protected by their inaccessible and fortified homes, they slaughtered the Sultan's forces, sent into the mountains to suppress them. Those who attempted to escape on foot were either taken and killed by Talib's men, or died from heat and exhaustion. Today, telegraph poles, lengths of cable along the ground and the sudden emergence of a section of tarmac road showed the advance into modern life of the more accessible villages.

Once again, we were approaching Rustaq. On this occasion, we had a close up view of the impressive fort that stands guard over the entrance to the Western Hajar. Originally built on Persian ruins, the imposing circular tower, rebuilt in the seventeenth century by the ruler of the first Ya'aruba Dynasty, is just one of over one thousand forts, watchtowers, and castles that stand guard over Oman's dramatic landscape. In fact, these defensive structures are as much a part of the landscape of Oman as the rugged mountain peaks and passes they guard. Persian invaders from the north and Yemeni invaders from the south are responsible for some of the earliest defensive structures, built to guard their settlements and lucrative trade routes through mountain passes that lead from the Mediterranean to the Indo-Mesopotamian regions. On the other hand, Oman's coastal forts are linked to Portuguese imperialism.

The protection offered by Oman's forts and castles was important, but equally, they served as points of convergence for political, social and religious interaction, as well as centres for learning. Often integrated with souks, mosques and residential quarters, they are a feature of the landscape overlooking wadis, palm groves, trade routes and ancient harbours. For today's travellers, they provide convenient and fascinating staging posts for exploring Oman's varied and dramatic landscape.

It is rumoured that a secret 17km tunnel connects the fort at Rustaq to Al Hazm Castle. Both make full use of traditional Omani defensive features: massive wooden entry doors, secret escape tunnels, dungeons, and cannon towers, as well as gun ports in the upper floors and machicolation above the entrance for pouring boiling oil or date syrup onto unwelcome visitors. Tradition has it that barbaric skills and despotism went hand in hand with education in many of Oman's forts, and the former capital of Rustaq was no exception.

In addition to the obligatory chute for pouring boiling date syrup on unsuspecting intruders, Rustaq Fort houses a prison with a section for women, an ominous 'final punishment' cell, as well as a Quranic schoolroom and a small mosque. Another common feature of the forts is a self-sufficient water supply from a well or spring, thus ensuring supplies of fresh water for the defenders while under attack. Whereas the fort at Rustaq contains a spring within its walls, the *falaj* flowing beneath Al Hazm Castle provides additional irrigation for its surrounding gardens.

Late afternoon sun provided the perfect play of light and shade for photographing Rustaq's old settlement. Although largely roofless, sections of the sand-brick walls, as well as elegant curved recesses and arched Arabic-style windows, were still in place. A separate but adjacent large and grand building boasted three doorways in the front wall. Crowned by a pointed plasterwork arch, the central and largest double door- decorated with traditional Islamic floral carvings – suggested that it had been the home of a wealthy and influential person. Commissioned by the head of the household, each door was made to fit a particular building; the quality and amount of carving reflected the status of the owner.

The tradition of carved doors in Oman is just one example of the exchange of ideas and goods from far-flung sea voyages of sailors from the Gulf region, throughout the centuries. As well as bringing back hardwood, the sailors were also influenced by the carved designs used for wooden doors in East Africa. Throughout the Gulf today, the designs used follow patterns discovered from two of the furthest points regularly visited by dhows: Tanzania and Basra, where European and Turkish architecture was adopted.

Today Omani doors, prized for their rarity and individually hand-carved designs, are taken from old settlements and sold in souks and antique shops for high prices. It is not unusual to see them converted into coffee tables, dining tables and even used to decorate walls in expatriate modern villas in the Emirates. It was satisfying to be able to photograph one that was still in place. Rustaq is also renowned for its souk where, if you bargain, traditional Omani wooden chests, silver jewellery and *khanjars* – ornate and lethal curved daggers worn tucked into the male's waistband – can still be bought for reasonable prices. My prized possessions include a carved, circular Omani rice storage table and a remarkable khanjar.

In her travels through the Hadhramaut (Yemen), Freya Stark describes her Yemeni guides as wild little men of an earlier world, each carrying a huge curved dagger, jammed into his waist band. These daggers – the famous *jambiyas* (*khanjars*) with handles made of rhinoceros horn – were thought to carry ferocious sexual powers. Both the daggers and the very best examples of silver jewellery were said to be the work of Yemeni Jews. I came across my khanjar – the curved blade engraved with Yemeni-Jewish writing and complete with a rhino-horn handle – while looking through tourist kitsch in Sharjah's Blue Souk.

We didn't feel in need of the protection of an armed guide but we were anxious to find a camping spot before dark, so once again, we found ourselves leaving Rustaq in a hurry.

On this occasion, we were making for Wadi Abyadh. Famous for its pools of milky blue water, this wadi would take us into the lower reaches of the mountains where they taper towards the ocean. Marked by a wide flat expanse running at right angles to the stony flood-plain, it was not difficult to identify the entrance. Scrubby bushes and the occasional acacia patrolled the rocky edges of the dried up river bed, while once again, pink oleander buds, glowing in growing darkness, added a touch of magic.

'Too open for my liking, but we have to stop soon,' Richard confided, confirming my belief that he was sharing my increasing feeling of vulnerability at our failure to find a secluded place before the swift fall of tropical darkness. Minutes later, a hollow in the hillside marked by a group of trees seemed to answer our prayers. On closer inspection, we found the entrance blocked by huge rocks and boulders. Choosing a circuitous route and attempting to avoid the largest obstacles, Richard eased the Musso over others and onto a ledge, marking the winter level of the now invisible river. We came to a standstill under an umbrella of intertwined thorny branches from gnarled acacias growing at the meeting point of several gullies.

It was while we were stretching our limbs that we noticed a collection of mud and reed shacks on the opposite bank. We remained silent and watchful, then since there was no sound and no lights, set up camp, built a small fire and put together a light supper from diminishing supplies. In crepuscular light, I imagined it was the sort of place where the last Arabian leopard was likely to suddenly appear and snatch me for his evening meal. Richard's comment that such a death, which would contribute to the preservation of the species, would be honourable was of little comfort. I resolved that nothing would make me leave the tent until morning light.

Our bodily rhythms adjusted to the fall of darkness and lift of light. We were up at dawn watching two swallows dipping and soaring over our heads. An hour later, trundling over the boulder-strewn wadi floor, we were making for the damp course and smaller stones of the now visible streambed. As we progressed, the stream fashioned itself into pools, before becoming a small river bordered by beds of six foot high rushes and grasses. Runnels from previous vehicles ran alongside for several kilometres, until the passage was blocked by massive boulders brought down by winter floods. At this point we abandoned the Musso and, donning our rucksacks, clambered and slipped our way over and between the barricade to a series of waterfalls leading to a network of translucent pools trapped in rocky hollows.

Light reflecting on calcite, suspended in the water and lining the bottom of the pools, turned the water exquisite shades of milky white or blue. Beneath falling water, the largest pool was both wide enough and deep enough to cool off and swim; I tested it and, although not numbingly cold, no amount of persuasion or pleading succeeded in tempting Richard to join me. Meanwhile, he had discovered a neighbouring shallow pool; water temperatures raised from flowing over rocks created perfect conditions for reclining. He lay back, enjoying the sensation of numerous small fish – like miniature piranhas – nibbling at the salt and dead skin on his shins and feet before poking about in hollows like an excited David Attenborough.

'See that leaf?' he asked, assuming a crouching position and pointing to a brown leafy cluster, flecked with white, where the streambed was shadowed by overhanging rock. 'It's no leaf,' he added. 'Scorpion fish. Scorpion leaf-fish.'

As I watched, I saw the movement of an eye and fashioned the outline of a fish. Like the stonefish, it was a master of disguise.

'Erects poisonous spiky dorsal fins when threatened,' Richard continued.

I hastened out of the water. It was my turn to sit on a rock and view the pool and its wildlife from a safe distance.

The Western Hajar

Forts, Castles and a Mountain Stronghold

... a cluster of seven villages mouldering peacefully between the mountains and the desert ... clusters of crumbling mud huts ... surrounded by a dark-green lake of date groves ... each had its tottering mud castle extruding from the sandy soil like monstrous ant-hills.

P.S. Allfree, War Lords of Oman

Such was the Buraimi experienced by Philip Allfree. His fascinating description resurrects the not so distant and colourful past of today's provincial, modern city. In spite of its former downtrodden image, for centuries past the oasis of Buraimi has been the most important market and watering place on the landward side of the Western Hajar. Before desert boundaries existed, it was a no-man's land, bordered by the salty coastal strip of the Trucial States – today's Emirates – the mountains of Oman proper and *Rub al-Khali*, the ocean of dunes of the Empty Quarter.

In fact in the past few centuries, Buraimi passed hands several times. In the eighteenth century, it was incorporated into the kingdom of Saudi Arabia. Then in the nineteenth century, Abu Dhabi's royal family moved into the oasis and ruled it jointly with the Omanis. It was the mid-twentieth century discovery of oil in Oman that renewed Saudi Arabia's interest in occupying and controlling the crumbling mud settlements. Overnight, it became a centre for major disputes of ownership between the three bordering countries: the Emirates, Oman and Saudi Arabia.

Today, the modernised settlement, awkwardly divided between Abu Dhabi and Oman, is the location of a border post that straddles the two countries. This was the first staging post of our foray into the western side of the highest mountains of Oman, the Jebel Akhdar, or Green Mountains.

Various explanations have been offered regarding the questionable use of the colour green to describe these mountains. Close-up they appear brown or slate grey, while from a distance they adopt various shades of dusky purple. One explanation is based on the interludes of date palm terraces and various green crops growing on precipitous terraced slopes; another is attributed to the narrow selection of colour references used by Arabs. This is not the only shortcoming of the Arabic language in describing Oman's natural features; neither jebel, meaning hump, nor hajar, meaning rock, do justice to the mighty mountain ranges that dominate the interior. Our plan was to explore some of the ancient forts, castles and fortified villages built in the lower foothills of these mountains to defend their territorial past.

Before the advent of tar roads in the Emirates, travel from the salt flats of the Gulf, along the only track across gravel plains to Buraimi, though less than 100 miles, was exacerbated by problems incurred crossing a four mile barrier of dunes of sand. Travellers using ex-RAF Bedford trucks had to allow for up to twenty four hours. On the other hand, the journey from the coastal sheikhdom of Abu Dhabi to the oasis could take up to five days by camel. By contrast, the first stage of our journey in the Musso, along a tar dual carriageway from Dubai to the border post, took the better part of two hours.

Since we were camping, our immediate plan was to complete the greater part of the 200 or so miles from Buraimi towards the former capital of Nizwa and find a safe spot in the foothills of the mountains to spend the night. This way, with the long weekend at our disposal, we could start our explorations at the furthest point from our home base and then continue working our way back to the border as time and circumstance allowed.

As the tar road burned beneath us, the monotony of a landscape of gravel desert plains, marked with the occasional thorny acacia, was finally broken, and the mauve silhouettes of distant mountains grew before us. It was the falling outline of the strangely distorted and swollen sun that provided the signal to head into the nearing foothills.

By error rather than judgement, we discovered that we were approaching the entrance to a gorge marked by the remains of the settlement of Tanuf. Once the capital of Suleiman, the formidable Lord of the Green Mountain, it was an intriguing place to begin our explorations. It was Suleiman's disguised support of Talib, the brother of the imam, as well as his power over foothill villages that strengthened the contest against the ruling sultan in the 1950s, for control over the mountainous interior. Finally in 1957, government forces backed by the UK's Royal Air Force, responded by blowing up Tanuf, along with the insurgent controlled castle of Izki and the towers and walls protecting the fortress-like settlement of Bilad Sayt. Taking control of these fortified settlements was the first step in a battle that lasted another two years before the heights of the impregnable Jebel Akhdar were seized.

Strategically set into the mouth of a huge gorge, Tanuf controlled not only the entrance, but along with it, access to tracks into the mountains. Like the settlement they once sheltered, the outer stone walls had quite literally been blown apart. Remaining sections – some twenty feet in height and several feet thick – contained arched pointed window openings affording splendid views across the plain for detecting and defending against intruders. The destruction of this stronghold was a prelude to the demise of the Mountain King and the Saudi-backed Imamate. We could not resist entering the remains of the former monarch's domain.

In evening sunlight, the sense of its ghostly past emanated from shadowed passageways. I picked my way past the occasional standing wall, complete with niches that once held personal possessions. Now, among pottery shards, a startled lizard, still as death, stared straight at me. Holding a statuesque foot in the air pose, he eyed me dispassionately before disappearing into a crack in the wall, leaving a length of tail exposed. At the far end of the settlement, a square and intact fortress, with neat arrow slit openings, stood guard over the gorge, while the remains of a great wall, crested by two rounded towers, followed the contour of the steeply sloping hillside. Marked by the angled distinctiveness of the range, the undulating precipitous edge severed the pale infinity of sky.

With limited time before the flood of darkness, we left the site and followed remaining sections of ruined battlements into the gorge where a huge dam has been built to control winter's flash floods. At the end of summer it was a dry wasteland, an open and uninviting place to contemplate spending the night. Since directions in our off-road guide didn't venture past the dam, consoling ourselves that we were true explorers, we set off following tracks that traced the perimeter. There was no sign of life as we rumbled towards and past a small shanty settlement of corrugated iron sheets with sacking draped across poles. The stony wadi floor took us towards a narrow canyon, leading directly into a cleft in the mountain wall. Entering the corridor of darkness reminded me of Lawrence's snake deliberately drawing itself into the 'burning bowels of the earth'.

We had no idea where the track was taking us, or if there was an alternative exit. On the other hand, we could not but believe that we had been heard and seen going in. Darkness thickened as we crunched and bounced and grumbled over the boulder-strewn floor. At times, the rock walls that stretched above us for some 500 feet were almost close enough to touch on either side. Over our heads, the cool stream of sky ran on a parallel track, twisting and bending with the shape of the canyon, opening and closing, leaking into fissures and cavities and leading us towards the mountain's very heart.

As on previous occasions, our hunt for a place to camp was provided by a circular bowl in the rock wall; a place where huge boulders, now lying dormant, swirled like marbles in the raging torrents of winter's flash floods until the five hundred foot high fortress, hammered and scoured over centuries, had been sculpted into the magnificent amphitheatre before us.

We trundled across an area littered with scrubby trees and bushes and then, deciding against an inviting sandy hollow, visible from the track, made for the protective covering of a sizeable acacia guarding the entrance to a womb-like enclave. Safely hidden and distanced from both the track and overhanging rock walls, where perilously perched boulders threatened to drop and crush like beetles everything in their path, we lurched to a halt and sat absorbing the silence and our surroundings. The remnants of a pale flag of sunlight draped over one side of the rock face. As it melted, the amphitheatre soaked darkness into its crevices and hollows.

Tacit and solemn, as if we were about to participate in some time-honoured ritual, Richard poured above room temperature Shiraz: a Jacob's Creek variety, it was one of a number of quality red wines available for expat residents in the Emirates. Armed with a government licence permitting the purchase of alcohol, we made regular visits to the most convenient liquor store in the Emirate of Umm al-Qaiwain. Now, with pewter tumblers in hand, we made our way across the cindery waste to a series of wide circular steps beneath the exposed rock face.

It was like the entrance to a magnificent cathedral, but everything was displaced. The great curved wall was adjacent to the steps and the steps adjacent to a series of vertical pillars, as if the entire place had been carefully crafted inch by inch, year by year, century by century, and then left on hold. Pink anticlines rested on grey vertical bands – black shiny buttresses shouldered a sandy wall, marked by perfectly spaced horizontal grey ledges. Where the steps ended, huge boulders littered the floor as if they too had been suddenly abandoned. Nothing was aligned. Then the half moon swung clear of the black lip of the crater – for now it was a crater – flooding the place with liquid light. Every tiny shape, each pebble and each leaf, had been sprayed with silver, highlighting its individuality.

Conditions were ripe for the imagination to take over. Mine did. On the far wall of the canyon darkness and moonlight conspired to release the contours of a face that was both monstrous in size and expression. Beneath a craggy brow, two eyes bulged from deep folds. One, set higher than the other, radiated a crazed agony that was reflected in its gaping, twisted mouth. It was as if the thing, trapped in the throes of struggle for escape, had been petrified into the rock face at its very moment of terror.

My moment of terror was yet to come. Standing under the acacia next to the tent we had just erected, I switched on my pencil torch. Instantly, the air filled with a vibrant rushing sound as if the tree itself were struggling to take off. Within seconds, a winged swarm descended upon my head and shoulders. Apart from crying out, my instinct was to switch off the torch, whereupon in a second uniform burst of flight, my invaders returned to the thorny branches.

'Locusts,' called my protector, strolling to my rescue. 'Locals love them. Highly nutritious. Best not use the torch,' he advised.

When we crawled into and zipped up the tent that night, the air was once again filled with the whooshing of wings.

'Bats,' my nature lover assured me. He was kneeling and peeking through a netted window. 'Dozens. Feeding on locusts.'

Crouching at his side, I watched a pair of huge wings lift and extend across star crazy sky. The swooping and munching continued into the night as locusts were plucked and devoured from branches over our heads. Decidedly nervous, I lay awake listening to strange nearby snuffles. Then, as silence descended, haunting cries tore apart the stillness of the night.

Morning held its own mysteries. Just as we were preparing to make an early start, three women appeared. Carrying huge bundles of wood on their heads, they were picking their way over the stony floor past the hidden entrance to our camping spot, and heading further upstream into the widening wadi. We remained hidden and silent. I watched intently, taking in details of their appearance. They were slight of build with finely chiselled features, and wearing metal necklaces, beaded bracelets and wide gold nose rings; silky bell-shaped skirts of bright green and burgundy swayed over narrow blue ruffled trousers. Red and burgundy veils of the same silky material covered their heads and shoulders, and fell to points reaching to below the level of their knees.

Imagination fired by the eighteenth century Omani author Sirhan ibn Said's account of a battle on the plain near Nizwa, I considered either Persian or Yemeni origins. Said tells us that when the Persians refused the Azd permission to settle – a Yemeni tribal group they controlled in Oman – a great battle took place. The Azd's calvary charge was led by the almost mythical figure of Malik ibn Fahm wearing a yellow turban and red cloak over his armour. Riding a piebald stallion, Malik ibn Fahm led his forces against the Persians, who were mounted on elephants. Over many years, battles between the two tribes took place until, in AD 578, the Persian forces agreed to withdraw to Sohar, leaving the mountains and deserts of western Oman to the Azd.

This did not, of course, herald the absence of Persians in Oman. Their thriving cities and ports on Oman's east coast survived until the fifteenth century, when they were destroyed by Portuguese invaders. Remains of the drum-like towers of their great castles throughout Oman are testimony to the strength of their presence. As recently as the mid-twentieth century, exiled Persians, who had rebelled against the Iranian Shah and fled to Oman for asylum, were operating as smugglers and slave traders. A number were employed as gunrunners for the late Sultan's forces against the imam's insurgents. Familiar with routes into the mountains, as they were with corrupt officials and cameleers transporting weapons and landmines into the interior, they remained loyal to the Sultan who had given them a home.

Was it possible, I continued to wonder, that the women disappearing between the trees were descendants from Persians, living in their mountain stronghold as their ancestors had done? Imagination and origins apart, their way of life was remote from the lives of the people in villages and towns just kilometres away. Even their slim build and colourful stylish clothes set them apart from black-cloaked village females. As intrigued as we were, we decided that an attempt to follow the women to see where they were heading would be impossible without being intrusive. Contenting ourselves with silent speculation, we watched their retreat until, unable to resist a shot of their receding back views, I reached for my camera.

Collapsing walls and towers held in the embrace of metal scaffolding; such was our first impression of the great castle at Bahla. Quite literally, it was sagging at its knees. Together with the forts of Izki, Nizwa and Rustaq, Bahla has stood guard at the foothills of the Jebel Akhdar since the thirteenth and fourteenth centuries. Then adobe walls and towers rose imperiously some 165 feet above Persian sandstone foundations. Cultivated gardens, protected and sheltered by seven miles of walls with defensive towers and gates, are said to have resembled the Sumerian city of Uruk in present day Iraq. At that time, the oasis of Bahla was prosperous and under the control of the Banu Nebhan tribe.

Today, as a Unesco World Heritage Site, the fort is under extensive renovation. Meanwhile, half-built modern villas, scattered at random throughout the date-palm grove of former splendid gardens, ensure that preservation of the past and modernity go hand in hand.

We cruised along the roadside until, from the brow of a small hill, we found the best place to capture some aspects of the fort's historic outline on film. Across a grove of heady date palms, against a background of low brown hills, stretched the extensive and crumbling ramparts of the castle. Neither walls nor turrets have stood the test of time. There was no shade, and the bald metallic sun that had taken its toll on the castle was having no mercy on us. Just standing outside the air-conditioned Musso while attempting to focus our cameras was enervating, and a stern reminder that we were not built of the same resilient moral or physical fibre as the Thesigers of this world.

The sheer size of the castle and the work needed to restore it was mind bending. To make things more difficult, whatever traditional skills local Omanis may once have possessed have been lost. To compensate, artists from Morocco had been employed to return the castle to its former glory. Their retention of ancestral knowledge, for using stone, mud or clay mixed with straw and dung for rebuilding walls, is reputed to be as effective as that of carving doors and ceilings from the trunks of palm trees. Just metres further along the road we were blessed with views over an impressive section of the original crenellated walls that once determined the castle's boundaries. Reaching to twelve or more feet in height, they traced a route over undulating hillocks of lose scree into the distance.

Serene and poised as a goddess, Jabrin Castle rose from a dark green lake of date palms. Massive spike-studded doors, guarding the entrance to this splendidly restored former palace, are a reminder that defence in the Dhahirah province (the back of Oman) was as necessary for the rich and mighty as it was for the village settlements in the foothills of the mountains (the spine). This message was reinforced by remaining grooves from a portcullis over the doorway, and the use of spiralling stairways for access to towers to prevent storming by enemies. Courtyards too were built to withstand attack: slits for viewing and firing at enemies; windows angled to look down and traditional chutes for pouring boiling water, oil or date syrup on unwelcome visitors were attached to random towers.

Head swathed in the traditional Kashmiri shawl, Hazim, our white-robed guide, led us towards and up a twisting stairway to a small lookout tower with views across the open plain to the foothills of smoke-blue mountains.

'Tanuf?' Richard asked.

Hazim signalled the direction with his arm.

'And Wadi Ghul?'

'Behind hill,' Hazim responded, indicating a conical hillock directly opposite. 'Cross road – turn left – find wadi. *Inshallah*!' he added, smiling.

Hastily unfolding our map we checked the route and a dotted line indicating a track from Wadi Ghul into the mountains; this, we believed, would take us to a place with clear views to Jebel Shams, once reigned over by Suleiman bin Himyar, The Mountain King. That he was a direct descendant of the royal line of the thirteenth century Banu Nebhan tribe supported bin Himyar's claim to be King of Nebhania.

With the proposed expedition in mind, we put away our map and descend to the castle's middle floor, where a corridor led to an arched doorway that opened onto a sunlit inner courtyard. A sheltered and peaceful place, it housed a well, niches with shaded seating and stairways to balconied areas at higher levels. For the castle's inhabitants, the huge and complex structure offered the luxury of multiple living and sleeping quarters, a mosque and a library. While admiring delicate floral designs in shades of green and rust covering the ceiling over our heads, Hazim explained that a team of Italian experts were responsible for restoring the artwork.

'Today, Omani people no good artist,' Hazim confided, confirming the lack of ancestral skills practised by local people.

Cameras working overtime, we were attempting to capture some degree of the elegance of lattice-work windows and the play of light and shade through doorways decorated with curvaceous overhead sculptured reliefs. Finally, a heavy door was unbolted, and we descended worn stone steps to a complex of underground cellars, store rooms and a dungeon. Confronted by stained blood-red walls and an equally blood-red grooved floor to the cellar, I stopped in my tracks. A smiling Hazim assured me that syrup, extracted from harvested dates, had caused the stain. I wanted to believe him.

Emerging from the cool interior to temperatures, verging on 40 degrees in the shade, was a shock, and a positive reminder of just how effective the castle's insulation was. Thick walls and relatively small windows provided a good start. Low window levels and the labyrinth of narrow corridors and spiralling stairways, acting as wind funnels, created a natural and highly successful system of air-conditioning.

It was time to dip into the mountains once again – this time into Wadi Ghul, a region known as much for its scenic beauty as for the character of it settlements. On our approach, we made a detour to the settlements of Hamra and Ghafat. Located on the south-facing side of the Jebel, they shared dramatic settings. In his book *Muscat and Oman,* Ian Skeet describes the position of Ghafat as sheltered in a crook of the mountain, with extensive date gardens, watered by flowing *aflaj*. Hamra is similarly positioned. We followed a road encircling walled gardens with sprays from lime trees and date palms spilling over them, and stopped to admire a flight of stone steps leading from an open piazza to the upper level of the town's elegant mud-brick houses, some several storeys in height.

Retracing our route and travelling in our own private dust cloud, we made for the track into the mountains. Within minutes, we were looking down on the abandoned settlement of Al Ghul. Once again, the walls of houses appeared to grow from the stone slabs of the mountain itself and crest a grove of date palms that reach to the wadi bottom. As if on cue, a woman appeared in an otherwise empty field of long green grass on the near side of the wadi. Calling to Richard to stop, I balanced my camera on the open window and focused on the figure of the woman. Wearing a loose, full-length dress of wide red and green vertical stripes, she obligingly lifted a bundle of cut grass onto her heavily turbaned head and walked towards a gap in the dry stonewall that borders the wadi.

From then on, both the steepness of the ascent and the switch-back nature of the route increased dramatically; at each bend a bridge of logs, balanced precariously over a dried up rocky gully, creaked and trembled as we trundled over it, suggesting that it would take less than winter floods to bring about its demise. As we ascended and the vista opened up, we made for a strategic viewing point, only to find it already occupied. Earmarked by local people, who make their living from selling rugs woven from goats' hair, they had set up some makeshift stalls and were making the most of an opportunity to do business with a group of tourists emerging from a minibus. Leaving the visitors to bargain with the enterprising locals, we set off to find a more solitary place for an encounter with the past.

Just a few kilometres further, a platform of rock, with clear views across a dramatic canyon to Jebel Shams, satisfied our needs. Reaching to 9,800 feet, the highest point in the Akhdar Range, the former domain of The Mountain King reared before us. From its topmost pinnacle, a dramatic escarpment fell in a vertical cliff wall to the foot of the canyon, ensuring its inaccessibility. Feeling both godlike and infinitesimal, we walked over a limestone platform, as neat and smooth as any paved street, to a precipitous edge. It was here, and on various similar peaks, that the Sultan's forces gathered to support the final and successful 1959 SAS assault on Suleiman bin Himyar's impregnable stronghold. It was visually and historically awesome.

Tombs of Fire

In the very same year, 1959, on an island off the coast of Abu Dhabi, with the evocative name of *Umm al Nar* – Mother of Fire – Danish archaeologists produced evidence of a 3rd Millennium BC habitation. Houses and tombs contained weapons, jewellery and pottery resembling 4,000 to 5,000 year old artefacts from Mesopotamia and the Indus Valley. Then in 1972, similar discoveries were made in the interior of Oman. From our research, we knew that some of the best preserved examples were to be found on the hillside close to *Al Ayn* – The Spring – a settlement adjacent to the very area we were exploring.

Leaving the realm of the former Mountain King, a stony track signposted to Amlah, took us through Wadi Al Ayn. At its widest point, an imposing pair of rock pinnacles, capped by watchtowers and standing guard on either side, formed impressive lookout posts. Just minutes later, we drew to a halt.

'Death row,' Richard announced, lowering the window to focus his camera.

Silhouetted against the majestic lopsided cliff face of Jebel Misht, twenty or so carefully positioned beehive-shaped tombs crested the curved brow of a hill. I stood outside the vehicle, absorbing the scene. Nothing had prepared me for this dramatic and lovely setting. The utter desertion of the place. The heavy silence, disturbed now by the crunch and slithering of our footfalls as we began to climb towards the burial chambers of ancient people – people who lived in prosperous villages with economies based largely on agricultural systems, irrigated by heavy rainfalls. By 3000 BC, wheat, barley and dates were grown, and the herding of sheep, goats and cattle was in full swing.

Further intrigue is added by the knowledge that the lives of these people were not confined to agriculture. According to evidence found in cuneiform writing, the name *Magan* (Oman) was connected with copper smelting industries known for making and trading weapons, tools and jewellery. The discovery of ancient smelting works, confirm that the trade in copper – flourishing from 3900-2500 BC, long before the Romans arrived – developed into a thriving industry.

Close up, the tombs appeared larger and even more impressive than from a distance. Reaching from between ten and twelve feet in both height and width, each had a circular base and small trapezoidal entrance facing east: 'Tombs of

Fire' catching and holding the early morning blaze of the sun. While some of the structures were collapsing in upon themselves, others remained remarkably intact. Painstakingly constructed from several layers of high quality dry flagstone, the curved walls inclined towards dome-shaped roofs. Based largely on respect and partly on safety, neither Richard nor I felt tempted to crawl inside a tomb entrance. Robbed long before they were excavated, they remain as impressive memorials to the people of the *Umm al Nar* period.

The last lap of our return journey through the foothills of the Jebel Akhdar towards Buraimi and Dubai took us past Ibri, the principal market town of the Dhahirah province. Ronald Codrai's mid-twentieth century description of the nearby village of Salaif confirmed our growing recognition that the fortification of villages, nevermind the preponderance of castles, forts and watchtowers, exemplified Oman's ambivalent and turbulent history.

Sited on a slope beside a wadi, Salaif's protective walls grow from rising levels, with one wall extending up the hillside beyond the town. The main gate and watchtowers, constantly manned, underlined the fear of attack that continued to prevail up until the time of Codrai's visit. His splendid photographs of Salaif show a fortified settlement that in a number of ways resembles a miniature version of Bahla Fort. The prevailing sense of insecurity is made clear in his narrative description of the harvesting of corn:

Softly intoning at a level that seemed suited to their halcyon task, women cut and gathered the crop and tied it in small bundles, while nearby men chanted louder and more competitively ... Still wearing their ammunition belts, and with their rifles close at hand, they pounded the corn with the wide ends of stripped palm fronds, urging themelves into faster and faster action.... Their day's work at an end they made their way across the wadi to pass through the gateway in the village's outer wall, to disperse to their mud-baked dwellings inside the fortifications. Some lived in tall, storied houses with crenellated tops, which doubled as watch towers.

– *Oman, An Arabian Album*

Preserving the Past

A tangible sense of the past was far less in evidence in the Emirates. In fact, it wasn't until after the discovery of oil that most of the rulers – with a little nudging from Western allies – realised that those vestiges of a past way of life that did remain were worth preserving. In most cases, as far as buildings were concerned, including those of the royal family, they were largely *barasti*, constructed from mud-brick with palm-frond roofing. Without continual renewal, these structures collapse into the sands on which they stand. Thus, apart from forts and wind towers, there was very little to preserve. In Abu Dhabi, only the fort is of any consequence; with its mix of square and round towers this ancient monument became the palace, home and office of the ruler, serving as a central bank and administrative centre. Today the fort is used as a Centre for Research and Documentation, with a library, archives and recorded oral histories.

Dubai's fort, now a museum, includes an excellent section on the pearling industry, highlighting the former importance of pearls as source of trade on the coastal fringes. Among the items on display are beautiful carved chests, used by pearl merchants to carry their stock; ropes and stones, used by the divers to reach the seabed, as well as nose-clips and cotton coveralls for protection against devil fish, and finally, copper 'colanders' with different size holes, once used to grade the pearls and scales to weigh them.

The nearby museum, the Bastakia, is where fifty or so windtowers, originally built by Persian immigrants from Bastak, have been restored and preserved. These impressive towers with mangrove pole skeletons projecting from walls, to act as scaffolding during building and for later repairs, are mentioned as long ago as Assyrian times. On his travels, Marco Polo noted the ingenuity of the wind tower, the *badgir,* open on all sides to catch the smallest breeze.

Sharjah has rather more to boast about on the heritage front. As well as the restored fort of 1820 – the previous residence of the Al Qasimi ruling family – former elegant houses of merchants and royalty who benefitted from trading in pearls, gold and slaves have been converted into museums. Restoration work to convert Al-Naboodah House, into the Sharjah Heritage Museum began in 1995.

The original house was built a century earlier by the late Obaid bin Eesa Al Shamsi (Al Naboodah) – one of the biggest pearl traders of his time, he is said to have had offices in Paris and India as well as business relations and connections with Africa. The two-storey building, comprised of sixteen rooms, had special parlours where Al-Shamsi met divers and traders. Another historic building is the *majlis* – gathering place – of Ibrahim Al Midfa, a respected scientist, poet and politician with a collection of four hundred books on religion and literature. A round windtower, decorated with small blue and white tiles – one of the most distinctive features of his former home – became a much-photographed favourite of mine.

If there is a star in the heritage crown, then for me, it has to be Al Bidyah Mosque. Set against a rugged hill alongside a road leading into Fujairah, this miniature mosque was to all intents and purposes unused and deserted until 2000. At this time, when tourism was on the rise and even the more remote Emirates were entering the preservation field, Bidyah Mosque was cordoned off and renovation work began.

On several occasions when en route to Fujairah, we were drawn to stop and admire this tiny abandoned mosque; with its four small cone-like domes made of mud and stone, supported by just one central pillar, buttressed walls and tiny ornate windows, it remained as an emblem and memorial to a forgotten past. When we climbed the nearby hill to view it from above, the top of the domes resembled curlicues of whipped cream.

Showing distinct Yemeni influence, and estimated to have been built in 1446 along with two nearby watchtowers, its origin remains something of a mystery. One persuasive account refers to a local man named Bidyah, who found one of the biggest pearls ever off the Fujairah coast and had the mosque built as a thank-offering. Like the mystery surrounding the founder, the mosque retains a secretive aura.

The Eastern Hajar

Merchants, Traders, Settlers and Invaders

What the Eastern Hajar lack in drama of form and height compared to the Jebel Akhdar, they make up for in the unforgettable beauty of their more isolated coastal position.

That was what we anticipated and hoped for when, in April 2000, we started planning a journey through these mountains to Oman's remote eastern coastline. Bordered by the Arabian Sea in the east, the Wahiba Sands to the north and west and by the desolate Jiddat al-Harasis gravel plain in the far south, has ensured that the lives of the people living in isolated coastal settlements where the mountains meet the sea have remained a step back in time.

Since we were travelling by road from Dubai, distance and time dictated that our first camp was to be in the foothills of the Jebel Akhdar. Our route through the Wadi Hatta Border Post took us onto the now familiar road south towards Muscat. Shinas, Sohar, Saham, Al Khaburah, As Suwayq – the names rang like bells, marking the hours of our passage to historic Rustaq. Once we had bypassed the fort and Wadi Bani Awf, we were on the lookout for the fortified villages of Awabi and Al Mahaleel: once notorious for affiliations with the imam against Said bin Taimur, the previous ruling Sultan.

Finally, as the falling sun slid behind the mountain we entered and were swallowed by Wadi Mistal. The track narrowed between canyon walls. Weaving round huge boulders brought down by previous floods, Richard guided the Musso through the now steep, smooth walls of a gorge, leading us into the wide expanse of the Ghubrah Bowl. We had camped in a variety of mountain bowls but, without a doubt, Ghubrah was the largest – so large that it denied us the safe pocket of overnight security we sought. Enveloped in a great cloud of dust, we bowled across a parched open plain to the shadowed feet of a vertical cliff face. Over our heads, the village of Wakan perched like an eerie on a ragged outcrop in the mountain's side.

Tired as we were, we could not resist the opportunity to visit the village. As lengthening shadows enveloped the bowl in a purple cloak, we set up camp; then Richard navigated the Musso up a twisting narrow track, hewn into the mountain's face. Heard long before we were seen, we were greeted by a straggle of smiling children. A small boy grasping a snake behind its head had my full attention; the boy was slight and the snake so long that its sinuous form was coiled about his arms and torso. In evening light, it was just possible to make out a distinctive brown pattern on the creature's pale body that culminated in a delicate crested design on its head.

'Diadem snake,' Richard explained. 'Like a crown. Harmless. Eats rodents, mainly,' he added as a comforting afterthought.

'*Thirwan*?' he asked, addressing the boy who smiled shyly, nodding his head in response.

Meanwhile, a wiry village elder had taken control. His deeply lined face creasing into a wide smile, he beckoned us to follow him towards the terraced slopes behind a collection of stone houses. Rows of vines on the lower levels were topped by orchards of apricot trees, pomegranates and a plantain of bananas. Water, flowing from irrigation channels cut into the hillside, ensured that the villagers were self-sufficient in their mountain home. As the last rays of the hidden sun faded and a sudden chill descended, we thanked our escorts and prepared to make our way down the slippery zigzag slope. Under a half moon and a night sky brilliant with a rush of stars, Richard steered the grumbling Musso to safety and back to our waiting tent. Once the engine was turned off, we stood for a time immersed in the almost forgotten, incredible silence of the natural world.

At the first sliver of dawn, the slow creep of light climbed the craggy cliff face towards the white walls of the village – so slowly that we could sense the turning of the earth towards the sun. As we watched, the cliff head and then Wakan village were bathed in gold. Dozens of desert white butterflies fluttered round parched and dust-shrouded shrubs and bushes as, once again, we crossed Ghubrah Bowl, this time in the direction of Nakhl Fort.

Beautifully restored and with a stunning setting against the backdrop of dark mountains, even metallic sunlight could not detract from the fairytale qualities of the castle. Located on a promontory of rock at the foot of a mountain of the same name, Jebel Nakhl, the walls and the rock from which the castle appear to grow formed a complete architectural whole. Pre-Islamic in origin, Nakhl's present combination of square and round towers testify to additions and changes that have taken place over the centuries. Nearby, mineral-laden hot springs, flowing all year round from clefts in the mountain wall, ensure constant supplies of water for the palm groves and castle residents.

In its more recent history, the castle was the home of the powerful Ya'aruba Tribe, who came to power in 1624 and were instrumental in expelling the Portuguese from Oman. In the mid-nineteenth century, during the era of Sultan Said bin Taimur, the *wilayah* – administrative region – included seventy four villages scattered over the hills, plains and wadis. The 1990 renovation and facelift, as well as its splendid location, have made Nakhl Fort a jewel in Oman's crown.

Anxious to begin our coastal journey, we headed in the direction of Muscat before turning south across a gravel plain onto a graded road, that gradually ascended into the lower reaches of the mountains until we were crossing a wide desert plain. Finally, the route led us downhill towards the east coast, and the fishing village of Dibab. An emerald inlet and a small lagoon, restless with vultures, heralded our approach to the Arabian Sea and the start of a track, heading once more along the foothills of the Eastern Hajar, to our goal: a dramatic and picturesque sinkhole.

At some 125km east from Muscat, situated on a plain between mountains and sea, the remarkable sinkhole of Bimmah holds a deep pool of intensely green water. Formed when underground water dissolved the limestone rock above a cave, causing the roof to collapse, the enclosed pool is home to sea and freshwater plants and animals unique to the environment. We made for a group of *barasti* huts that signalled the approach, and arrived to find newly erected shelters providing shaded parking.

'Cordoned off,' Richard called as he strode ahead.

A wrought iron fence, circling the outer edge of the cavernous hollow, and a set of some fifty concrete steps leading down the steep slope to the water's edge, confirmed rumours that it was now a tour group attraction. Looking down on translucent water that darkened mysteriously beneath the curved ridges of its rock sides, revived memories of a slippery descent and unplanned up-to-the-thighs immersion on a previous visit. On this occasion our stop, primarily with photographic intent, also served as an excellent place for a caffeine top up.

Our journey continued, following the ragged coastline where fingers of mountains penetrate into the sea hiding isolated wadis in their folds. Where there is water there is life, and each wadi, with its own natural flow of sweet water, housed a settlement. We had set our sights on finding Wadi Tiwi. Previously reached only by sea or a narrow donkey trail through the mountains, the recently built gravel road has provided an accessible coastal approach. A photo stop at the mouth of Wadi Shab – a ravine of intense green water between treacherous cliffs – then, as we rounded the next promontory, the track turned inland and ran alongside a wide open plain crossed by a stream flowing from a pool of water.

'Has to be Tiwi,' I declared. 'It's a colour replica of Codrai's black and white photo.'

The place and the scene before us was a reminder of the quality of Ronald Codrai's splendid selection of photographs taken in Oman in the 1950s. Processed in an improvised darkroom in his Omani home and washed in the sea as he swam on the following day, their quality – composition and reproduction – more than match any modern day, high tech digital efforts.

Announcing our presence, the Musso trundled over the stony floor towards dappled shade, where grazing cattle paused to watch our progress with soulful gaze, and then across a streambed between further pools of deep green encircled by beds of rushes. The edges of the rock sides, previously festooned with trees, were now bordered by plantations of dates, figs, bananas, papayas and more. Smiling villagers emerged from stone houses set among the trees, while the sound of water flowing through the channels of the ancient *aflaj* recreated the tranquil scene experienced by Ronald Codrai; a scene of serenity, endorsed by his comment that the shepherd he met on his visit was gentle and unarmed, unlike the mountain people he encountered inland.

Modern life was visible in newly installed electric and telephone power lines, football goal netting on a field of green and pick-up trucks that used the graded road to the coast instead of donkeys through the mountains. Advances into the modern world have arrived without destroying the sense of harmony and culture.

As we left the wadi and the sun disappeared behind the mountains, finding a camping spot was a priority. A succession of rocky promontories, holding isolated inlets, provided tantalising glimpses of inaccessible coves of white sand.

Finally, a rough track over the side of a hill took us to a platform of rock. Backed by a cliff face and overlooking the sea, it was sheltered from the track, and came complete with remarkable ocean views. It seemed heaven sent. It wasn't until we prepared for sleep that we discovered the downside; whether in or out of the tent, the heat radiating from rocks beneath was unbearable. In fact, lying in a prone position was tantamount to presenting oneself to be roasted. I was certain that I could feel myself cooking. Giving up on any attempt to sleep horizontally, I sat outside on a rolled up sleeping bag, nodding off and waking until – dispensing stars in its wake – darkness faded.

As first light pearlised sea and sky, I watched Richard making his way over the rock-strewn headland towards the ocean. His mission was to collect oysters for his breakfast. Returning with a satisfied smile on his face, he explained that while wading in the shallows and sampling his catch, he had been delighted to find that he was sharing the inlet with two green turtles feeding on sea grass. Such was his delight that he felt fully recompensed for the restless night. As we sipped morning tea, we watched the first of the day's dust-devils whirl its way between barren slopes, across a desert plain – a stern reminder of the journey that lay ahead, this time to the remains of the ancient coastal city of Qalhat.

Former home to the Yemeni, Al Azd people, at its height in the fourteenth and fifteenth centuries, Qalhat was the premier port associated with the city state of Hormuz, on the island of the same name, near the mouth of the Gulf of Oman. Records tell us that Persian, Indian and Ming Empires, connected to Qalhat by an umbilical cord of seaways, made it one of the most fantastic cities of its time.

On the final approach, we rounded a peninsula housing a new settlement. There, on a parallel headland, set against peerless blue sky, was the unmistakeable outline of the most distinguishing feature of the ruined city: the tomb of Bibi Maryam. Even from a distance, the square coral-built mausoleum, crowned by the remains of a central dome, was more striking than photographic images suggest.

Close up, with daylight seeping through beautiful shell-shaped designs over each of the four arched entrances, its fragility was more apparent. Round the doorways, fragments of glazed tiles hinted at the splendid blue ceramics that once covered the walls. Today, the mausoleum is open to the sky. Inside, all that remains is a set of worn steps leading down to the long-ago raided burial chamber. Darkness, a sense of intrusion and then a skittering – lizard or rat, maybe – kept us at the foot of the steps from where we could make out a head and footstone, marking the position of a grave. A layer of resin that covers the floor of the vault – said to be from candles burnt by devotees of Bibi Maryam long after the destruction of the city – bears witness to the strength of belief in her outstanding and pious reputation.

In AD 1330, the great Moroccan explorer, Ibn Battuta, walked the streets of Qalhat and marvelled at its grandeur: 'Were the world a ring,' he wrote, 'this would be a jewel in it.' He praised the city for its markets and for having one of the most beautiful mosques in the world, and a remarkable tomb. He attributes both to Bibi Maryam, the wife of Bahauddin Ayaz, Prince of Hormuz and son of the founder of the Hormuz Empire. Bahuaddin Ayaz retired to Qalhat, from where his family originated, and he died there in AD 1312. He was buried in the splendid mausoleum, built under the patronage of Bibi Maryam. The people of the city, he describes as merchants who brought many goods from India.

It was Qalhat's favourable position with respect to dominating winds and currents that allowed relatively easy maritime connections within the region, enabling it to become one of the most important ports. Such was its significance that it featured in the stories of great explorers, including Pliny the Elder, Marco Polo and Alfonso de Albuquerque. In the thirteenth century, Marco Polo described the city as noble, and the people as Saracens subject to the King of Hormos (Hormuz). At times of danger, the king took refuge in the fortified city of Qalhat. Polo goes on to expand on the city's advantages for trading in goods and merchandise, and in particular, the export of many horses. His account of how the horses were shipped to the sultans of Delhi, the Rajputs in Rajasthan and the kings of southern India conjure fairytale images and fuelled our intention to visit Ibra – the ancient pivotal centre in Oman for the breeding and trading of horses.

The colourful and fascinating accounts of Qalhat are of the city at its zenith but its history goes back much further. The discovery of Neolithic flints suggest human habitation some seven thousand years ago. It is believed that *Ichthyophagi* – fish eaters of the Indian Ocean – probably developed into the early maritime communities that were a crucial link between the Indus Valley and Mesopotamian civilisations. Access to fresh mountain water and to the legendary deep sheltered harbour were just as vital to ancient man. Links to settlements in Wadi Tiwi and Bani Khalid are believed to have followed the same narrow track that crosses the mountain behind the tomb to this very day.

At the end of the fourteenth century, Qalhat was struck by a heavy earthquake that destroyed many of the city's buildings and its *aflaj* system. Then in 1507, the Portuguese arrived in Oman. After ransacking Quriyat and Muscat, in the following year they set their sights on Qalhat, destroying the city, killing the local population and burning all the ships and buildings. Braz, the son of Alfonso de Albuquerque, described the tragic and systematic destruction of the town including the legendary mosque:

… which the Moors much took to heart, for it was a very large building with seven naves, all lined with tiles and containing much porcelain set in the walls … Doors and ceiling of the mosque were all made of carved timber … They did not stop to put fire to the building until it was completely burnt down …

Philip Ward, *Travels in Oman*

Although recent excavation has not been carried out on the site, an Australian team of underwater archaeologists found a remarkable selection of Indo-Arabian anchors in the sea nearby. Along with a Greek anchor, dating from the sixth to fourth centuries BCE, they are thought to be the largest collection of Indo-Arabian anchors known anywhere in the world.

From one of the arched doorways of the mausoleum, we could make out the boundary of former defensive city walls, running from the sea up the side of the mountain. Size alone, was indicative of its extent and importance. Today, amidst a landscape of rubble, apart from the mausoleum the only other identifiable remains are a stone-covered water reservoir and a grave with an ornate dome-shaped head and footstone at each end. Successive earthquakes have taken their toll, uplifting the coastline and destroying the old harbour and buildings that may have survived attacks by the Portuguese.

The elegant outline of the tomb of Bibi Maryam, standing atop a landscape of rubble, is a tribute to the lady whose spirit has survived the ruins of the city. It is also a potent reminder of the fragility of life, whether of early man, of mighty civilisations or of remarkable individuals. On that day, the only sound was that of the cry of a lonesome bird of prey and the relentless hammering of the sea on the coastline.

Just seventeen kilometres further south and east, we were approaching Sur. Once a magnificent port, trading with India and East Africa, it was famous for its shipyards throughout Arabia. During the sixteenth century, the Portuguese benefited from its sheltered harbour and ideal trading position before Arabs of the Ya'aruba dynasty reclaimed it. Throughout the nineteenth and early twentieth centuries, large ocean going dhows were built here, for use on trading routes to the Gulf, India and East Africa. The dhows sailed on the aptly named Trade Winds to East Africa, bringing back gold, ivory, cloves and slaves.

We made a brief tour of the headland, cruised along the shipyards, housing *sambuks* – fishing dhows; the traditional design is the same, but they are now powered with diesel engines and carry refrigerated tanks for ice and fish. A circuit round the huge curved bay to Ayja and its labyrinth of narrow streets, guarding the entry to the inlet from the opposite side, took us into the old part of Sur. Home to former shipbuilders and merchants, a display of modern villas now interlace with old merchant houses, notable for their lovely hand carved wooden doors and Arabesque windows. By chance, we came upon the Sur Beach Hotel, providing a welcome stop for freshening up in modern toilet facilities; coffee served in comfortable surrounds and supplies of fresh ice for our coolbox added to the comforts on offer.

Once hailed the 'Gateway to the East' and celebrated for fearless horsemen and the breeding and trading of fine horses, the inland settlement of Ibra stands guard over the main route to the port of Sur, as well as those north to Muscat and Nizwa. First sighted across a sunbaked plain, the old settlement's conglomeration of towers and fortified buildings – some three storeys high, with arrow slit openings in the walls and mounted cannons – stood squarely before us.

Leaving the Musso, we made our way towards and under an imposing entrance arch, into welcoming shaded quarters; turreted forts, castles and the former homes of wealthy merchants, boasting imposing entrance porches, bolstered by stone pillars, stood solidly shoulder to shoulder. Interlaced between sections of the old city, an invasion of new villas stand alongside the ruins of old. A walkway took us through a grove of date palms. The silence was broken only by bird song and water flowing through a *falaj*. Echoes of the past were as transient and fragile as the shadows of trees.

We knew that Ibra was pre-Islamic in origin. What was even more surprising was the revelation that people from the *Umm al Nar* period had once inhabited the area. An amazing by chance discovery of their legacy of tower and beehive tombs on a hillside overlooking nearby Wadi Naam, testifies to this. Although local people have always known of these tower-like structures, they weren't discovered by outsiders until the early 1990s, when a Professor Yule recognised the tombs from an aerial photograph in John Nowell's book, *A Day Above Oman*. Thought to be from the Bronze Age – some 4,500 years ago – photographs and descriptions of the beehive structures show them to be remarkably similar to the beehive tombs we had visited in Al Ayn.

The news was made even more exciting by the additional discovery of some eighty tower tombs. The inner structure of each tomb – formed by the use of successive ceiling stone slabs gradually stepping inwards – was 'corbelled' as the chambers in the pyramids. These in turn were protected by a large tower, built round the outside, and forming an outer shell. Like beehive tombs, each tower has a small entrance at ground level, just large enough for an adult to crawl through. These discoveries added yet another dimension to the historic importance of this ancient settlement.

We were on the trail of a different legacy from the past – a wall of prehistoric rock art. Leaving Ibra, our plan was to follow a track through the Eastern Hajar, formed by three adjoining wadis: Dima, Tayin and Dayqah. Within minutes of turning into Wadi Dima, we were following the bed of a stream that circumnavigated the stony floor, linking pools of water and winding through small settlements. Date palm plantations gave way to groves of bananas and papayas; stone houses grew from the wadi sides; smiling friendly people – collecting water or crops – paused to wave; a man, dressed in a sarong and carrying a heap of alfalfa on his head walked into a shady avenue between rows of overhanging palms. Around us, the bare, unforgiving sides of mountains rose brown and dusky purple, contrasting with the pockets of intense green of the oasis connected by the streambed.

By the time we reached and bypassed the settlement of Al Ghayyan, the village marking the meeting point with Wadi Tayin, the sun was low and the wadi had become a wide, dried-up river bed between vertical slopes of loose scree. We carried on until trees and rushes, growing at the foot of a river cliff, provided the invitation to stop we were hoping for. In spite of the shade, the place was like a furnace. Heat from the rock walls and floor kept temperatures high and seeped through bedding, ensuring another uneasy and restless night.

Woken by a sudden burst of wind and bird calls from nearby trees, we surfaced in time to watch a group of children making their way to the school in Al Ghayyan; then, a boy on a camel, a man on a donkey and a second elderly man, khanjar in his hand, came to inspect our tent, before smiling quizzically and moving on. Electric power lines and a pick up truck took Al Ghayyan into the modern world.

Before the sun had risen over the rock face we continued following tyre tracks along the deeply shadowed side of the increasingly wide wadi floor. Hugged by huge limestone walls, created by water slicing through solid rock for millions of years, it was beginning to resemble a mini Grand Canyon. Wider than a ten-lane motorway at the start, as we progressed the walls closed in, the pebbles on the floor increased in size and the going became increasingly hard. Suddenly, we jolted to a halt.

'Eagles,' was Richard's explanation, as he left the vehicle and trained his binoculars skywards on a pair tracing lazy circles in the peerless dome.

Some 13km from the start, we came upon a good-sized pool of water so clear it was like looking through glass. Set in a hollow at the foot of the rock wall, it signalled our approach to a fork in the wadi bed. Keeping the place in mind for cooling off and a picnic stop on our return journey, we took the left-hand branch and prepared ourselves for a further 16km joint-jolting ride.

Finally, as our notes dictated, the pale tones of the rock wall gradually darkened, and then a gnarled tree, standing before a great panel of dark smooth rock, marked the spot. It was extraordinary. In the middle of nowhere, an open-air exhibition of rock art was right before us: white silhouettes of huntsmen and warriors, pecked with flint stones onto the exposed rock surface, stood out against the dark background. Scenes of groups of people hunting, warriors, with outstretched arms, riding horses and camels with single humps, covered the rock wall. If confirmation were needed that prehistoric people, from this region, were breeding and trading in horses all those centuries ago, it was right before us.

Just 150 odd km by tar road from Ibra, Oman's capital city of Muscat was a world away from the places we had been visiting. Rescued, in 1970, from 20th century descent into international oblivion under Sultan bin Taimur, by the progressive leadership of his son, HH Sultan Qaboos bin Said, Muscat has grown into the thriving modern city it is today. For a start, a hole was driven through city walls that had remained as barrier to the outside world; then an archway replaced the locked city gates, allowing goods and services to flow into and out from the city. By imposing a ban on high rise structures, in favour of traditional white-washed buildings, the sultan also ensured that the modern city retains its integrity of character. And so it remains a welcome contrast to the glass and concrete structures that dominate the skyline of the neighbouring Emirates; it has become a favourite weekend retreat for discerning Arabs and ex-pats alike.

It was to the older part of Muscat that we were heading; dominated by cliff-side forts and ancient city walls, it retains substantial and visible links with the past. First mentioned and described by the second century geographer Ptolemy as a settlement with a concealed harbour, Muscat's location – surrounded by mountains on three sides – made it all but inaccessible from land. Its very name Muscat, derived from *Masqat:* a place of anchorage – supports the claim that the original Yemeni settlers discovered its secluded position by approaching it from the sea.

The start of the 15th century heralded the gathering momentum of the city as a trading port. At the same time a race was on by European powers to discover a sea route to break the Arab's monopoly of overland and sea passages between Europe and Asia. Ironically, the famous Omani navigator, Ahmed Majid, guided the Portuguese explorer, Vasco da Gama's ship around the Cape of Good Hope to reach India in 1498. This marked the beginning of change. The arrival of the Portuguese in these waters, dramatically altered the political landscape of Oman. Rivals for the lucrative maritime trade, developed by the Omanis, they invaded Oman and took Muscat.

History tells us that when the Portuguese explorer, Alfonso de Albuquerque, was appointed Viceroy of the Portuguese in 1507, he immediately led a small fleet of seven ships and 500 men to capture the Persian stronghold of Hormuz, at the entrance to the Gulf. Its thriving markets for pearls and horses made it, along with Aden, one of the two strongholds on the trade route between the Arab world and Asia. On the way to Hormuz, Albuquerque captured not only Muscat but other coastal towns as well. As Muscat grew in importance the Portuguese made it their major naval stronghold. The need to build the twin forts of Mirani and Jalani, at either end of the harbour, and further forts along the coast is evidence of the fierce resistance they faced – not just from the Omanis but from other emerging European powers, including warring Ottoman Turks.

While the two Muscat forts were built to overlook the horse-shoe shaped harbour, a third was built at neighbouring Mutrah. To this day the forts of Muscat, built into, against and on the cliffs some 50 metres above sea level, remain as impressive citadels dominating the shoreline. We knew that our viewings would be strictly from the outside: Fort Mirani, now housing the offices of the Royal Court, forbids the entry of outsiders while Jalani, formerly a much feared prison and now serving as army barracks, remains open but for guided tours only. We had to be content with history between pages instead of between walls.

The innovative design of the Muscat forts – to accommodate the use of cannon fire – was a stepping stone in the history of warfare and instrumental in affecting change. Mirani, the first fort to house cannons, was built with round towers instead of the traditional square ones: better to deflect cannonballs. Jalani and the other coastal forts, adapted to follow a similar design; the resulting mix of round and square towers remain in evidence throughout Oman and the Emirates. Despite some renovations, the Muscat forts have stood the test of time and remain virtually unchanged. Even Mirani's chapel, with its dome and holy water basin, has survived. The inscription at the inner gateway leaves us in no doubt of its 1588 origin:

> In the reign of the very high and mighty Philip, first of this name, our sacred king, in the eighth year of his reign in the crown of Portugal …

Finally, with the help of a cunning Indian merchant, Milani fort was captured by the Omanis. The story told is that the Portuguese commander was enamoured of a merchant's daughter. The merchant managed to convince the lovesick commander that the rations and gunpowder, held in the fort, had become spoilt and needed replacement. Once the stores were removed, the Indian informed the Omanis, who quickly besieged the fort. Rather than face surrender, the Portuguese commander jumped into the sea and was dashed on the rocks.

We cruised around the perimeter taking long-distance shots, including some of upmarket graffiti on the rock-strewn, cliff face: the names of naval vessels, painted on the rocks, include that of HMS *Seahorse* – a record of Nelson's visit in

1775; this legacy of 'artwork' of the sailors, who scaled the cliffs, has been graciously referred to by the Sultan as a picturesque 'visitors' book.'

On a beach, on the outskirts of Muscat, we came upon fishermen 'dragging' their nets as their predecessors had done for thousands of years. Suddenly, among the catch, we saw one and then a second turtle trapped in the netting. Our initial fear for the turtles was unfounded. As we watched, we saw that the fishermen were working to free the turtles before releasing them into the sea. In fact, Oman is a haven for turtles. Their east coast nesting sites are protected nature reserves and open to visitors.

A small gold dome – like a clenched fist – repeated in miniature on the spire of a slender minaret – each capped by a crown that tapers skywards to uphold a slim crescent moon.

Framed in the curve of an archway, at the far end of an avenue of palms, the simple and elegant silhouette of Zabeel Mosque stood before us like a perfectly executed painting. Then a figure in white and the scene came to life. Dressed in the traditional crocheted fitted skull cap and a flowing white *dishdasha,* a muezzin was making his way beneath the crown of palms towards a pair of gold arched doors, marking the entrance to the mosque. As he walked he swung an incense burner, leaving a trail of fragrance in his wake: a poignant and lovely reminder of the frankincense trade and its long associations with religious belief in all its forms.

The Saiq Plateau

O Man, the Last Stronghold!

He who holds Nizwa holds Oman – he who holds the Jebel Akhdar holds Nizwa.

An ancient and memorable saying that neatly sums up the contest for control of this mountain stronghold and the ancient capital of Nizwa.

It was in the autumn of 2000 that whispers of a graded road leading to Oman's 7,000 foot high Saiq Plateau reached us. Rumour had it that not only was there a graded road but an hotel. Although the arrival of an hotel, accessed by a gravel road, on the previously impregnable heights of the Jebel Akhdar, spelt heresy – if it were fact, then a head start was imperative. Thus triggered into action, we booked a room at the appropriately named *Jebel Al-Akhdar Hotel* for a weekend visit; checked the validity of our Omani multiple entry visas; filled the Musso's tank with diesel and were on our way. An expedition into the previously inaccessible kingdom of the former Lord of the Green Mountain was an opportunity not to be missed.

It was the belief in the presence of oil at Fahud, in Oman in the 1950s, that heightened the contest for control of Nizwa and the heights of the Jebel Akhdar between Said bin Taimur, the ruling sultan of Muscat and Oman, and the Saudi backed Trinity of the interior. Composed of Suleiman – the Mountain King – the imam and his insurgent brother Talib, the Trinity was a force not to be taken lightly.

Situated at the foot of the Jebel Akhdar, Nizwa's strategic position enabled it to control routes to Muscat, Salalah and Buraimi while an imposing 17th century fort, built by the second Ya'aruba Imam, guarded the settlement. We had passed Nizwa's great stone walls and enormous drum-like stone tower, rising to 35 metres, on various expeditions between the Western and Eastern Hajar. Strong military and defensive fortifications, at the summit of the tower, are said to include 24 cannons, placed at equally spaced openings around the perimeter; 480 gun ports – allowing for a concentrated barrage of fire when under attack – and a protective wall for the 120 guards armed with muskets and flintlocks. It was and is impressive.

Serving as a combination palace, seat of government and a prison for 300 years the fortified castle was the primary seat of the *imams* (religious leaders) who ruled the country's interior with ferocious fanaticism. Such was the reputation of Nizwa that, as late as the mid-twentieth century, it was a place feared by travellers. Even Wilfred Thesiger took the advice he was given to avoid it. Since 1970, under the reign of Sultan Qaboos, Nizwa has become a thriving modern city, a hub for education, medical facilities and a growing centre for tourism. Today, the labyrinthine castle is connected to a fort and carved wooden doors open onto courtyards and shops in the adjacent souk.

Just over four decades ago, when the imam and his followers were in control, it was a very different scenario. Then in 1957 Sultan Said bin Taimur called upon the British Royal Air Force to assist him in taking control of the fort and the settlement. A task that proved to be beyond them. Their anti-tank rockets exploded on impact with the stone walls of the tower, doing no more damage than dislodging lumps of plaster. It wasn't until the surrounding fortified villages had been taken that the imam's supporters moved out of the tower and the sultan's men moved in. Subsequently, the foothill villages of Izki, Mutti and Bilad Sayt pledged loyalty to the sultan. Taking control of the fort and the foothill villages was one thing but taking control of the impregnable Green Mountain was another story. Once Nizwa had been taken, the Trinity and their followers retreated into their mountain stronghold.

The most vivid description of the Jebel Akhdar that I have come across, is that of an unknown 1830s British explorer; his poetic vision of a massive limestone block, a mile thick and several miles wide, forcing its way up between several other layers which 'open like the petals of a flower' stays with me. Roughly triangular in shape and reaching to some seven and eight thousand feet these 'petals' overlook the flat top of the plateau. Equally visionary, is his portrayal of the capital Sharaija and its sister rock-clinging villages 'tumbling down a thousand feet of sheer cliff-face terraces'. Further colourful accounts of the inhabitants of this plateau, with its Mediterranean-style climate, include a reputation for being ill-mannered and an addiction to the wine they made from their grapes to while away the cold of winter nights.

Following the capture of Nizwa it took a further eighteen months – backed by various British army and air force brigades – for the sultan's forces to take control of the Jebel Akhdar 'in only way possible – the impossible way'.[3] The SAS walked up one of the impregnable petals. After a glance at the sheer limestone wall dropping from the apex of the triangle on the far side, the force calmly knotted ropes and lowered themselves commando fashion down onto the plateau. Talib's supporters were outflanked, resistance all but collapsed. The impregnable fortress had been stormed. With this relatively recent and dramatic history in mind, it was no wonder that we were excited at the prospect of being among the first to climb to the mountain's dizzy heights, albeit in a 4x4.

With the long tar road - some 280 miles from Dubai - behind us, we skirted the walls of Nizwa Fort and the adjoining mosque and headed into the Sumail Gap. Just 25km to the east, hidden behind the settlement of Birkat al Mawz where two mountains converge, a great wadi emerges. This was the starting point for 32 kilometres of gravel road. Until the birth of the road, the plateau was accessible only by foot along a treacherous ravine and then in single file up a series of steps cut into the vertical rock-face by long ago Persian inhabitants.

Attempts in the late 1950s, by Sultan Said bin Taimur's forces, to reach the plateau were thwarted by armed insurgents perched on their rocky stronghold;

---

[3] P.S. Allfree, *Warlords of Oman*

would-be assailants attempting to reach and take the plateau, accompanied by the vital convoy of donkeys carrying supplies of food and water, were easy targets for supporters of the imam. It was this sheer inaccessibility that made the capture of the plateau, before the arrival of the SAS, impossible.

Navigating our way to the village of Birkat al Mawz we followed the wadi for some seven kilometres until it forked, before parking under some trees on the fringe of a date-palm oasis. As the passenger-cum-navigator on our expedition, I was more than ready for a caffeine top-up. As the driver, with several hours under his belt and no more than one brief roadside stop for a snack lunch on the edge of an inhospitable desert plain, Richard took some persuasion before agreeing to a further stop before tackling the steep ascent. I had come to the conclusion that Richard had been born without a body-clock.

While mine went off at regular intervals, signalling various needs including those of caffeine, food, sleep and alcohol, his was inoperative. We had learnt to compromise.

Now, in late afternoon, relieved to find that temperatures, if not humidity and flies were on the wane, we sipped the remnants of tepid coffee.

Just a few hundred metres further into the wadi a military check point, marking the start of the ascent to the plateau, was a reminder of the continued importance of retaining control over the interior. Once our passports and identity cards had been inspected and approved we were given the green light to continue; almost immediately the wadi narrowed and disappeared between sharp-angled folds in the vertical rock walls that surround the fractured mountain.

The newly made gravel track gravitated between rock structures rearing to infinity; one leaning in towards the plateau, the other tilting sideways on reminding me, once again, of the 19th century explorer's vision of the limestone mountain bursting opening like the petals of a gigantic flower. A landscape that must have posed some interesting conundrums for road planners and road workers alike and proved disastrous for a truck we caught sight of: upside down, it was hanging from a tree, growing from the precipitous cliff-face.

For the next hour we climbed and zigzagged uphill leaving a great trail of red dust in our wake; rounding hairpin bends of slippery sandstone, with vertical sides plummeting out of sight, stunning views across mountain ridges and down into the Sumail Gap presented themselves; these tantalising snapshots appeared and just as swiftly disappeared as we swerved to take the next bend before twisting and growling into action once again. Road warnings, at the start of the trail, included: 4WD only/low gear/headlights on. The wisdom of the advice struck home when we came face to face with an oncoming dust ball, encircling a Toyota truck, and skidded to a halt within a hair's breadth of a drop to infinity.

By the time we reached the hotel, to compensate for a dramatic drop in temperature, we were pulling on layers of clothes. The one adequate sweater we had between us – belonging to Richard – was loaned to shivering me. Although on this visit, in late November, temperatures didn't fall below eight degrees, they can drop to minus five in winter; below zero temperatures and snow for Christmas are not unexceptional. On the other hand, summer temperatures do not exceed 30 degrees with no more than 25% humidity. The Mediterranean-type climate, plus the annual summer rainfall, averaging 300 millimetres, has made farming in this region unique for The Arabian Gulf. Renowned for the cultivation of summer fruits on mountain terraces, villagers grow peaches, apricots, figs, grapes, plums, almonds, walnuts and pomegranates. Weaving sheep's wool and goat's hair and the production of rose water from pink roses, using ancient techniques, are inherited occupations.

Fronted at each end by a domed entrance, the single storey hotel promised both comfort and the simplicity we preferred. Like a window in the sky each blue glass dome was embellished with scenes from the natural world. The warm welcome we received and the extraordinary surroundings made it difficult to believe in the way of life that had existed on this plateau just forty years ago. Before the loss of his kingdom, Suleiman bin Himyar, the unchallenged and tyrant King of Nebhania, stalked about his domain asserting his power. His dominance and reputation as a womaniser did him no favours with the people from the surrounding settlements.

As far back as memory takes them people from the villages 'tumbling' from the plateau have taken their produce by foot and on donkeys, on a journey of several days, to the markets in Nizwa. Now, the main settlement has graded roads, electricity, modern houses, a school, banks and shops; the ultimate luxury was, without doubt, the possession of a 4WD Toyota pick-up truck to take owners and friends to Nizwa and back in a matter of hours.

Donkeys, the earlier and alternative form of transport, are now free to wander about the plateau enjoying their newfound leisurely existence. In the weeks before the final assault on the plateau, platoons of the sultan's forces took up positions on craggy mountain peaks overlooking the stronghold. To keep them supplied with water and food three hundred donkeys were brought over from Somaliland. A useful legacy for the villagers at that time.

The following morning, armed with a hand-drawn map from the hotel, we set off past the military camp at Qatana through a winter landscape of scattered rocks bejewelled with hundreds of sea fossils, thorny shrubs and gnarled bare trees. This surrealistic and even hostile landscape contrasted with the green terraced fields of cliff-side settlements. Each time we stopped to admire a view it was apparent that the plateau ended on all sides in deep wadis, chasms or vertical cliff edges and was overlooked by the impressive peaks that surround it.

We knew we had arrived when the track ended abruptly at a dry stone wall. Over staggered hillsides, terraced fields of green and gold fell from the mud-walled former homes of the people who worked them. One village stood out. While the majority were perfectly camouflaged to melt into the background – as if celebrating its presence – this one was painted white. While we were taking this in, it struck us that the complete absence of forts and castles, so prominent in the foothills of the mountains, was testimony to the natural security and safety provided by the landscape.

We guestimated that the settlement immediately opposite, was the recently abandoned village of Bani Habib – the village we hoped to visit. We had learned, from hotel staff, that although some villagers started moving out as soon government housing on the plateau was provided, others resisted and that the final exodus, of an elderly couple from Bani Habib, had taken place just weeks ago. Villages may have been abandoned but the same is not true of the orchards and fields on the slopes around them; the people return to tend and harvest the trees and crops. At that very moment, an elderly man with a kindly face drew up in his Toyota pick-up.

'*Salaam,*' he called, after depositing a bag of fertilizer at the roadside.

'Come!' he instructed as if he knew of our intentions. Beckoning us to follow he set off down a flight of steps leading into the steep-sided wadi. Pausing at the bottom, he pointed to the row of stone houses, set into the hillside, opposite.

'*Ahlan wa sahlan,*' (welcome) he said. Then raising his hand in a farewell gesture he set off along a track between a row of fruit trees.

'*Shukran.* Thank you,' we called after his departing figure.

At the foot of the steps, a *falaj* of flowing water – channelled through an orchard – was ashen white in winter sunlight. Handfuls of dead leaves shivered and rustled in the breeze – a ghostly reminder of the past while branches tipped with tight bud-nodes promised new life. It was the perfect setting for an encounter with an ibex or even a leopard. Finding I was alone, I looked anxiously over my shoulder before hurrying through a vine trellis to catch up with Richard only to find him crouching, camera focused a tumble of rocks. Then I saw it. The tail end of a snake protruding from the rock pile.

'Side-winder,' was his explanation. 'You can see its trail. Over there!' he directed, pointing towards some twisting runnels in the sand. 'Won't come out now. Prefers darkness,' he added ruefully as he switched off his camera.

Leaving the snake in peace we followed a trodden uphill pathway to the lower houses of the settlement. Deserted rooms, resonant with the recent past, had shuttered windows overlooking the hillside – providing perfect views for families to admire their crops and fruit trees; watch the comings and goings of neighbours and give warning signals of the presence of strangers or predators. The rasping of dead leaves, water running along the *falaj* and the haunting cry of a bird were magnified in the still air.

The plateau had more tracks and places to explore than we had time for. Whatever direction we chose we were surrounded by jagged peaks and turrets of rock, some rising to over 10,000 feet while vertical rock walls fell dramatically, from our feet, to the wadis and plains below. On a rocky outcrop, against a vertical cliff face, sunlight and shadow had conspired to create the perfect profile of a sombre faced Indian. Focusing my camera I called to Richard to stop. On this occasion, there was more drama to come. It was early evening and we were following a narrow track towards a lookout point, on the edge of the plateau, just as a black predatory cloud was inching its way towards the fast sinking sun.

'Grab you camera!' Richard called, screeching to a halt and wedging the Musso against the rock wall.

Scrambling from the vehicle we stood, silent and spellbound, to watch the drama unfurl: suspended between a dark cumulus layer overhead and black serrated mountain peaks below, a night-dark cloud was fringed a blinding silver-white by the hidden sun. Above, the sky turned molten gold, below deep sienna. Then, as the dazzling globe slipped behind the black edge of the mountain ridge, the sky erupted deep, deep red. It was like standing on the edge of the world.

South of Wahiba Sands

Duqm, Qahal, Khor Ghawi

As we jolted and bounced some 250km over dried out wadis and inhospitable gravel plains we focused on the curvaceous outline of the Wahiba Sands growing and then receding before us. After an early start we had reached Nizwa by 2.30, completed the remainder of the journey through the Sumail Gap towards Izki, then headed south and inland to Sanaw before sunset; this gave us the head start we wanted to tackle the off-road section to Filim that would take us past the impenetrable barrier formed by these magnificent dunes of sand.

180km from north to south and 80 from east to west, the dunes climb to 100 metres; woodlands stretching along the western and eastern margins are home to former wandering but now largely settled Bedouin tribes. Where the sands reach the sea rich fishing grounds are exploited by local people, who continue to live in small *barasti* dwellings along the coast as their forerunners the *Ichthyophagi* did in centuries past.

For hour upon hour a heat mirage dissolved the graded road ahead and behind us. It was as if we were travelling in space. The increasingly distant outline of dunes, fringed by a line of trees on one side and the equally distant cliff-edge of a limestone ridge on the other, was all that the eye could focus on to bring relief from the vast emptiness of our surroundings. With no more than one brief stop, after crossing the border at Buraimi, we were tired and we were hungry and our plan to find a sheltered camping spot was not materialising.

In vain, I searched the map and then the horizon for a change in terrain. As daylight and our hopes faded Richard pulled onto the roadside among hillocks of gravel and sand; while he collapsed onto the stony floor I set about erecting the tent, all the while vowing to myself 'never again' and wondering why we undertook punishing journeys instead of taking the five-star breaks that our friends in the Emirates indulged in. Almost immediately my question was answered.

The descending sun had dissolved and melted into a band of fire on the horizon. Exactly opposite, the full moon, swollen and glowing copper red, rose majestically into a star-studded sky lighting our surroundings in ethereal light. In this magical ambience, tumblers of warm red wine added piquancy to a hastily prepared supper of bread, cold chicken and tomatoes; then, as darkness thickened, we prepared for an early night.

Whether our bodies were now adjusting to the heat or we were too weary to notice we couldn't decide. We slept soundly. Awake at first light, I was aware of an incredible stillness. Unzipping the door flap I gazed in wonder.

'Wow! Mist. Thick mist.' I called to the prostrate form beside me.

'That,' a drowsy voice began. 'That is how desert creatures survive. They drink the dew that settles on plants and trees and rocks.'

Following that astute explanation, the owner of the voice turned over and pulled the sleeping bag over his head. I decided to follow suit. We took our time resting then making and drinking tea while waiting for the sun and a light breeze to lift the mist and dry the tent. The reward – the appearance of two gazelles. They viewed us curiously for some minutes before disappearing as quickly as they had appeared, giving just sufficient time to capture fleeting images on camera.

Apart from an imperious eagle, watching us from a roadside rock-pile, we could boast of seeing nothing to break the monotony of the gravel plain surroundings on our journey south; as hour, after monotonous hour passed we understood the absence of other travellers. Finally, the appearance of low hills and stretches of *sabka* – salt-flats – signalled a change, and then a small roadside filling station provided fuel and directions across mudflats towards the headland and bay of Ras Duqm.

It was on the track past Duqm that we suddenly came upon isolated outcrops of rock that appeared to resemble the contours of people and creatures – so much so that curiosity demanded we stop. Close up they were even more remarkable: to my imagination, and not for the first time, some appeared trapped and struggling to be free as if caught and solidified in a lava flow. In fact, the entire place resembled a unique sculpture park with larger than life forms strangely reminiscent of surreal Henry Moore-type sculptures in an equally surrealistic landscape.

Finally, the white cliffs of a headland, guarding a horseshoe bay, signalled our approach to the coast. On our left, low-lying mudflats, with literally hundreds of wading birds, stretched into the distance: spoonbills, herons and gulls were easily identifiable; the immediate shoreline was crowded with modern fibreglass fishing boats while a line of dhows, anchored in the bay, stretched to the pointed headland. It was a relief to be out of the vehicle and to feel soft white sand underfoot. Before us the stretch of beach, separating two bays, was no longer smooth but crowded with pointed domes of sand.

'Ghost crab towers,' Richard enlightened me. 'Males build them to attract females.'

We wandered across mudflats sending the nearest birds wheeling into flight. They circled and settled at a safe distance from the intruders. Just minutes later, from among tidal deposits of seaweed and debris, Richard retrieved and thoughtfully inspected what appeared to be a carefully shaped rock.

'Whale's vertebrae,' was his considered response as he offered it to me.

My surprise and pleasure could not have been greater if he handed me a huge desert diamond. In fact, it had diamond shaped sides, some 20cm across at the widest point; the base was flat while, at the top, a handle-like projection was marked with a neat round opening that once held the nerve cord. Although I knew that whales, dolphins and turtles were frequent visitors to these shores I had never imagined such a find. It was strangely moving to be holding part of the skeleton of one of the gentle giants that had once swum close to this beach.

Richard had a sixth sense for finding invaluable and interesting objects, as well as locating hidden wildlife in all its forms. On the first day of our present trip, in the shade of an acacia, on a desert plain we stopped for a coffee break. While my mind was bent on more practical things, Richard was busy investigating and photographing a lizard in the tree's upper branches; when I reminded him that his coffee was getting cold he opened his hand to reveal a small copper object he had found beneath the tree.

Fashioned from a single piece of copper, it had the unmistakeable appearance of a cigarette holder; the gentle curve of its length – some 9 cm – was held and decorated by delicately interwoven concentric copper bands, with a smooth wider band marking the mouth piece. A central motif of a flower head, with six petals, was in place between the bands. Apart from some minor indentations, its condition was good. In fact, this tiny and beautifully worked copper object had the distinct look and feel of something genuine from a past way of life. If it were a holder for some form of tobacco, who was the owner and what did he smoke? Like the whale's vertebrae, the origin remains an enigma – a memento from Oman and its fascinating past.

Sidarah and Nafun are just two of a number fishing settlements along this coastline; bordered by the inhospitable desert plains of Jiddat al Harasis and cut off from each other by headlands, these villages are more remote and inaccessible than those in the heights of the Jebel Akhdar; their advance into the modern world remains limited to the acquisition of fibreglass fishing boats and, for some, the possession of a pick-up truck. The people may be poor and unused to visitors but, on occasions, when we approached them they were eager to help, especially when it came to finding a place. They spoke no English and our Arabic – limited to pleasantries and greetings – wasn't much help. All we had to do was show them a picture or name a place and they responded by using sign language or jumping into our vehicle to act as a guide.

On this occasion, when it was understood that we were looking for Sidarah, our guide accompanied us by balancing on the step of the Musso, outside the driver's door; with a grin, he demonstrated that knocking on the roof was the signal to stop. Arriving alongside a *barasti* settlement, with washing strung across thorn bushes, the signal was given and he hopped down. Waving him goodbye and intent on finding a camping spot, we followed a track towards the coastline, trundled across several adjacent wadis finally coming to a rock bowl, protected by a half-circle of jagged hills and overlooking the sea. On one side a magnificent headland – with a face chiselled by wind and waves, like the figurehead on the prow of a ship – was silhouetted against the sky.

Tempted to explore, we set off dodging incoming waves and clambered round a jagged peninsula into a wide empty bay. Fear of being cut-off by the incoming tide sent us scurrying back just as the sun dipped behind the headland. Minutes later, the copper disc of the full moon rose over the sea. Pure magic.

First light. The sea was a silver strip humming with a line of fishing boats, moving across the water like birds in flight. Within minutes heavy mist rolled inland, chilling the air as it slowly and purposefully engulfed us and the entire the coastline, before turning and rolling back over the sea to smother the rising sun.

From Sidarah, the coastal track took us to the fishing village of Nafun – memorable for rows of shining fibreglass boats adorning a sweep of white sand – while abandoned traditional wooden boats lay disintegrating beneath overhanging cliffs. Further along the coast, beyond the mist clad limestone stack of Hamar an Nafur, we hoped to find the inland lagoon of Khor Ghawi. Stretching for six kilometres, Khor Ghawi was the planned high-point of our visit to the east coast. Separated from the sea by a sandbar, the lagoon is famous for algae turning its waters and wintering flamingos pink: the plumage colour so vital in mating flamingos. What is more, our off-road guide recommended the bar as an excellent place both for camping and bird watching. It sounded too good to be true.

We set off across the Jazir Plain, an eagle hovering overhead; then through a heat haze, between intermittent patches of thorny scrub, we were surprised by the sudden appearance and disappearance of gazelles as they took off with incredible lightness and speed. The shade beneath a lone acacia tree was the invitation to stop for a picnic lunch. Intense heat and suddenly ticks all over us sent us scurrying to the Musso to pick them off. Finally, a row of white flat topped cliffs marked the edge of the plain. From this point we dutifully followed guide-book instructions to pass the village of Qahal and 'take any one of a number of tracks towards the coast to the lagoon (5km)'.

Somehow, it all went horribly wrong. The sea was glinting tantalisingly beyond hummocky sand-hills and there were numerous tracks criss-crossing the area but each one we chose led us on a convoluted route and back to where we started. We could not find a way to the beach. Giving up on the guide-book we decided to try local knowledge; heading back to a collection of *barasti* dwellings, we remembered passing en route, we chanced upon a local fisherman.

Sign language and a hand-drawn map did the trick. The man pointed to a bottle of water. Payment made, he hopped into his pick-up and beckoning us to follow drove ahead on a circuitous route until the tip of the sand-spit and the ocean were in sight. Raising his arm in a farewell gesture, he turned and took off in a haze of smoke. Engine off, we paused for a while absorbing the silence and the sight before us. The lagoon was pink but, after the long hot summer, the water was receding and one lonesome flamingo was picking its way through the shallows. Then, a shushing of wings. Over our heads, a flock stretched in flight across gossamer sky.

Back to the guidebook; with romantic notions in mind we set off driving along the coastline, following the six kilometre length of the sand bar, searching for the elbow and a point of entry. Eventually, coming upon an abandoned boat we followed tracks across tufted hillocks of sand onto the bar and started making our way along the inner edge of a line of dunes. Within minutes the sand became alarmingly deep and soft; to find an easier and firmer passage we knew we had to cross the dunes to the coastal side. As the Musso reached the crest it growled and juddered to a halt. The sun was setting and we weren't going anywhere. A cursory inspection revealed that not only were the wheels deeply embedded but the entire body was resting on sand.

Travel-weary and feeling mildly suicidal I joined Richard; knee deep in sand we scooped armfuls from under the vehicle until a clear passage showed beneath the chassis. We then set about clearing sand from in front of and behind the tyres; finally, with an assortment of driftwood wedged as far under the tyres as we could manage, we felt we had a chance of escape. The engine roared and pieces of wood cracked and flipped skywards as they took the vehicle's full weight. Moments later, all four wheels gripping and slipping and dispersing driftwood and sand on all sides, we trundled free. We continued driving along the beach, on the seaward side of the bar, searching for a spot to park the vehicle and put up the tent. But now it was all too clear that the incoming tide reached to the edge of dunes. What is more the entire dune area, above the tide line, was completely covered in pyramidal sand-hills.

'Ghost crab towers.' Richard reminded me. 'A colony.'

It was obvious that camping on the spit was neither viable nor safe. Somehow, Richard navigated a turn and began re-tracing the route. By now the sun was down, the moon was up, the tide was coming in and we were becoming increasingly anxious to find a safe crossing beyond the reach of the tide. Headlights full blaze, Richard was attempting to dodge between ghost-crab towers, while displaced frantic crabs scurried for their lives.

'There!' I shouted as our headlights picked out the abandoned boat and track pointing inland; alongside the track we found what appeared to be a vehicle turning point: a flattened area looking firm enough and large enough for the tent and vehicle. Relieved, we set up our tent and took our collapsible chairs onto the beach. Mugs of coffee in our hands, we sat under the full moon marvelling at the silver spread of sea and sky and the capacity of the human spirit for recovery. At that moment, Richard shone his torch onto the beach. My heart lurched. We were not alone.

Literally, hundreds of crabs crowded the beach. Momentarily mesmerised by the spotlight, they were motionless. Richard switched off the torch. As if joined at the hip, they set off on a sideways dance, moving en masse across the beach. Suddenly it became clear just why they are called ghost crabs. The entire army was in motion, silently gliding over moonlit sand so that the beach itself appeared to be on the move. Shining his torch in the opposite direction, Richard then turned it off and we watched a repeat performance. Unnerved, I turned to examine our tent. It too was surrounded. We were marooned in the centre of a colony of ghost crabs performing a moonlight ritual.

Sunrise over the sea; flamingo silhouettes stretched against pale sky and a lone ghost crab, suffering the indignity of being dragged from beneath his tower. This was the scenario before me as I crawled from the tent. In a state of shock, the sand-freckled crab remained where Richard placed it, holding a statuesque pose while his portrait was taken. He then underwent the further ignominy of being washed in the sea in readiness for a second portrait. Finally, unharmed and left to reclaim his freedom, he beat a hasty retreat.

Morning looked good but, after camping for three nights and travelling for four days, all our ice had melted and supplies were running out, deteriorating or undergoing profound changes. Bananas and tomatoes had become soggy breeding grounds for various moulds. The contents of a carton of long-life milk had reached a stage somewhere between yoghurt and cheese; when I removed the lid from a plastic bottle of fruit juice it exploded louder than the cork pulled from a bottle of champagne. Deciding to veer on the side of caution rather than enterprise, I emptied the contents.

There was neither the time nor did we have supplies to sustain us on planned visits to the volcanic rocks and unspoilt beaches of Ras Madrakah, or the white limestone canyon of Shuwaymiyah with promised sightings of hyena, ibex, oryx and gazelles. On a more practical level we had been unable to find bread of any variety in a nearby village and a diet of dates and camel milk did not appeal. To reach our planned destination of Salalah, we had to travel some 400km across the desolate gravel plain of Jiddat Harasis. 'Allow half a day' the guide-book advised. Sustained by the thought of ablutions, food and a night of comfort at the Holiday Inn, in tropical Salalah, we set off.

Land of Frankincense

I will get me to the mountain of myrrh, and to the hill of frankincense.
- Song of Solomon

Jiddat Arkad. The very sound of the name suggests something bleak and without life. In fact, the only form of life apparent on this desolate overheated plain, crossing southern Oman from the Arabian Ocean to the dunes and plains of the Empty Quarter, were nodding donkeys, gas flares and the occasional truck criss-crossing between the gas and oil stations of Shelim and Marmul. After a fuel stop at a road-side filling station, we negotiated a route across an escarpment; on either side, occasional flat topped ridges marked our passage until we headed inland across the Jiddat Arkad Plain for the start of an uncomfortable and long ride through an empty, endless landscape that shimmered before and around us like a great void of water. I lost count of the bone shaking hours; then, just when we thought things couldn't get worse, they did. We had a puncture.

The heat from above and beneath was such that the only way in which I could assist Richard, who was either crouching or lying on hot gravel while changing the tyre, was by standing over him with a sun-shade in one hand and a bottle of water in the other. Then, in answer to my prayers, an Angel of the Lord drew alongside in a Toyota pickup; without hesitation the kindly Omani insisted on driving ahead of us to a – in the middle of nowhere – makeshift, desert garage to get the tyre fixed. Thanking our guardian angel, we sipped warm water while a temporary repair was carried out. Just one hour later we were victims of puncture number two. We had already used the allocated 'half a day' to cross the plain; we estimated another 160km to the exit and start of the tar road and we had no working spare tyre. Apart from distant images of remnants of the British army on exercises in the desert, we encountered no other travellers on the desolate track from Marmul to Thumrait.

It was as the route began to wind its way downhill that the occasional wandering camel and an increasing number of dry wadis, decorated with thorny acacia, provided the first signs of life. Finally, Thumrait and the miracle of a tar road. We were truly bone shaken and so was the Musso. In fact, the smooth road surface revealed that the spare tyre had developed a serious wobble. The Musso was suffering from a severe limp. Consoling ourselves that Salalah, civilisation and help were less than 80km away we focused on the changes of scene that were now unfolding as we began the climb into the Jebel Qara.

On the landward side, this mountain chain that separates desert from sea, is as barren and brown as the Hajar. Then, as we crossed the watershed to begin our descent to the coastline, it was as if a curtain had been drawn back. The ocean-facing mountains were a life-saving green. Fed by monsoon rains, green interlocking spurs unfolded into the distance. That was only the start: crossing the plain at the foot of the mountains and approaching the coast, we found ourselves in a tropical haven of plantations of coconuts, papayas, mangoes and bananas.

As the sun dropped below the horizon we were congratulating ourselves on surviving the journey and anticipating the long awaited, pre-booked night of comfort at the Holiday Inn. There was a surprise in store. We were late arriving. Our room had been given to soldiers from a platoon of the British army. Stationed somewhere on the wastes of the Jiddat Arkad they were allocated recovery periods at the Holiday Inn. Panic was replaced by relief. Not only had we been saved from another overheated night under canvas but we had been upgraded to the Hilton on the other side of town. We were in for 5 star comfort.

We may have looked like down-and-outs but as we signed in at the Hilton, not an eye-brow was raised. Greeted and treated like royalty, we were then left to enjoy the unadulterated luxury of hot water, fluffy towels, exquisitely clean cool sheets on exquisitely comfortable beds and room service at the touch of a button. If this hotel was 5 star, then it was the sort of five star that we approved of: luxury without interference. Memories of sharing the beach at Qahal with a colony of ghost crabs, on the previous night, seemed like a clip from somebody else's life.

The day started with some 5 star attention for the Musso: new tyres and wheel balancing before heading east through tropical plantations; stopping briefly to buy bananas and coconuts – at just one of many fruit stalls lining the coastline – we continued across an increasingly desert-like coastal plain to the fishing settlement of Taqah. Here, too signs of progress were evident: the beach was crowded with fibreglass boats. Traditional vessels, constructed from wood and held together with coconut fibre instead of nails – abandoned, along with the craft of making them – were disintegrating into the sand. Some traditions continue: the beach was glittering with the reflections from hundreds of sardines, drying in the sun to be used as fodder for the cattle and camel farms of the Jebel Qara. As we continued our eastward journey the plain narrowed and spurs from the mountains projected into the sea forming natural harbours and headlands, sheltering pristine bays of pure white sand.

A brief detour into the foothills of the mountains to Wadi Darbat ended abruptly opposite a sheer wall of limestone, the surface worn into hollows and intricate shapes; during the monsoon, cascading floodwaters thunder 100 metres to the wadi floor. Today, the wadi was silent but evidence of life surrounded us: a weaver bird's intricately woven honey-coloured nest, hung from the branch of flowering tree; tiny orange butterflies flitted among scented blossoms; meanwhile

Richard was busy focusing his camera on a blue long-legged spider hovering over its perfectly executed web.

During the monsoon water, from the falls, flows to the sea via Khor Rori. 2,000 years ago this ancient creek was the port for the bulk of the trade in frankincense from the Dhofar region. We followed a track through the ruins of an ancient civilisation that led to a headland, overlooking the creek.

Control of the incense trade and its routes was such a coveted prize that, in the first century BC, the King of Shabwa sent a group of colonists to establish a port close to the source of the frankincense. They discovered the splendid Y-shaped creek of Khor Rori and there, on the cliff, they built the city of *Sumhuram*: The Great Scheme. The palace-cum-port is reputed to have been the home of the Queen of Sheba, who once ruled over the entire Hadhramaut kingdom, including Dhofar (Southern Oman). Centuries ago, from this small bay, boats and rafts took frankincense to Qana, 640km down the coast to, what is today, Yemen on the first stage of a journey to the bazaars of Damascus and the Temples of Rome.

A further 66km took us to Marbat, another important frankincense port and once home to wealthy merchants. The renovated former homes, noted for carved doors and windows, have been carefully crafted to capture the architecture of the past. The settlement was quiet and still in afternoon heat making it difficult to grasp that in the late 1960s, Marbat had been the centre of the Dhofar Rebellion: communist guerrillas from Yemen were fighting to take over the region: a movement that was put down by British Special Air Service, requested and backed by the Omani government.

From 1968-1970, Sir Ranulf Fiennes served as captain in the army of the sultan, commanding a reconnaissance force of Omani volunteer soldiers – none of whom spoke a word of English – to assist in taking and keeping control in the region. In an interview with The Independent: *My Life in Travel* (February 2005) – when Fiennes was asked what place from his travels had seduced him – his unhesitant response was:

Oman. I spent two and half years in Dhofar and it was utterly unspoilt. There were people who hadn't seen non-Dhofarians before. I found the area to be the loveliest place on earth.

Furthermore, he declared that his dream trip was to fly to Muscat, catch an internal flight to Salalah, rent a 4x4 and then take a two week self-drive tour of southern Oman.

We, too, had a dream of more leisurely travel in the region. Just now we had to make the most of what was left of the remaining 36 hours, at our disposal. The scene before us endorsed the belief that today serenity rules over Marbat: fibreglass fishing boats lined the village wharf and the air was filled the haunting cries of gulls.

The coastal road, linking small fishing villages, took us to the turn-off to access another remarkable mausoleum. Famed for its Yemeni-styled, twin-domes, the tomb was built over the grave of Bin Ali, a descendant of the son-in law of the

Prophet Mohammed; Bin Ali set up a *madrassa* – religious school – in Marbat and died there in 1161. Enhanced by austere desert-like surrounds, this distinctive twin-domed tomb stands guard over a cemetery where engraved headstones, with crenellated tops, mark the position of raised graves – dramatically different from the unadorned anonymous Islamic graves and grave yards we had come across in the Emirates. In terms of medieval architecture, Ben Ali's tomb, like the mausoleum of Bibi Maryam, is unique and captures the imagination.

By mid-afternoon we were heading back to Taqah for the start of a round trip into the Jebel Qara. Known as *jabali*, the mountain people have their own distinctive style of dressing – a wrap around sarong-type garment and head band – speak their own dialect and are rarely seen without a stick and a gun. Their complex ancestry includes Hamitic Cushites from Egypt and Semitic Qara from Ethiopia – hence the Qara Mountains; travelling by way of Yemen they were part of the Joktanite invasion. The book of Genesis states that descendants of Joktan – himself a descendant of Shem and son of Noah – advanced as far as Yemen and those, under the prince of Ophir, eventually reached the mountains of Sephar – now Dhofar. A past that has created reverberations within the region.

Nevertheless, young *jabali* are increasingly becoming integrated into the modern ways of Salalah and hill farmers are succumbing to improved amenities. Modern houses replace the original circular houses made from stone, while pick-up trucks, farm machinery and tar roads make life easier.

On the ascent, round wooded hillsides, we discovered tracks that detour from the main road providing excellent lookout points across severed mountains and to the coastline – in particular to Khor Rouri, the ancient frankincense port we had visited that morning. We stopped to admire the view, alongside a grove of frankincense trees. Low and thorny, they have no pretensions to beauty. Fat, twisted branches, with crinkly leaves, spread out from a central base. The beauty and worth is revealed when silvery bark is pared off and drops of white resin ooze from the incision. Known as *luban* these drops are left to dry into semi-translucent globules of resin to be collected before the monsoon.

The importance of frankincense in religious ceremonies – the belief that its smoke carries prayers to heaven – reached its peak at the time of the Roman Empire; in the first century BC the Emperor Nero burned it by the ton at religious ceremonies. The Roman historian Pliny described it as, 'brilliant white and gathered at dawn in drops or tears in the shape of pearls'

These pearls were so prized that Alexander the Great planned to invade Arabia in order to control the trade; a plan thwarted by his death. Its extraordinary value at religious ceremonies is matched by its use to embalm corpses: the tomb of Tutankhamun released a perceptible aroma of frankincense when opened after 3,300 years. In addition to its healing powers which are said to range from psychological to physical, it was and is, a major ingredient in Arab cosmetics and perfumery.

I was fascinated to read – in the summer 2010 edition of *Exeter Living* magazine – that the use of frankincense in cosmetics is now acclaimed in the West:

Try adding a few drops of essential oil of frankincense to a bath to rejuvenate the whole body and best-selling frankincense nourishing cream can help to reduce fine lines and wrinkles.

In the past, when most of the frankincense caravans started out from Dhofar for Jeddah, the domestication and breeding of camels became pre-requisite for arduous journeys across parched desert plains and wastelands. After harvesting the frankincense, 150-400 camels were loaded up with 50 tons. One trail went north-east across the Arabian Peninsula to the Persian Gulf and another followed the Red Sea via Jeddah to Petra in Jordan. From there, the routes diverged to Alexandria and Mesopotamia.

When these ancient trade routes declined so did the ports and cities through which the traders passed. Just 4km to the east of Salalah, the ancient port of al-Baleed is currently being excavated. Once surrounded by a trench and defensive walls with gates in the west, south and east sides, this remarkable settlement, boasting rows of 148 rectangular pillars – similar to those found at the port of Sumhuram – is undergoing restoration.

The search for the legendary city of Ubar or *Irem* – the City of Pillars – has proved to be more elusive. Shown on Ptolemy's first map of Arabia and mentioned in the Bible and the Koran – according to legend, Ubar grew incredibly wealthy through its control of the frankincense trade and was known as: 'the finest city in Arabia, built like Paradise with pillars fashioned from gold …'

Legend also has it that because the people were decadent and had turned away from religion, God destroyed Ubar causing it to sink beneath the sands. Great Arabian explorers including Thomas, Philby and Thesiger sought Ubar. It eluded them and has continued to haunt and evade modern explorers; over the years, Ranulf Fiennes returned many times on archaeological digs attempting to unearth the lost city.

Then in 1981, satellite images picked up caravan routes in the desert which had been covered in sand. At first, excavations of a watering place near the main intersection of ancient caravan routes, 200km northwest of Sumhuram, on the edge of the Empty Quarter, seemed to confirm the truth of the existence of Ubar. However, further investigations demonstrated that the city – once the nexus of routes bringing the incense 90km north of Dhofar and thence in three directions across The Empty Quarter – was considered to have been a crossing and resting place but not a settlement. A decade later the undeterred Ranulf Fiennes believed he had succeeded in locating the one-time frankincense centre of the world. In the first year of the dig, archaeologist, Dr Yuris Zarins, traced much of what was believed to be the ancient city's walls and recovered over 3,000 artefacts.

The Ubar route is said to have been used to avoid the extortionate taxes demanded by the powerful Yemeni kingdom of Shabwa. Successive Yemeni kings decreed that all incense carrying caravans should travel by way of their capital and anyone attempting to leave without paying tax was executed. An effective deterrent. The Ubar Museum holds a variety of artefacts from around 2,000 BC which bear witness to the ancient traders who visited this region:

ceramics from Syria, Rome, Greece and even China, as well as stone tools used by settlers from 5,000 BC onwards.

Higher into the mountains we came across camels strolling freely over the road. Unperturbed by our presence, they ambled round and in front of the Musso ensuring that our progress was as leisurely as theirs. At an especially dramatic viewpoint, alongside a pyramidal ant hill, we pulled over to watch the red sun slide between distant mountain ridges.

The overriding sense of space and peace was one that we associated with Oman. A country that continues to move towards changing ways of life in the 21st century but with no sense of urgency; a country where past and present remain at ease with each other; a country that we had grown to love and hoped to return to. Tomorrow, was a different story: we planned to take the fast route by tar road from Salalah to Nizwa – eight hours if we were lucky – overnight in Nizwa and head back to Dubai, so that Richard could return to work on the following day.

Five Stars in Fujairah

A weekend for two at the recently opened, five star Meridien Hotel in Fujairah. This was Richard's reward, for his prize-winning portrait of a ghost crab, in the annual photographic competition run by Abu Dhabi, Natural History Group.

For convenience, we took the recently built tar road that cuts through the Hajar Mountains – an alternate and faster route than the customary track through Wadi Bih we used when camping or to reach the then one and only hotel in Fujairah: The Oceanic. With its port-holed windows, unspoilt beach, and off-coast diving facilities it had become a favoured weekend retreat. Now we were destined for Gold Star treatment. In spite of using the fast track, we were late arriving and swiftly diverted from the main reception area to the check-in desk reserved for Gold Star guests. Not only did we have Gold Star check-in but a Gold-Star bar as well. It was on the top floor with lovely views over the ocean but, apart from one other couple, intent on each other's company, it was empty and devoid of atmosphere. We retired to our Gold-Star room. Within minutes a succession of staff tapping on the door to check everything from the bar fridge, laundry, tea and alcoholic beverages to turning back the beds, drove us downstairs to the dining room.

The following morning, books in hand, we made our way to the pool-side hoping for a quiet read and swim. Music filled the air, drowning the sound of waves lapping onto the beach. The place was a hive of organised activities and the pool so bedecked with waterfalls, fountains, urns of flowers and decorative lights that swimming was impossible.

We exchanged 'what are we doing here?' glances, returned to our Gold-Star room, packed our bags and made our way to Gold-Star check-out.

'Arrived late, leaving early,' was the comment from the member of staff on duty.

'Back through Wadi Bih?' was Richard's rhetorical question, as we climbed into our beloved sand-crusted Musso.

Musandam

The Rhino's Horn Jutting up into Persia
December 2001

On one side a vertical wall of rock towered out of sight, on the other the rock wall fell away to the deep blue of the Gulf. Gouged into the side of the mountain the road wound round hairpin bends that, at times, followed natural folds in fractured walls of uplifted rock and, at other times, headed along paths bulldozed straight through the rock face. We swung round successive bends, one minute heading perilously towards the ocean and the next into the mountain wall. Overhead, great blocks of undercut stone balanced precariously on ledges. Below, smashed boulders littered the roadside – a warning of untimely avalanches. We were approaching Khasab, the capital of Oman's northern stronghold – just a few hours by road from Dubai.

Ruus Al Jibal – Peaks of the Mountains – is the Arabic name for this isolated mountainous peninsula. Situated at the northern extremity of the Hajar range, jutting into the narrow neck of the Arabian Gulf, the region – evocatively described by Philip Allfree as 'the head of a rhinoceros, with its nose poking into the Arabian Sea and its horn jutting up into Persia' – is known today as Musandam, a derivation of *Sanadin* or Anvil's Head, after a craggy islet at the peninsula's tip.

In the 16th century the Portuguese made Hormuz into a great trading centre, receiving pearls from Bahrain and the coastal towns, dates from Mesopotamia and incense from inland tribes. Today, this former stronghold of the Persian kings of Hormuz belongs to Oman and offers spectacular mountain scenery and a coastline of magnificent fiords, scattered with isolated villages accessible only by sea. Relatively unknown to the outside world and still in the early stages of organised tourism, Musandam remained wondrously unspoilt

Our objective was to reach the Golden Tulip Hotel before sunset. Set on a peninsula of rock, overlooking the Strait of Hormuz, the hotel's spectacular and isolated setting provided a luxury base for the steadily increasing flow of travellers. We were not new comers to Musandam; we had been regular visitors to the *Khasab*: a comfortable guesthouse with a central courtyard and swimming pool, fringed by a row of palms, silhouetted against a backdrop of mountains. We had enjoyed its informality and lovely setting. Now, that its solitary reign had been challenged by a new resort and the advent of tourism, it was under renovation. We couldn't complain. Sundowners on our balcony at the recently opened hotel, overlooking sea and mountains and sky – it was the perfect place to plan tomorrow's expedition.

The winding track, that took us from sea level through Wadi Khasab, continued on a steep zig-zagging course finally cresting a ridge that overlooked the wide bowl of the Sayh Plateau. Cradled within the mountains at 1,800 metres, rust-gold, ready for harvest fields, spread before us. Walled terraces of crops, cut into the hillsides, led down to a lake of green criss-crossed by fences dividing fields of wheat, alfalfa, onions and other root crops. A long tradition of trapping rainwater in cisterns for the cultivation of crops, as well as the ancient *aflaj* system of channelling water, is still used. From time to time – especially during the hot dry summer months – farmers, from the plateau, migrate to the coast to supplement their diet with harvested dates or freshly caught fish, returning to their mountain habitat in time to plant winter crops. Though many villagers have migrated permanently to larger coastal settlements, well-tended fields and some sizeable villas indicated the continuing presence of a successful and established farming community.

Our route into the mountains continued to wind uphill reaching to 1,980 metres at Jebel Harim. It was in this less than hospitable, yet magnificent rugged terrain we first noticed neat stone walls that marked the entrances to cave dwellings once inhabited by the Shihuh. An ancient mountain tribe, said to be descendants of prehistoric immigrants from India, they used caves or simple stone structures as shelters and to store their supplies of food. Feared by other tribal groups, as well as by sailors seeking shelter in rocky inlets on the coast, the Shihuh developed a reputation for fierceness.

On his mid-twentieth century travels in Oman, Ronald Codrai met and lived with members of the Shihuh. He believed their reputation was unjustified and that their fearsome behaviour was brought about by their own fear of potential enemies who threatened their frugal existence. It was the threat of attack that led them to remain out of sight exchanging eerie warning calls, which reverberated like the cry of wolves. When they appeared from the mountains brandishing *jirz*, distinctive traditional axes, it was to protect their families or meagre supplies.

Such was the isolation of the Shihuh that until a decade or so ago, when the convention still existed, if you wanted to approach a Shihuh village, you fired your rifle while some way off as a way of knocking on the door. The Shihuh people would look to see who was there before coming to greet their visitors. Nevertheless, their grunts and shrill calls, whether warning or celebratory, did instil fear. One story told is that a group of Shihuh sent to help the Sultan's forces against the imam's insurgents in the late 1950s, so terrified local people with their calls that they were relieved of their duties and sent back to their mountain stronghold.

To this day, the older generation of Omani males walking the streets of Khasab continue to carry the small axe head, or *jirz* – a metre-long stick with a blade at the tip. Whether used as a walking aid or a tool for cutting or for protection, it is as much an Omani tradition in Musandam as the decorative curved dagger, the khanjar, is in the rest of Oman.

On the far side of Jebel Harim, we followed a narrow ridge that descended to the Rawdah Bowl, a lovely open valley scattered with acacia trees and home to people still living in traditional mountain villages, but with the undeniable asset of owning a pick-up truck or 4WD. Long before the sound of an engine can be heard reverberating through the mountains, a whirlwind of dust heralds its approach. We watched a dust ball bowling across the plain towards us on a lower track. At its closest crossing point to our own cloud of dust, a friendly arm was thrust through the open window to wave. The mountain ridge continued following the course of the deeply gouged Wadi Bih through the Hajar range to Fujairah.

Among the most outstanding views is one that looks down on a range of bare mountains, their sides marked by concentric bands of jutting rock like perfectly executed contour lines. Even more remarkable are the locations of ancient agricultural sites situated either at the very bottom of an apparently inaccessible wadi floor, or crowing an equally inaccessible hilltop. Oval in shape to accommodate their oval shaped surroundings, levelled sandy floors, outlined by neat stonewalls are a testimony to an abandoned way of life. Once, ancient tribes shared these mountains with the Arabian leopard. Today, the tribes have migrated and settled in more hospitable terrain and goats outnumber by far the few remaining critically endangered leopard.

We knew that the mountains were lived in by prehistoric tribes long before the arrival of the Shihuh and were intent on finding evidence of their lives. Just a few kilometres from Khasab on the coast road, we followed a track into a wadi leading to the village of Tawi. Opposite a natural well – *tawi*- from which the village has taken its name, stood a tumble of massive boulders. Right before us, on a smooth-faced wall of rock, was the legacy of rock art left by ancient people. Camels, boats and warriors or huntsmen on horseback were clearly marked and easily accessible from ground level.

Within minutes, we were surrounded by curious villagers. The younger girls spoke some English and pointed to the position of further engravings on rocks, not visible from the ground. I followed in Richard's wake as he climbed to a viewing point between precariously balanced boulders. Pecked with flintstone on rock walls the engravings confirmed prehistoric man's use of boats and horses for trade and travel. Equally remarkable and thought-provoking was the similarity between these engravings and those we had seen in the Jebel Akhdar, some two hours drive south of Muscat. Scenes of people hunting and warriors riding horses appeared identical to the petroglyphs before us now: confirmation that the same people travelled long distances through desert and mountains, and from Tawi continued their travels and trading by and from the sea.

On our return, we stopped to admire the shadowed outline of Khasab Fort. Overlooking an inlet and against a backdrop of barren mountains, it stands guard over the old settlement as it has done for centuries past. The irregular shape and appearance of the four corner towers and adjoining walls, built by the Portuguese in the seventeenth century, is supplemented by the massive central tower in the main courtyard. Like that of Nizwa Fort, the tower is believed to be of Persian origin and to predate the castle itself. Ceilings, filled in with plaited palm fronds and mud and supported by teak timbers brought from India, are just one more reminder of the trade and interchange of goods made easier by the fort's optimum coastal position. Once an essential supply point for dates and water for Portuguese trading ships, it has remained in constant use, serving as residence for the *Wali* – the local governor – and as a jail for prisoners, before becoming the museum that it is today.

Mist and clouds from the mountains greeted us on the following morning. Nevertheless, we were determined to take a dhow ride into one of the many isolated inlets on the coast.

A bay next to the port, quite literally filled with small speedboats, was a reminder that Khasab was and is an Iranian smuggling den. Sheep and goats are brought into this bay and exchanged for American cigarettes and electronic goods. On the return trip, assets wrapped in black plastic, the smugglers head back after dark, some 55km across the strait in their high-powered boats. Iranian coastguards, as well as other shipping, have to be avoided. With so many oil tankers, passing to and fro, the crossing is hazardous. Both Omanis and Iranians are said to be quite open about and to benefit from this 'illegal' trade.

Finally we located our dhow and, given the poor weather conditions, decided on a half-day trip into the nearby inlet of Khor Ash Sham. Ali, our skipper-cum-owner, a native of Kumzar, a remote village set in an isolated cove on the most northern tip of the peninsula, was familiar with every secret inlet in the fiords. A gentle and courteous man, he smiled and shrugged his shoulders when we asked if there was truth in the rumour that the people of his village were descendants of shipwrecked sailors. Traditionally a fishing village and isolated from outside human contact for thousands of years, the inhabitants still speak a language of their own.

'Today,' Ali said, 'my people speak Arabic and our language – some Persian, English, Portuguese, French. They have school, small hospital and electricity. To my village by boat, two hour.'

Furnished with Persian rugs and floor cushions, Ali's dhow was his prized possession. He treated us like honoured guests, offering us miniature glasses of hot sweet tea, water and fresh fruit. On a day trip, barbecued fish is served with salad and Arabic bread for lunch. In common with most converted dhows, an engine replaced sails and an upright coffin in the stern housed primitive but adequate toilet facilities.

Rolling mist and cloud continued to hold sway over mountains and fiords. Temperatures apart, it could have been Scotland or Norway itself. On sunny days, the crystal waters are so clear that coral and tropical fish can be seen from the deck. Then it is not unusual to be accompanied by turtles, reef sharks or dolphins, while many other exotic varieties of tropical sea-life can be seen while snorkelling. However, there was something mysterious and appropriate about the mist-clad *khors*, creating an atmosphere well suited to tales of smugglers and pirates who once hid in these secret inlets.

Isolated villages fringing the sound have taken strides into the modern world. Concrete square houses with satellite TV receivers replace the ruins of former stone-built homes that blend into the rugged background. Pylons, miraculously striding over mountain peaks, carry electric power to the village.

'Children have school in Khasab, by boat,' Ali explained, 'and water for village come by boat,' he added, pointing to a huge blue tank strategically stationed on the stony beach.

Our tour took us to a barren and isolated rocky outcrop. Situated in the inlet of Khor Ash Sham, on a bend on the tip of a remote peninsula invisible from the sea, it was the notorious Telegraph Island. A flight of worn stone steps led to the remains of stonewalls that marked the former British Telegraph Station. It was from this remote outpost that engineers passed the first telegraphic message from London to Karachi in 1865. The achievement took its toll on the engineers. Assigned to this barren outcrop for tours of duty lasting for six months, the men suffered from a form of isolation madness that became known as 'going round the bend' – a saying used, to this day, to describe the onset of varieties of madness.

As we left the inhospitable island, sunlight filtering through cloud gave shape to the mountains and depth to the water. A touch of magic was added when the resident school of dolphins broke the surface to greet us, and then escorted us back to the port.

One minute we were climbing a steep sandy track, and the next we crested a ridge and drew to a sudden halt. Below us, stretched between the arms of a ring of mountains, lay the aquamarine waters of a magnificent fiord. It was the sand spits and khors of the Musandam Peninsula and the adjacent coast that enabled pirates from the seventeenth to the nineteenth centuries to escape capture. Hiding in concealed inlets they fell upon their prey, escaping there again when chased by warships.

Today, great fingers of green merged with blue and reached between amber slopes to distant hidden coves that sheltered isolated villages, before opening to the jaws of the Indian Ocean. Before us lay Khor Najd, the only fiord accessible from inland and a photographer's dream. I knew that attempts to capture the sheer size and wonder of it were bound to fail. So it remains, imperfectly reproduced on film, a living memory of the magic of Musandam.

Villa amidst Dunes
February 2002

A villa, set among crested dunes; a desert garden, transformed into an oasis, attracting bulbuls, bee-eaters, desert larks and the occasional hoopee. Lizards of various sizes were completely at home as were geckos on the villa walls, both inside and outside. Scorpions, colonies of ants and mosquitoes were less welcome, but set up camp anyway. Finally, a family of carpenter bees made their home in the dead limb of a tree. The tree stump, along with a range of Omani date pots and drinking vessels, added artistic touches to the patio. This, our new home, was our final staging post in the Emirates.

Richard had been transferred from Sharjah to Dubai International Airport. Over the intervening years, since our first meeting and travels together, I was having increasing success as a travel feature writer for various Gulf-based newspapers and magazines. Thus, abandoning my students, along with Shakespeare, Virginia Woolf and other literary companions in their desert surroundings at the Cambridge High School, I took up residence with Richard in Mirdif, a new development in Dubai – so new that a network of roads led to a handful of newly built villas amidst a sweep of dunes.

Meanwhile, Richard had become the co-photographer for my travel features. In addition, he was my adviser and practitioner in all things technical and practical, including the setting up of a website to advertise 'Images of Arabia', a series of blank cards and mounted prints from our photographs that were on sale throughout the Emirates.

The transfer to Dubai had several advantages. Not the least was the upgrading in accommodation. Richard installed an irrigation system to transform our desert garden into an oasis; constructed vine trellises round the villa's huge windows; set up a birdbath for chattering bulbuls and a pole attached to the side of the house as a collection and look out place for visiting bee-eaters. A gap under the side gate was used by a desert lark, who came and went at his leisure. Jacaranda trees, bougainvillea, hibiscus and a grove of frangipani all contributed to a garden that was good to look at, though generally too hot to spend time in. Views over the eight foot surrounding walls to crested dunes satisfied our love of the wilderness. We had a new and lovely home and, for added excitement, Africa was on the horizon.

Unspoilt Coastal Islands, Umm Al Qaiwain

Al Badiyah Mosque, Fujairah

The Blue Souq, Sharjah

Jebel Al Faya (Fossil Rock)

Dhow at sunset, Dubai Offshore Sailing Club (DOSC)

Racing dhow, Umm Suqeim, Dubai

Racing camels, Nad al Sheba

Keeping in Touch, Al Awir

Camels on dune, Tawi Assaman

Racing camels, Tawi Murrah

Ruus al Jebel, Ras al Khaimah

Islamic graveyard, Fujairah

Round wind tower, Sharjah
Heritage Centre

Wind sculpted dunes,
Sweihan

Camel trail past Rustaq Fort

View to the fortified settlement of Bilad Sayt

Women in fields below Al Ghul

3rd Millenium Beehive Tombs, Al Ayn

Nakhl Castle, Jewel in Oman's Crown

Bimmah Sinkhole

Mausoleum of Bibi Maryam

Green Turtle feeding on sea grass

Sunset from the Saiq Plateau -
like standing on the edge of the world

View to the Sumail Gap from the Saiq Plateau

Flamingos at Sunrise, Khor Ghawi

Ghost Crab, Khor Ghawi

Rescue by a kindly Omani, Jazira Plain

Bin Ali's Yemeni-styled Tomb, Mirbat

Ancient Frankincense Port, Khor Rouri

Richard enjoying Ali's hospitality, Khor Ash Sham

Working dhow, Khasab

Shihuh shelter and look-out, Jebel Harim

Ancient rock-art, Tawi

Dramatic headland known as Hell's Corner,
Fish River Canyon

Fleeing ostriches, the only sign of life on the desert plain

Quiver trees mark the route across the desert plain

The utterly deserted landscape could have been Mars itself

Silhouettes of people climbing the ridge of Dune 45 at sunrise

Self rescue in deep, loose sand

Springbok, springing into action

The magic of elephants approaching a waterhole at sunset –
bathing and indulging their thirsts

A giraffe meets its reflection in the diminishing water of the pan

Oryx viewing us with regal indifference

Moringa tree, 'the upside down tree'

Entrance to Tsodilo Hills – believed, by the San, to be the place of the first creation

Ancient rock-art attributed to ancestors of the San Bushmen

View of Eagle Island Camp from the Cessna

Formidable hippos guarding the channel entrance

Elephant warning us to keep our distance

Malachite kingfisher, brilliant jewel of the reeds

Mighty and Adrienne taking a breather where lions swim to the island to hunt

Lioness, the morning after an elephant hunt, Savute Elephant Camp

Lions taking it easy after feasting on elephant flesh

Elephant at the water hole at sunset

High society wedding, Ghion Hotel, Addis Ababa

Musicians playing *krar* (lyre)

Solemn Orthodox priest

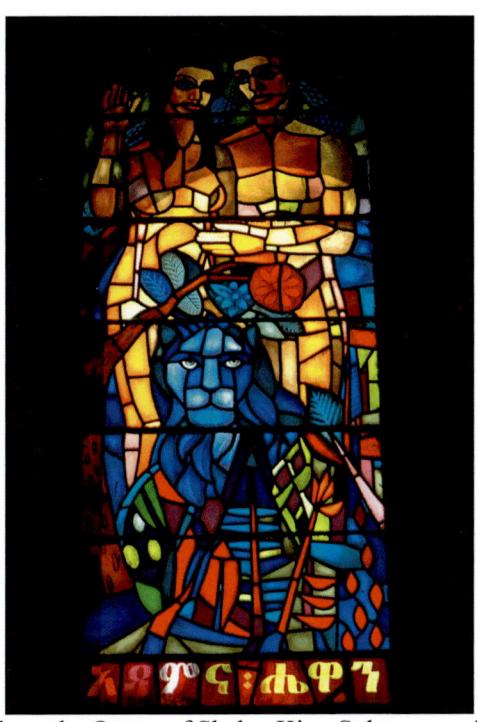
Stained glass window: the Queen of Sheba, King Solomon and the Lion of Judah

Lake Langano, men cutting reeds

The Guge Highlands: untimely breakdown overlooking Lake Abaya

Dorze women appear over the ridge

Mursi women with full size lip-plates posing for photographs

Mursi men armed with obligatory Kalashnikovs

Hamer woman with iron torques welded round her neck

Hamer man eating coagulated bull's blood

Abore village elder: former slave traders now peace-makers

Dassanech villagers gather hoping for money for photographs

Cattle waiting to drink at the Singing Wells of Borena

Borena men sing as they pass buckets of water from the well

People walking to the local market

Church bell, Adadi Maryam

Women leaving the rock-cut church of Adadi Maryam

Ancient stelae of Tiya: carved swords, each marked with a cross suggest a possible former boundary between the Christian north and Islamic south.

Aerial view of estuary of the Gambia River

Woman collecting oysters, Palm Grove Hotel, Banjul

Cashew nuts, Jinack Island

Mandinka woman caught between two worlds, Jinack Island

Jola women dancing at Sindola Camp

Kankurang: masquerade associated with Mandinka initiatory rites

Remains of European trading station, Kuntaur

Richard and Mark waiting to board Janjanburay Ferry

Alpha male chimpanzee

African Connections

*The British imperialist and entrepreneur,
Cecil John Rhodes had a dream of a railway running
from the Cape to Cairo – a dream
that was never fully realised*

Rhodesia

While travelling over the undulating veld of that part of Africa which bears his name, Rhodesia (Zimbabwe), Cecil John Rhodes had a dream to extend the fortune he had made in the Kimberley Diamond Fields of South Africa in newly discovered territory north of the Limpopo River. Rhodes envisioned a great corridor of British owned land, linked by a railway running from the Cape to Cairo, on the mouth of the Nile. In 1890, he occupied and established control over what was to become Rhodesia. The Union flag was raised over Fort Victoria (Masvingo), Fort Salisbury was established and named after the British Prime Minister, Lord Salisbury and Umtali (Mutare) was made the eastern headquarters on the new frontier with Mozambique. Richard's African beginnings in Umtali had their roots in Cecil Rhodes' dream.

Mozambique 1926

The opportunity to settle and work in acquired British territory persuaded Richard's maternal grandfather, Arthur Paul Proudfoot – son of the wagon train survivor – and his wife Annie Florence to give up their life on a farm in Mozambique, and to set up home in Rhodesia. A near quarter of a century later, a similar opportunity was taken by Richard Wilson Chapman. Returning to post-Second World War Britain after fighting the Japanese in Burma, Richard Chapman was keen to start a new life overseas. Work on the Southern Rhodesian Railways, in this now fast developing part of the British Empire, provided the answer. It was in Umtali, Southern Rhodesia in 1950, that he met and married Kathleen Florence, daughter of Annie Florence and Arthur Paul Proudfoot. Their firstborn child, Richard Wilson Chapman (2nd), arrived in 1951.

Umtali 1951-1980

Joan (Bekker), Richard's closest sibling, shares some glimpses into her brother's early life in Rhodesia and his love of the wilderness that was to stay with him for the rest of his days.

As children, we loved to visit our surviving grandparent, Annie Florence Proudfoot. Grandma Annie lived on 'The Plot' – the name we gave to the wood and iron house built by Grandpa on the plot of land given to settlers working for Southern Rhodesian Railways. The house was raised from the ground on stilts to protect it from termites and keep it cool. We soon discovered that termites were not the only insect invaders: a colony of wild African bees had set up home in the chimney. This was fine until one day, when the heat from the sun melted their honey. Suddenly, angry swarming bees were everywhere. Terrified, we all fled through the house to find places to hide. Sadly, the family cat became the victim of the bees' anger and was stung to death.

Inside, there was no fridge, only an old fashioned mesh-covered 'meat box' hanging in the pantry. A wood-burning stove served as the cooker, while the iron was operated by means of burning coals. A favourite place for family gatherings was on the verandah overlooking the garden. Shaded by avocado, mango and paw-paw (papaya) trees, it also housed a well and a long-drop toilet, dug by Grandpa. Best of all was the location; nestling at the foot of Murahwa Hill, with its caves, rock paintings and a spring, it was one of Richard's favourite haunts.

On one occasion, Dad arrived home from 'down the line' – the place we children were told he was when working on the railway. In his arms, he was cradling a red-brown furry bundle which turned out to be a lively eight week old Rhodesian Ridgeback/German Shepherd male pup. As he grew, the pup's favourite place was the kitchen, where he quickly developed a habit of stealing food, earning him the name of Pincher.

Richard and Pincher became constant companions, and were forever climbing Cross *Kopje* – a small rocky mountain with a large cross on top, a memorial to Rhodesians and Mozambicans lost in the First World War. Just a couple of miles from the house, the *kopje* could be seen from the kitchen window, and was the place the pair went on the lookout for wild birds. As a youngster, Richard would try to shoot the birds with his 'catty' (catapult), but more often than not, he had to use it to defend Pincher from attack by baboons.

Fishing was another of Richard's passions and Old Umtali Dam, a popular location. It was also the haunt of African Giant Toads, who took exception to their space being invaded. Richard would arrive home with hilarious tales of being chased by these twelve inch high aggressors. At other times, he rode his bike, loaded with camping gear, to meet up with friends and spend the weekend camping and fishing at Fern Valley Dam. They took no food, but relied on catching bream and cooking it on a stick over an open fire.

Hunting exploits extended to constructing a gun from a piece of conduit pipe and a wooden butt carved from a tree. The most dangerous and disapproved of activities were the making of gunpowder and setting up a target practice in the back garden. In his teenage years, Richard progressed to a pellet gun, snares and traps, and converted his bedroom into a collection place for taxidermied birds and small mammals. These were later donated to Umtali Museum. As an adult, binoculars and a camera replaced weapons and snares.

In 1980, when Southern Rhodesia became Zimbabwe and Robert Mugabe took power, the Chapman family decided it was time to make plans to leave Africa. Resigning from his position as an officer in the Royal Rhodesian Air Force, Richard became a Moses-like figure; he was instrumental in leading his 'tribe' into South Africa before making arrangements, over the years, to bring them to the safety of his father's original home in Blyth, Northumberland.

Tremors from the legacy of European, Arabian and Omani people trading and colonising in Africa were to surface from time to time on our African travels, as were those from Richard's more immediate African connections.

Dubai, November 2002

With the help of Judy Fell from *Africa Connection, Dubai*, preparations were made for a month long trip. The plan included return flights from Dubai to Johannesburg to collect a Land-Cruiser Camper (4x4) from *Ashton's Explore Africa/Self Drive*. Sadly, Zimbabwe was not an option, but neighbouring Namibia and Botswana were. Our intention was to travel in a loop through Namibia and Botswana, stopping at key places known for their history and/or outstanding natural features, as time and circumstance allowed. The climax of the journey was to arrive at Kruger National Park, South Africa, in time for the total solar eclipse on December 4th 2002.

South Africa

Nairobi, Johannesburg to the Augrabies Falls

The descent to Nairobi through towering cumulus clouds and falling rain, the sky full of circling swallows and hovering birds of prey, conjured strangely symbolic life and death images for the start of our impending journey. The airport itself, a shabby concrete two-storey building with flimsy doors, cluttered with heavy chains and locks, as if expecting violence, added to unsettling first impressions of Africa. Then as the connecting flight soared into swallow flecked sky, the image of the twin snow clad peaks of Kilimanjaro, thrusting through layers of towering cumulus cloud, conjured a wonderful sense of relief.

Arrival in Johannesburg brought further anomalies. Free of the airport's chaos, our taxi swung through jacaranda-lined streets: cascading mauve blossoms smothered graceful limbs reaching into peerless sky. Wide streets from wagon train days, and an absence of traffic created a sense of space as well as desertion, while the distinctive and elegant designs of Dutch buildings were offset by the unnerving presence of metal bars across windows.

Safely deposited at Ashton's, we were delighted to find our 'home on wheels' for the next month ready, waiting and fully equipped with all mod cons to sustain us throughout our travels. After a swift visit to a local store to stock up on food and drinks, with Richard at the wheel and me as chief navigator, we set off in the direction of Pretoria. Here too, jacaranda trees were in full bloom, bestowing an air of celebration on suburbia. Caught up in nose to nose traffic, we drove straight into the eye of the setting sun. Then, as the sun melted on the horizon, we headed for Buffelspoort in Magaliesburg Valley, our first overnight camp. Hunting and killing buffalo may have been sport for man but not much fun for buffalo that once lived and roamed in the region. Not surprisingly, there was not a buffalo to be seen, but the camp was spacious, set amongst huge trees and with upmarket toilet facilities – an excellent place for recovery and preparation for the next leg of our journey: a 400km drive that would take us to Upington on the Orange River.

Delareyville, Vryburg, Kuruman, Olifantshoek – names on a map that marked our route and evoked the history of trekking Boer settlers. Row upon row of eucalyptus trees replaced fragrant jacaranda, then a landscape, reminiscent of the Australian outback gradually gave way to open farmland, dotted with the distant tower-like forms of massive grain silos. Each pinpointed an isolated cattle ranch, connected one to the other and the outside world by a single rail track. Fortified by a roadside lunch break, we arrived at the small and deserted settlement of Delareyville, and made a brief stop to photograph its grey stone church.

It wasn't until we were approaching Kuruman that the monotony of the landscape was broken by a chain of hills. Then, *Olifantshoek* – Elephants' Corner – named after the tusk of an elephant used for payment for the farm on which the town was built. Today the settlement is memorable for a sign pointing to the graves of the victims of Galeshewe's War, one of a series of battles over land between settlers and native people – on this occasion, between the inhabitants of the old Transvaal and the Tswana tribe. Described as an ill-defined and poorly protected area of the northern Cape in the mid-eighteenth century, the region also had a reputation as the stomping ground of cattle rustlers, gunrunners and river pirates.

From a stronghold near Upington, fierce Korana chiefs rustled cattle from all across the region. Then in 1879, Sir Thomas Upington, the first Attorney General of the Cape Colony, visited the region to establish a police station which, in the accepted colonial manner, he named after himself. With this potted history in mind and estimating that Upington, on the banks of the Orange River, was still some 165km away, we had just decided to look out for a camping spot when we chanced upon Mala Lodge.

A lakeside setting under huge trees was complemented by the presence of numerous birds and their songs. Transported to the bush surroundings of his home and garden in Southern Rhodesia, Richard surprised both me and nearby winged associates by responding to various calls with a remarkable range of similar notes. The final rendition, that of a guinea fowl searching for a mate, was so realistic that a flock was lured from surrounding scrub into the clearing where we were enjoying sundowners. They inspected the area for some minutes before coming to the unanimous decision that the caller was not one of their kind. Then, loudly voicing disappointment and disapproval, they made a speedy exit.

Named not for its colour but after the Dutch monarch, Prince William of Orange, the Orange River, which forms a natural southern boundary between Namibia and South Africa, was the location of our next stopover: the celebrated waterfalls of Augrabies. Known as the Great River by the San Bushman, it was a favoured place to hunt. Among riverside reeds, the Bushman dug pits with a cunningly covered spike in the centre – a trap to catch the nocturnal hippopotamus. Dutch trekkers and wagon pioneers kept advance patrols to look out for these lethal pits. A memorable Laurens van der Post Bushman tale is that, of all men the Bushman was unafraid of lions; he would come and go unharmed, while those armed with guns feared for their lives.

Now the Bushman and lions have long departed; vineyards, stretching for kilometres along the banks of the river, replace wide plains of desert scrub and mark the greater part of the route to Upington. We arrived to find a green, spacious and elegant town serving as a holiday centre. For us, it was a convenient stopover to replenish supplies, before heading to Augrabies National Park.

Set among trees within the roar of water plummeting 56km into a ravine, it is hardly surprising that the falls take their name Augrabies from a derivation of the Khoi word *Aukoerebis*, meaning 'place of great noise'. Boasting fifty varieties of mammals, sixty three of amphibians and reptiles and more than one hundred and eighty recorded species of birds, the park offers safari-type drives, as well as canoeing and trekking. During our two night stay in boulder strewn moonscape surroundings, circled by swallows, we were content to watch the coming and going of multicoloured lizards, foraging rock rabbits and baboons, and to make the most of exquisite evening light to photoshoot rainbow clusters caught in spray cascading over the falls.

Namibia

Fish River Canyon

Imagine an uplifted desert plain, stretching from horizon to horizon, split by the great wound of a canyon that twists and turns for over 160km – reaching, at times, up to 27km in width. Namibia's Fish River Canyon, said to be second to America's Grand Canyon, shares its dramatic landscape – albeit on a reduced scale – but lacks its celebrity status. This is part of its magic. The knowledge that to this day it remains unspoilt and largely unknown to the world at large, gave it priority status at the start of our journey through Namibia.

Separated by vast tracts of desert, rugged mountains and bare plateau, the spectacular landscape of Namibia was reminiscent of Oman, but on a far grander scale. Stretching for 2000km along the coast, from *Oliphants* – Elephants' River in the south to southern Angola in the north, its attractions are as incredible as they are diverse. We knew that we could have arranged to fly from place to place and dip into the heart of each, rather like a butterfly taking nectar from flowers. We concluded that although such experiences would be memorable, we had learnt from our expeditions in Oman that it is the very act of travelling and being a part of the landscape that makes arriving and standing before the destination worthwhile. To reach these jewels, scattered across Namibia's great desert wastes, by overland journeys of exploration would take us on an inner journey as well.

Once we had crossed the border into Namibia, we set off on the greater part of a day's bone-shaking drive across the gruesome gravel plain, fringing the Karasberge Mountains to the southernmost of Namibia's outstanding landmarks.

Alone and poised – quite literally – on the northern edge of the canyon's outer rim, absorbing the view of magnificent exposed rock walls was pretty awesome. Reaching 550 metres in places and dating back some 2 billion years, a succession of cliff faces and tabletop surfaces mark the river's tortuous route to the distant horizon. Immediately before us, a dramatic headland, named Hell's Corner, has been carved. In the very bottom, pools of water glinted, hinting at the rush and hurl of summer torrents that had twice washed away the hot-spring resort of Ai Ais at the far southern end.

Legend imbues the canyon with romantic beginnings. The early San believed Koutein Kooru, a frenetic snake scrambling to escape hunters, gouged the canyon. In fact, like the Grand Canyon, it is a canyon within a canyon. Around 500 million years ago, a period of tectonic earth movement caused layers of ancient rock to rift apart and tilt at an angle of 45 degrees, creating the outer canyon. The inner canyon, first carved by glacial action, became a natural watercourse where powerful currents forged a meandering gorge deep within the outer walls. Thus the Fish River began, increased in momentum and continues to flow – intermittently during the dry winter season – but with impressive erosive force when heavy summer rain, on surrounding mountains, feeds its tributaries.

One of the main attractions of the canyon is the five day hiking trail to Ai Ais. This can only be achieved in winter. High temperatures and dangers of flooding make it impossible to attempt in summer. Now, in the southern hemisphere's early summer we could see wide sandy stretches on either side of the limpid river; in places the water level was so low that it appeared no more than a succession of limpid pools. Although daytime temperatures were reaching over 40 degrees, unlike Oman where we knew – only too well – that night heat can make camping intolerable, it is believed that the lack of water in Namibia allows temperatures to fall to bearable levels – a theory which was about to be tested. We were determined to spend a night in the canyon.

Armed with sleeping bags, sunhats, and quantities of water, as well as other essential supplies all crammed into our backpacks, we set off. Knees and thighs locked, our descent over loose scree triggered small avalanches that propelled us between boulders, down a polished trail at unexpected speeds. Sideways on and leaning towards the rock wall we discovered to be the safest method of descent. The slope was west-facing, but the sun was already losing height and throwing great slabs of shadow across the canyon floor.

At a guestimated halfway point, we made for the shade of overhanging rock disturbing a klipspringer, also hiding from the sun. As camera shy as the flock of ostriches we had surprised earlier, he took flight on delicately pointed hooves. Below, the serpentine remains of the river glinted tantalisingly, while over our heads, a vulture drew lazy circles across an ocean of sky. Cavernous walls, held between towering rock pinnacles, revived images of the long ago tilting of the earth's crust, wrenching these ancient walls apart.

It was a relief to finally arrive at the bottom, to find level sand underfoot and the ultimate luxury – cool green river pools. Now in complete shadow, we followed the damp course of the former river on its intermittent meandering course until, rounding a wide u-shaped bend, the distant outline of a clump of heavy-headed date palms came into view. Hopeful that this was the legendary Palm Springs we were making for, we quickened our flagging pace.

The early San's knowledge of the springs and their restorative powers goes back thousands of years. In more recent history, it is claimed that the waters cured two escaped German prisoners of war, both of whom suffered from life threatening diseases while hiding in the canyon for a period of two years. When they emerged, they were found to be suffering from no more than vitamin deficiencies. Legend has it that the date palms, near the sulphur pools, grew from stones discarded by the two men.

A sandy cove alongside one of the pools was the chosen place to spend the night. Refreshed and revived from ablutions in the therapeutic waters, we collected driftwood, conveniently left over from last summer's floods. Before long a fire was burning, and our senses responded to the smells and sounds of barbecuing *boerewors* – spicy African sausage. Once a speciality of South African farmers, it was Richard's favourite camping food; he confessed to stocking up on a supply from a store near Augrabies Falls.

On summer leave at our Poole base in the UK, he would drive for miles to discovered outlets selling *boerewors* and *biltong* – strips of dried meat – to introduce to family and guests at summer barbecues under the pine tree in the garden. Now, as darkness drained into the canyon, absorbing the last of the sun's vermilion light and flames from the fire threw shadows on the rock walls, Richard filled tumblers with red wine. It tasted like the nectar of the gods.

Cocooned in sleeping bags beside the dying embers of the fire, we watched the pale river of sky collect its stars. Then as a half-moon slipped over the lip of the canyon huge figures, towering over us like the carved effigies of a mighty civilisation, grew from the rock walls. In the all-prevailing silence, occasionally broken by wind-stirred flames or the shifting of charred wood, the poignant cry of a bird filled the night sky.

Sesriem

Another bone-shaking, teeth-rattling gravel plain from Fish River Canyon took us towards and through the Tirasberge Mountains, across the Nanamia Plateau, then north through the Naukluft Mountains to the start of a long descent into a wide bowl. Keetmanshoop, Helmeringhausen, Maltahohe – the accumulation of Germanic names was a reminder of the strong German colonial presence and influence and the establishment of Rhenish mission stations throughout Namibia. On the other hand, the names recalled heated battles in the region between platoons of heavily armed German soldiers and the local Nama people. In 1894, the defeated Nama surrendered to German sovereignty on the condition that the leader, Witbooi, could retain his chieftaincy and his people keep their land and weapons.

On the descent, the sudden appearance of pale grassland and vivid green trees was the reward for our soul wearying travels. Then the sight of distant mountains rising from a sea of pale grassland, as if rising from mist or cloud, reminded me that it was a photograph of giraffe drifting through sea mist along the coastline fringing the Namib Desert that had first captured my imagination; it was this image that had awakened my interest in Namibia and its magical and diverse scenery. Held between grave distances of empty landscapes, where horizons curve to infinity, the magic is intensified.

Now rugged mountains were replaced by the smooth outlines of low-lying hills, which opened out until we were surrounded by carpets of blond grass that 'clothe the world and meet the sky' until the entire vista appeared to be floating in an ocean of pale gold. In this landscape of the imagination, an encounter with Tennyson's knight in shining armour, riding towards Camelot, would not have seemed out of place.

We were heading for Sesriem Gorge, the entrance to the oasis of Sossusvlei: an oasis celebrated for dunes of red sand that tower some 200 metres above the valley floor. The 30m deep gorge of Sesriem and the oasis are linked by the River Tsauchab, which emerges from the gorge before making its way to the oasis. Here, the river follows a meandering intermittent course to one side of a plain, crossing to the opposite side approximately halfway to the *vlei* – open place – before disappearing without trace. At this point a second river, the Aub, arrives and follows at the foot of steep dunes, until it too disappears into the sea of sand. On occasions when summer rains are heavy, the rivers are said to flood the oasis, creating an ethereal vision of red dunes, mirrored in a still lake.

Our plan was to overnight at *Sesriem* – six thongs, referring to the number of ox-wagon thongs once needed to draw water from the gorge – and be ready at first light to reach the foothills of the dunes at sunrise. In failing light, a signpost directed us to an overgrown field, delegated for the use of self-sufficient campers. A row of 4x4s and camper vans confirmed our arrival. That we were there, on the very doorstep of the highest dunes in the world, was as unreal as it was exciting.

Sossusvlei

The pre-dawn sound of another vehicle starting served as an early morning call. A tar road took us from the camp, across the oasis for some 60km to end abruptly. At this point, deep sand heralded the start of the Great Sand Sea that covers over 32,000 square kilometres of western Namibia. From behind us, fingers of light from the not yet risen sun were streaking grassland white-gold. Surprised springbok paused long enough to size us up, before quite literally 'springing' into action and racing to a more distant spot. At this end, the oasis was an open plain of blond grass cupped by low-lying dunes of sand. On our left-hand side, green trees and vegetation followed the course of an intermittent river. Where it changed direction or disappeared, the skeletal outlines of trees, marking a former channel, assumed dramatic postures.

By the time we had reached the start of the 200 metre high parabolic dunes, the sun was highlighting eastern facing slopes, creating a dramatic contrast with the shadowed western sides. Between them, a fine line traced the pure wind-sculpted ridge. As the sun rose higher, shedding its light, so the colour of the dunes changed from violet to red to orange and cream. Our photographic frenzy satisfied, we headed for the foot of the 150 metre high Dune 45 – so named because it is 45km from Sesriem. Intrepid explorers had arrived before us; the crest of the dune was marked with silhouettes of tiny figures struggling to the summit. The reward: a spectacular view of the sun rising across some of the most dramatic and picturesque dunes in the world.

Where the tar road ends, at the start of the vlei, the rolling dunes of the Namib Desert begin and stretch for over 300km until they reach the Atlantic coastline. Here, the River Tsauchab meets its demise and disappears into the Sea of Sand. It never reaches the Atlantic Ocean where the cold Benguela current creates swirling sea mists that roll inland, blocking out the sun. In this surrealistic setting, elephants follow chocolate brown seasonal rivers surging across dunes towards the ocean, giraffe drift through shrouds of mist, and lions prey on unsuspecting seals.

Preoccupied with driving through deep sand, we were attempting to follow a firmer route along readymade tracks. From experience, we knew that the safest policy was to keep going. Even so, at one point we were forced to stop and let more air out of the tyres to avoid the ignominy of needing rescue.

Finally, we arrived at the near-centre of Sossusvlei, an enchanting open desert landscape of sand and trees, kept alive by the hidden river and surrounded by red dunes. We were faced with the choice of scenic walks into one of two remarkable vlei, each surrounded by its own impressive circle of dunes and renowned for unearthly but stunning scenery of dead trees in secluded settings. The problem before us was daytime summer heat: to reach either vlei required a walk of several kilometres. Soaring temperatures dictated that a hike, lasting for several hours over heat-absorbing sand, was not advisable. Deciding to forego unique photographic opportunities, we contented ourselves with tackling the early part of the trail to Hidden Vlei. Lined with starkly picturesque trees, it provided some aesthetic compensation: dark skeletal outlines against intensely blue sky and the sweep of red dunes.

The dunes and the oasis are equally stunning in evening light. The entire place, including wildlife, had taken on a rust-gold appearance. A perfectly camouflaged giraffe paused to give us a cursory glance, while the coats of springbok that had melted into blond grass in morning light appeared now to reflect the bronze of their surroundings. Even the oryx, with his distinctively marked head and impressive horns, glowed copper-gold. The more subdued colour of the dunes changed to deep creams and shades of caramel before our eyes. In the tangible silence, the oasis was as achingly beautiful to the senses as it had been at sunrise.

Walvis Bay

The long and lonely graded road to appropriately named Solitaire took us through two river gorges – the Gaub and the Kuiseb – into Naukluft Park, then west across a stony plateau towards Walvis Bay on a deteriorating gravel track that ensured slow progress. Surrounded by endless desert plain, occasionally broken by *inselbergs* – isolated and dramatic outcrops of rock – I had the recurring feeling that we were travelling across the surface of the moon. Then a gradual descent towards the Atlantic Ocean and all at once the desolate scene was transformed and enhanced by the outlines of crested dunes that announced our approach to Walvis Bay.

Its complex history includes discovery by the Portuguese explorer, Bartolomeu Dias. It was in 1487 that Dias sailed into the bay naming it: *Bahia da Santa Maria da Conceicao*: Bay of Our Lady of the Conception. By the mid-18th century, as a result of the large amounts of plankton in the waters attracting whales, whalers and an increasing number of international fishing vessels, the bay became known as *Bahia das Baleias* – the Bay of Whales; annexed by the Dutch in 1793, it was renamed Walvis Baai before Captain Alexander – the Commander of a British fleet – claimed it as Walvis Bay for Great Britain in 1795. The bay's strategic value, including a natural harbour, salt extraction, offshore guano platforms and rich fishing grounds, sparked a two hundred year political battle of ownership. This ended in 1994, when the Namibian flag was raised.

First impressions of wide wagon train and grid patterned streets, thinly peopled and with little traffic, seemed promising. But even from the confines of our vehicle, there was a tangible eeriness to the place. Veering on the positive side, we set out to locate Lagoon Chalets, the place we had earmarked to spend the night. With its nearby lagoon location favoured by breeding flamingos, it sounded our sort of place. It was when we drew alongside the compound's entrance that our premonition of 'something not quite right' was reinforced. Before us, a pair of wrought iron, padlocked gates guarded an enclosure, encircled by an eight foot high metal fence. Gates were unlocked, opened, clanged shut and locked behind us.

'For your safety,' a tall, elderly African man assured us. 'Too many armed gangs,' he added. 'This way we can all sleep at night.'

Thus comforted, we made the most of the upmarket prison camp facilities, including an excellent restaurant, before retiring to our home-on-wheels for a night of the sound sleep we had been promised.

The explanation for the emptiness of the streets was confirmed on the following day by an African lady running the local launderette. She and her fisherman husband had recently bought the premises from a Chinese couple, who fled after being robbed twice by armed men. We managed some shopping, and even used the Internet in the local library before collecting our laundry and paying a brief visit to the lagoon: a wide, shallow bay that stretched and widened towards the wave-torn grey Atlantic Ocean. Foraging flamingos were present, but they were made of sterner stuff than we were. A stiff Atlantic breeze, with a cold edge, sent us hurrying back to the comfort of our prison camp surrounds for a second night.

As much as we wanted to, time did not allow us to explore further up the mist shrouded Skeleton Coast, notorious for the skeletal shipwrecks that litter its rock-strewn shore. In fact, we were regretting the detour to Walvis Bay, which had taken up days of valuable time. From now on, in order to achieve our dream, we needed to plan our route more carefully.

'Eclipses,' Richard reminded me, 'wait for no man!'

The Waterberg Plateau

The plan that emerged was to take an inland route to the Waterberg Plateau. This isolated island of sandstone, rising 150 metres from an ocean of desert with an abundance of freshwater springs, also had a reputation as a repository for wildlife. We estimated that it would serve as a resting place, as well as a prelude to further wild-life viewing at Namibia's *piece de resistance*: Etosha National Park.

Waterberg's European-involved history added further interest. The site of a Rhenish mission station, it was destroyed in 1880 by Herero-Nama wars. This was finally resolved when German colonial forces took it from Herero resistance fighters in 1904 – an event commemorated each year by local Herero people to this day.

First, more desert plains and barren mountain lowlands had to be crossed. Like travelling through Oman, distances could not be measured in kilometres. Without roads, time was dictated by a featureless landscape. As the hours rumbled by, we passed isolated ranches and safari lodges usually accessed by air, while the occasional threadbare acacia or quiver tree, adopted as home by colonies of weaver birds, formed picturesque sign-posts lining the route. Finally, I persuaded Richard that my needs – including stretching my legs and drinking coffee in the shade of a solitary quiver tree taking shape on the quivering horizon – were imperative.

Named by San hunters, who use its lightweight branches as quivers, the tree's extraordinary capacity to store water in succulent leaves, fibrous trunks and branches is what enables it to survive harsh desert conditions. It also provided a convenient nesting site for a colony of innovative weaver birds, busy coming and going from an intricate cluster of nests 'woven' between its branches.

Around us, the great panorama of desert plain reaching from horizon to horizon was utterly devoid of life. The sky was molten gold. Searing heat rose from sand and rocks underfoot. A feeling of great aloneness swept through me. Apart from a startled group of fleeing ostrich, we had seen no other sign of life since leaving Walvis Bay early that morning. It was as if we were the sole survivors in an endless rock-strewn wilderness. It could have been Mars itself. Boasting great Barcan crescent dunes, volcanoes and canyons, the surface of Mars is said to resemble Namibia. Such was the silence that I was aware of the beating of my heart. I could imagine being transformed into a desert rose or becoming part of the landscape, like the stone figures of my imagination, held in rock walls or trapped in rock-strewn surroundings. After all, we had no means of communication, and apart from return air tickets from Dubai to Johannesburg and our plan to end our travels in Kruger National Park, no one knew of our whereabouts.

Preoccupied with focusing his camera on the comings and goings of birds to and from their tightly woven nests, Richard was as at home in this desert terrain as he was in the bush. Joining me for coffee, he brushed aside my concerns as nothing more than 'heat maddened imagination – over 40 degrees in the shade,' he added. As usual, his stoical calm, whatever the situation, was all the assurance I needed. Minutes later we were underway, and an hour further into the journey, he was pointing to the first shadowy outlines of the plateau. As we drew near, the solidity of the green treed top, supported by vertical red walls, grew before us. At the base of the cliffs where fresh spring water emerges, a lush mosaic of trees and scrub savannah took shape. Giant-sized anthills lined the route to the camp. Cradled beneath the cliff-edge and amidst a belt of trees, its lovely setting was further enhanced by a swimming pool and selection of upmarket restaurants. It was a true oasis.

As evening approached with the promise of panoramic views of the swollen sun receding on the distant horizon, we decided to follow one of a number of tracks that wound uphill, over huge boulders and between trees, to the top of the plateau. As I trailed Richard and darkness increased, I was reminded that this was leopard territory. Nervously looking over my shoulder, I examined overhead branches and the underside of shrubs until tiredness and imagination took over. Giving up, I made my way back to the camp for a cool dip in the pool.

A late morning was followed by a leisurely walk through trees with the intention of identifying some of the two hundred or so varieties of birds. Big cats still on my mind, I followed in Richard's stride. Surmising that even the biggest are usually sleepy in the morning, the anticipation of a surprise sighting of a dozing leopard or cheetah was overriding my evening fears and adding excitement to the expedition. Before long, increasing heat and elusive wildlife meant that we had to content ourselves with fleeting glimpses of bird silhouettes in distant treetops. Expectations were put on hold for the camp's guided evening safari on the plateau.

In the end this turned out to be a leisurely drive through bush, stopping from time to time to watch baboons wading in the shallows of a number of purpose built waterholes. Further interest was limited to the occasional appearance of a wide eyed dik-dik – the smallest variety of antelope – viewing us from scrubby bush. Although not on the driver-cum-guide's itinerary, I was about to suggest a photo stop at the location of a set of dinosaur footprints marked on our map – an opportunity we secretly entertained – when we had a surprise encounter.

It was the last waterhole stop, and we were second comers. Our unexpected arrival surprised a female black rhino and her calf. The result was electric. First she challenged us with her 'don't even think about it' stare, then she took off, charging to within inches of the vehicle, before making a dramatic 90 degree turn and heading into the bush. Her offspring followed at a leisurely gambol. A mock charge. A convincing 'Don't mess with me!' message that gave the evening and the Waterberg Plateau, gold star rating.

The regret we shared was not so much the lack of wildlife, but missing the opportunity of a close encounter with fossilised animal tracks, preserved on the plateau for more than 150 million years. The largest footprint – that of a two legged, three toed dinosaur – is said to measure as much as 25 metres in length. Our interest was heightened by the achievements of a distant namesake of Richard's: Roy Chapman Andrews, traveller and scientist. The expeditions of Chapman Andrews and his team into the Gobi desert between 1920 and 1930 marked a significant place in the history of palaeontology. Numerous new species of dinosaur and very early mammals – whose remains had been hidden in the Gobi desert for 75 million years – were discovered.

Crossing continents was no problem for the dinosaur. The discovery that these prehistoric creatures were as at home in polar regions as they were in tropical swamplands raises the possibility that, like the mammoth, the dinosaur developed 'a type of biological anti-freeze enabling it to endure Arctic temperatures.'[4] It was frustrating to be so close and yet, metaphorically so far from the prints on the plateau. Like the artwork of ancient people, they were an historic emblem of the living past, but now darkness was taking hold. Headlights full blaze, the driver-cum-guide was making for the camp. The following day, we were heading north on the trail of wildlife in Namibia's largest wilderness park. Dinosaur prints were 'on hold'.

Etosha National Park

Savannah grasslands and trees surrounded the gravel road that took us along the edge of Etosha Pan. Beyond this a broad band of white like driven snow, stretched and reached to distant horizons. The place was deserted. Or was it? Long sword-like horns and a handsomely marked black and white face bestowed a regal bearing on the oryx that gradually took shape, and was standing before us. Statuesque and unafraid, he paused, assessing the visitors and heralding our approach to Etosha Wildlife Park.

'The Great White Place Of Dry Water' – this lovely and enigmatic description of Etosha arises from the park's origin. 12 million years ago, Etosha Pan, an immense, flat saline desert covering 5000 square kilometres, was a shallow lake, fed by the waters of the Kunene River. Over the intervening period, climatic and tectonic changes have lowered the water level and created a salt pan, which occasionally holds water. When the rainfall is sufficient, this vast shallow depression is fed by incoming channels. For a few days each year, the pan becomes a shallow lagoon, teeming with flamingos, white pelicans and varieties of bird life.

Although as far back as memory takes them indigenous people have known of this wildlife oasis; the first Europeans to set eyes on it were the traders Charles Andersson and Francis Galton, who arrived by wagon in 1851. It was McKiernan, an American trader, who in 1876 drew worldwide attention to the area when he observed: 'All the menageries in the world turned loose would not compare to the sight I saw that day.'

In fact, Etosha didn't attract the attention of hunters and tourists until the turn of the century. Such was the effect when it did that at the turn of the century, the German Governor of South West Africa, Dr F. von Lindequist, concerned about diminishing animal numbers, founded a 99,526 square kilometre reserve; by 1970 Etosha had been pared down to its present 23,175 sq km.

---

[4] Lewis Smith, *Anti-freeze evolved in mammoth blood*

Okaukuejo

Known to the Haikom Bushmen as 'the woman who has a child every year' – Okaukuejo is the most westerly of three upmarket camps in the park. Originally the site of a German Fort, built in 1901 the camp now houses the Etosha Ecological Centre and provides thatched self-catering chalets or roomy pitches for camping, each with its own *braai* (barbecue), with the additional luxury of not one but three circular swimming pools.

It was evening when we arrived. As tempting as it was to relax and take full advantage of the comforts on offer, we had other things on our mind. Moringa trees, to be precise. Not just any moringa trees, but a ghostly forest. As soon as we booked our camping space, we set off on a 32km trip to a find the mysterious forest. Although moringa trees, growing world wide throughout Africa and Asia, are largely known for their medicinal properties, the unusual gnarled and misshapen appearance of these particular trees has given rise to their ghostly reputation. Unlike the regular smooth stemmed species which occur naturally on rocky hillsides, those of the Ghost Tree Forest are said to not only look unusual, but to congregate in large numbers.

En route, springbok and giraffe wandered between herds of zebra and wildebeest, roaming purposefully and elegantly across savannah grassland as if on cue for a film set. Then, in evening's shadowed silence, as vegetation thinned and wildlife disappeared, we came upon the forest. The bizarre silhouettes of swollen joints and leafless branches of the mysterious baobab-like trees before us gave credence to a Bushman legend:

After God had found homes for all the plants and animals on earth he discovered a pile of leftover moringa trees. He flung them into the air and they fell to earth with their roots pointing skywards.

Cameras about necks, sundowners in hands we were strategically positioned at the camp's floodlit waterhole, watching the sky's diminishing light cling to the pool's still surface. Beyond the water, stony desert disappeared into a belt of woodland. A lone giraffe glided to the water's edge. Legs splayed, she stretched her long neck to meet her reflection as she drank. The evocative cry of a giant eagle owl echoed across the lake.

Then as if in a dream, from out of the distance huge dark silhouettes were taking shape. Soundless and majestic, fourteen adult elephants and six youngsters emerged from the woodland and crossed the desert plain. Striding purposely and magnificently towards us, they raised incandescent clouds of dust, their momentum increasing with their eagerness to reach the water. Oblivious of the spellbound audience, they siphoned water into open mouths, and showered and bathed in obvious delight until the dying sun turned the sky molten gold. Finally, content and immensely self-contained, they turned – using their trunks as vacuum pumps to powder themselves in dust – made their way across the plain and disappeared into the deep darkness of the forest. Magical moments in time, captured on film to adorn the wall of whatever place was our current home.

Halali

Waterholes are stage sets for drama and at midday latent drama was on the menu. We were en route to Halali, Etosha's central resort, which lies midway between Okaukuejo and the most easterly camp of Namutoni. Hollows of stony wasteland on the periphery of shallow pools tempted us to stop. At first, the place appeared to be without life. The stage was empty. Then a handful of zebra, tentatively approaching the water's edge, halted some metres away in statuesque poses.

Suddenly, we saw them, four well-camouflaged lionesses, slouched like abandoned sacks at the water's edge. First, a sandy-coloured head, ears pricked, lifted. Sensing our presence, a second inert shape stirred, slowly stood and turned to stare intently. Satisfied that there was no immediate danger, she flopped down again. Occasionally one stirred, lifted a head and stretched, before succumbing once more to sleepy stupor. We watched as more unsuspecting creatures approached, then stopped dead in their tracks. Finally, two well-tuned springbok, alert to danger, sprang into action and headed off. This was a signal to the others who wasted no more time before fleeing too. The quenching of thirsts would have to wait.

Guarding the entrance to Halali's camp, the fort is marked with the emblem of a horn, a reminder that today, the German word *halali* – previously used to describe the ritual sounding of the horn to signal the end of the hunt – now signifies that within the park, sport hunting and the needless killing of animals is over.

In evening light, we climbed Tsumasa Kopje, a rocky limestone hill, to the perfect lookout spot alongside the diminishing waterhole. Once again, our timing coincided with the arrival of a family of elephants; this group, preoccupied with reaching the water and quenching their thirsts, ploughed through a herd of zebra and were soon noisily indulging. Minutes later from the opposite direction, a second group of elephants appeared. As they drew near, the leading adults, aware that they were second-comers, stopped in their tracks. At this point, a large bull came up from behind, bellowed loudly and led the group forward. Unnerved, the zebra scattered and waited at some distance, watching. Not impressed, the first group of elephants stood their ground, especially a huge bull that had taken up a firm position guarding the fountainhead of the waterhole.

Fully occupied in preventing others from using this favoured spot, he was pulling intrusive trunks away and, on one occasion, deftly kicked an inquisitive youngster with his back leg. While both parties were in their element, drinking, spraying themselves and bathing, two young bulls from opposite camps tussled with each other in a friendly display of bravado. Finally, as the red ball of sun disappeared behind the tree line, both parties retreated in the direction from which they had come, leaving the pool for thirsty onlookers.

Namutoni

A spectacular and desolate landscape of startling white stretched to the horizon. Waterholes fringing the pan had either evaporated, or were reduced to shallow pools where thirsty wildebeest and springbok gathered. The discarded ribcage of a giraffe, a foraging jackal and a vulture perched in a skeletal tree added to the desolate and dramatic scene of drought. Temperatures were in the mid 40s. A distant rumble of thunder disturbed the heavy silence.

Our first sighting of the distinctive white towers and walls of the fort guarding the entrance to Namutoni grew from a mirage on the distant horizon. 70km east of Halali, it was built by German cavalry in 1899 to control the fierce resistance of local tribes. Today the fort provides an impressive camp entrance and a convenient place for sighting wildlife at sunset.

As afternoon drifted into evening, we gravitated to the thatched awning, overlooking the reed fringed remains of the waterhole. Utterly deserted by fellow travellers and equally deserted by wildlife, the place was engulfed in an eerie prevailing silence. As we dabbed sweaty brows and quenched our thirsts, Richard reminded me of the tale of the onlooker who fell asleep and was taken by a lion at this very place. I resolved to remain wakeful. Slowly but surely, the sky grew ominously black. Then a momentous clap of thunder, followed by lightning, tore the floodlit sky apart, heralding a storm and the long awaited rains that would transform desert to wetland once again.

Angola Border

Set on bluffs alongside the Okavango River, Rundu was to be the place of our long-awaited meeting with this life-giving, life-saving waterway. Starting life on the Benguela Plateau in Angola, the Okavango forms a border between Angola and Namibia before flowing southwest into Botswana. Here it soaks into the sands, creating the 15,000 square kilometres of convoluted channels and islands of the Okavango Delta, a haven for wildlife and wildlife viewing.

With an estimated 350km of gravel plain before us, it was far too soon to get excited. The first signs that we were entering the more hospitable Kavango region didn't appear until after a lunch-time stop when *kraals* – villages of thatched circular houses and cattle enclosures – in a landscape that was becoming increasingly green, gathered along the track. It had the feel and smell of the Africa of my imagination. From our homework, we knew that nomadic cattle herders had become settled agriculturists and cattle raisers, and that before the Germans moved into Namibia, it was home to descendants of three main tribal groups – the Khoi Khoi (Hottentot), the San (Bushmen) and the migrating Bantu (Herero).

The more aggressive Herero, largely displaced, not only the Khoi and the San, but other smaller descendant groups as well. They did not fare as successfully against the Germans, either in battles or on the social front. The latter is evident from the depletion in numbers, as much as for the dress code of the women, derived from Victorian-era German missionaries, who took exception to what they considered was a lack of modesty. To this day, Herero women are recognisable for their voluminous crinoline dresses, supported by a series of petticoats and elaborate horn-shaped hats or headdresses.

Now fuller, taller trees punctuated the scenery and swathes of cultivated fields increased as we crossed the lowlands towards the river. A series of shanty settlements, growing alongside the route, heralded our approach to the outskirts of Rundu. By the time we located Sarasungu River Lodge, an overnight retreat on the banks of the Okavango, the sun was nestling behind a fringe of trees. Just as we were congratulating ourselves on finding such a peaceful overnight haven and were drifting towards sleep, disco-music from an early pre-Xmas party throbbed from the nearby lodge.

Rundu

The need for fuel, food and funds dictated a visit to Rundu. Warnings from our host, that large numbers of immigrants and refugees fleeing from warring Angola hang about the streets, were not to be taken lightly.

'Robbery is common place. You must be vigilant. Leave nothing on view. One foolish couple left passports on the front seat. All it takes is a brick through the window. In fact, don't leave the vehicle unattended!'

Fuel and food accomplished, we parked in an overgrown lay-by alongside a tourist information centre: a safe and convenient place with easy access to the bank, or so we surmised. It didn't take long to realise that the centre was not only rundown, but closed. A straggle of men, lounging and smoking near some broken railings that once guarded the lay-by from the river increased my growing nervousness. The prospect of being alone on vehicle duty while Richard visited the bank was not a happy one.

'Just wait beside the door,' was the final instruction as the Cruiser was locked. 'I'll be as quick as I can,' Richard promised, as he pocketed the keys. He paused briefly to look back, before adopting a fast stroll and disappearing into the main street.

Obediently standing alongside the vehicle, I was attempting to look nonchalant while silently praying, 'Dear Lord, protect me,' over and over, with no idea what I would do if He didn't and I was set upon by an armed gang. Then, just as I was becoming conscious of my increasing heartbeat, prayers and panic were over.

'Let's go!' was the greeting as we boarded the Cruiser. Map and guide book in hand, I was dictating a route that would take us south, past the celebrated Poppa Falls to a lodge overlooking the Okavango River, close to the border with Botswana.

Huge baobab trees and lush vegetation greeted us – a welcome contrast to weeks of desert landscape. We arrived to find another treat in store. Fronting the lodge, a balcony overlooking the river provided a perfect wildlife viewing platform. A magnificent sable antelope with sweeping twisted horns paused eyeing us with an air of cool appraisal before disappearing into a belt of trees; crocodiles idled in shallow water, resonant with old man grunts of hidden hippos. As the descending sun turned the river blood red, we watched fishermen passing in dugout canoes and the comings and goings of varieties of brightly coloured birds. Finally, attracted by my white T-shirt, a bombardment of huge moths and increasing humidity sent me inside for a cold shower.

A quiet night was followed by a breakfast of scrambled guinea fowl eggs in the open-sided thatched dining room, accompanied by an orchestra of bird calls. A place to dream about.

Botswana

The Tsodilo Hills

'Some of trickiest off-road in Botswana. You're mad to consider it. Why suffer when I can arrange the comfort and convenience of a flight?'

Such was the response of Jake, the lodge owner, when we explained our travel plans. After a second night of pampered luxury, we were determined to regain our independence and were preparing to set off following an overland trail to the Tsodilo Hills, to find some of the oldest Bushman artwork in Africa: a legacy of over 3500 rock paintings, estimated to be dated from AD 800-1300. Ancestors of the 'San' – an ancient people, who decreed that the hills were the site of the first creation – are believed to have executed the earliest paintings.

Nowhere in Botswana is said to have a stronger sense of the past than the Tsodilo Hills. Derived from the Mbukushu word *sorile*, meaning sheer, Tsodilo accurately describes the rock faces on which the artwork is found. Situated in the Kalahari Basin to the west of the Okavango River, these outcrops of quartzite schist rise abruptly from an ocean of desert. Like Australia's *Uluru* – Ayers Rock – the hills are imbued with myth, legend and spiritual significance associated with the tribes who inhabited the area.

The Bushmen believed the hills were the home of ancient spirits, who inhabited separate sections; the master spirit lived in the central Female Hill, near a pool of water that never dried up. Beside this pool, grows the tree with the fruit of knowledge and, close to the tree, marks in the rock were made by the master spirit who knelt to pray on the day that he made the world. There, among the 'Slippery Hills' – as they were known to the San – their ancestors gathered, once every year, for a short season.

A number of circuits or trails through the hills lead past walls of rock containing panels of paintings. Of these, the most famous is named after Sir Laurens van der Post whose book, *Lost World of the Kalahari,* brought international attention to the hills.

It was during his explorations of the hills that van der Post and his party suffered a series of misfortunes, including being attacked by a swarm of bees on three successive occasions. When he learnt from his local guide that the party had upset the gods by killing wildlife in the vicinity of the hills, in an attempt to appease the gods, van der Post buried a note of apology beneath the panel now bearing his name. The utopian society of San Bushmen, so revered by van der

Post and immortalised in the film *The Gods Must Be Crazy,* has long since disappeared, but their artwork remains as a living testimony to it.

Leaving Namibia's ultra-casual tin-hut border post and entering Botswana's more formal concrete equivalent, we then joined an off-road track through Kalahari Sandvelt to a ridge of dunes where the track split into three. From our map, the shorter and more direct middle track seemed the obvious choice. After some 30km, the red sand was so loose and so deep we feared becoming entrenched. Somehow, Richard negotiated a turn and retreated to the start before setting off on the longer, lower trail. This too quickly deteriorated, and we began to question the sanity of our decision to drive alone to such a remote and isolated location. By the time we had voiced our shared concerns, we decided we faced more danger by attempting another retreat, and anyway, we had gone too far to turn back.

For the better part of three hours, we ploughed through loose sand along a deeply rutted track that swung unnervingly towards and between trees, so closely set that passage through without damage to the vehicle or ourselves was a miracle. Teeth-clenching tension was intensified by speed. We couldn't afford to lose momentum for fear of being bogged down. However, the gods must have been with us. Feeling both physically and mentally shaken but mildly heroic, we realised we were on *terra firma* and approaching the Mbukushu village on the outskirts of the hills.

Symbolically named for their size and appearance, Male, Female and Child Hill, the main outcrops, lie roughly in line on a north-south axis. By chance, we had located the airstrip – used for the coming and going of guided tours – and were following the perimeter on a track leading to the site. From our approach, the conical outline of Male Hill, neatly framing the thatched roof of the entrance gate, came into view first. Just visible in its shadow was the lower and prostrate form of the Female Hill. Renowned for its creative forces, it is said to harbour the most impressive paintings. Overall, the belief that the paintings have religious or spiritual significance is what gives the hills a vibrant sense of the living past.

'Makoba Woods', carved onto a plaque and nailed to a tree in a wooded enclave, was the only evidence that we had arrived at our overnight camp. The Visitors' Centre was locked. There was no sign of life. Once the engine was turned off and the ticking of cooling metal subsided we were enveloped in heavy silence. Then the rustling of dried grass made us both look round; a klipspringer, balanced like an overweight ballerina on delicate tiptoes, eyed us nervously before taking off into surrounding bush.

By now it was mid-afternoon and we had but a few hours of daylight to explore the more accessible sections of the Female Hill. Armed with reason over apprehension, cameras and a map, with a plan of the prime locations of the artwork, we set off along the foot of the Female Hill to explore a section of this extraordinary and extensive open-air gallery. Within minutes, panels of smooth rock of varying pastel shades rose before us. As in a number of places we had explored in Oman, they seemed to have been purpose-made for the artists to do and exhibit their work.

'Over here!' Richard called. He was striding ahead and had stopped before a series of adjacent walls covered in red ochre wild life images. On a panel of blue rock, three long-necked giraffe were facing to the right, while on an adjoining panel of buff coloured rock the form of a lion, poised on two legs, was positioned over a row of left facing rhinos. Images of cattle, various antelope and rhino – one with three horns and another resembling a kudu with long twisting horns – appeared on successive panels of smooth rock.

The male kudu, armed with formidable horns, is one of the few creatures depicted in the earliest paintings reported to still live in the hills. The Bushman used the horn of a kudu to adorn the head of a painting of a serpent; this was a warning of the danger posed by a legendary serpent said to live in a well found in a natural hollow in a rock-grotto on the northeastern side of the Female Hill. It was believed that if a stone were thrown into the water to warn the serpent of your approach, it would not harm you.

Although the local Mbukushu tribe have been in the region for no more than two hundred years, they too believe that the Female Hill is the site of the first creation of their tribe. They claim that the set of footprints discovered on the summit – said to be the prints left by dinosaur and claimed by the Bushmen as the prints of their master spirit – were prints left by cattle when the Mbukushu god Ngambe lowered the tribe and their cattle onto the hill.

Shimmering heat, glancing from sheer rock surfaces and from the ground beneath our feet, sapped depleting energy. We knew that we had followed one of the trails through the Female Hill but we weren't at all sure which one, or quite where we were. In evening's uneasy silence, as shadows lengthened and fell upon the rock walls, the sense of isolation increased. Thirsty, and plagued by insistent flies, I followed in Richard's footsteps as he navigated a route back to the campsite. I reassured myself that we had done nothing to upset the gods. We were under attack from flies, not bees. Nevertheless, convinced that we were not alone, I found myself constantly looking over my shoulder.

Then a pleasant surprise: a Bush Camper, 4x4 was parked near our vehicle – we had been joined by fellow travellers. We were greeted by Ivan, who was confined to a wheelchair. Unable to access the sandy uphill trails leading to the artwork, we learned that he had parted from his companion and returned to wait at the camp. After acepting his invitation to join him for sundowners, he explained that he was here with his Swiss friend, Eric. Inveterate motorbike travellers, they had crossed continents together until an accident left Ivan with a damaged spine and unable to walk. Determined to continue their travels they swapped motorbikes for a Bush Camper. Before long, Eric returned, and we exchanged stories about our equally hazardous rides to reach the hills.

'We were warned,' Richard confessed. 'We're not inexperienced, but it was something else.'

Eric explained that since it was too difficult for Ivan to follow the trails to the rock art, their intention was to leave early the following morning.

'If you're prepared to join us, we could travel in a convoy,' he added.

'It will mean missing out on dinosaur footprints as well as dancing penises!' Richard responded, referring to our remaining objectives. 'But, I guess survival is the priority,' he continued, sensing my agreement.

'That's good news for us,' Eric replied. 'That way we can take the shorter middle route. There are literally miles of deep soft sand, feasible if we let down the tyres and keep a steady momentum. We can look out for each other. Sorry about the missing out on dinosaur prints,' he added. 'Must admit, dancing penises intrigue.'

'Adrienne will explain,' Richard volunteered. 'She's the Bushman enthusiast.'

'I'm no expert, but Laurens van der Post is. He grew up with them, and then years later returned to make a documentary. In his book he explains just one of the ways in which the Bushman and woman are remarkable. While the women are born with a piece of loose skin that acts as an apron to preserve their modesty, men are born, live and die with semi-erect sexual organs. The Bushman celebrates this by painting himself naked in silhouette. One of the panels shows a dancing crowd of sexually excited male figures. Hence the dancing penises.'

'Here's to the survival of the remaining Bushmen,' Eric responded, uncorking a bottle of red wine and refilling empty glasses. 'And here's to a safe journey.'

That night, a full moon, howling dogs and my imagination kept me from all but fitful sleep. I thanked God for sending Eric and Ivan. Splendid isolation, I was learning, is not without its drawbacks.

Nguma Lagoon Lodge

Our companions not only safely guided us across miles of deep sand, but took us to yet another luxury lodge, surrounded by lush forest and on the banks of the Okavango. The waterside setting provided a magical ambience for an afternoon reclining on the decking and watching crested water birds, egrets, bee-eaters, kingfishers, snake-birds and so many more. An evening fishing trip with Ivan and Eric had the added excitement of sharing the river with crocodiles and lordly hippos, eyes and noses visible amidst papyrus reeds. Richard, in very heaven, caught two Okavango bream, which were barbecued for supper.

Maun

The 'Gateway to the Delta', neatly sums up the importance of Maun to the tourist industry in Botswana. The comparative comfort of travelling over 300km of tar road to get there was offset on arrival at the campsite. It was entirely surrounded by an electric fence. We soon learned that, like Walvis Bay, the place attracted gangs of migrants, and robbery was commonplace. Unlike Walvis Bay, this campsite was rundown, there were no other campers, and a basic toilet block was the only on-site facility. Feeling decidedly uneasy, we locked ourselves into our Land Cruiser for the night.

In daylight, Maun appeared an open and friendly place with good facilities for shopping, laundry and checking emails – that is, if you had the patience to wait half an hour to download just one. Once the chores were complete, our priority was to book a two night stay at a lodge in the delta. 'Game Trackers' from Orient Express Safaris soon had us sorted. Khwai River Lodge, with game viewing, at Moremi Game Reserve, was on the cards.

On the doorstep of Moremi Reserve, Khwai River Lodge has the distinction of being formally opened in 1969 by the first president of Botswana, the late Sir Seretse Khama. Added to this, the promise of up-market accommodation and a range of 'wet' and 'dry' safari experiences in a wildlife sanctuary where the likelihood of encountering other safari vehicles is rare, was everything and more than we had dreamed of.

Brimming with excitement we were attempting to leave Game Trackers to find a group of women blocking our exit onto the pavement. Dressed in voluminous crinoline ensembles and colourful wraparound headwear, with two ends sticking out like horns, there was no mistaking their identity. There was something incongruous about Herero women fleeing from the Germans in Namibia and settling in Botswana, yet to this very day, continuing to wear the imposed Victorian dress code that is so unsuitable for their life-style and the climate. They looked entirely out of place, and wonderfully eccentric. I longed to capture some images on film, but our cameras were locked inside the Cruiser at the campsite. Even if we had had them with us, they were of the large Nikon variety that appear so intrusive. I was also struck by the women's strong build and imperious manner. I wouldn't have wanted to upset them.

To avoid spending a second night at the Maun camp and to prepare for our wilderness encounter, we made our way along a trail through savannah and woodland, and set ourselves up to overnight by the Khwai River, close to the North Gate entrance to the Moremi Reserve. That evening, while birdwatching along the river, Richard became aware that he was the one being watched. Dozens of hippo eyes, trained on him as they began to emerge from their watery stronghold, sent him striding back. From the safety of the Land Cruiser, we listened apprehensively to the increasing volume of their grunts as they took their night-time stroll.

Khwai River Lodge

An amazing assortment of birdsong and croaking frogs heralded morning. Things livened up when a monkey slipped into the open Cruiser, snatched and ran off with a bag of recently opened muesli. Unabashed, he sat just feet away, indulging and watching us watching him. When Richard gave chase, the infidel swung into overhanging branches and continued to stare and munch on his ill-gotten goods. Finally, when a stick was thrown into the tree, the miscreant dropped the bag, spilling the contents over the forest floor. A hornbill quickly took advantage of an easy snack. It was time to give up on breakfast and head for the comfort of the lodge.

We couldn't have arranged more perfect timing. Brunch, the traditional late breakfast/early lunch prepared for guests returning from the morning safari, was about to be served. In the open-sided dining area overlooking the floodplain of the River Khwai, talk was of a sighting of a pride of lions – in particular, of two males reclining alongside the remains of a recent kill. My mission was a close photographic encounter with a lion. I was all ears.

Afternoons are set aside for relaxing by the pool or indulging in a siesta, so I had to wait. Our tented air-conditioned retreat, set on stilts and under a thatched awning, had an open verandah with splendid views towards the river. Richard settled with his binoculars. Seduced by the cool interior, I wallowed in the comfort of the four-poster. Vaguely aware of the distant calls of hippos, I drifted towards sleep. This, I drowsily reminded myself, was their stomping ground. Above and beyond floated the magical sound of the wilds of Africa – the haunting cries of fish-eagles.

A dramatic thunderstorm and heavy rain shower provided an unceremonious wakening and an early lesson: nature does not operate to order. Consoled by the thought that the parched landscape needed water and a drop in temperature would be a welcome relief, we lingered over afternoon tea, and then, in lightly falling rain, resolutely set off on a vehicle-safari with two fellow enthusiasts from Holland. Like us, the Dutch travellers had work-related connections to Dubai. The owners of a company, currently engaged in dredging the Gulf, they were responsible for the groundwork (or was it underwater work?) for the creation of the two Palm Islands and the latest waterside venture, the Arabian World.

'They are also responsible for ruining my fishing,' Richard muttered. 'No king fish and no barracuda for weeks.'

Just then we had other things on our minds. While my thoughts were centred on big cats, our companions were focused on birds. With literally hundreds of varieties at large and accompanied by Mothupi, a knowledgeable local guide, they were not to be disappointed. As I suspected, conditions for sighting lions were not good. An hour or so later, under leaden skies, I was having less than charitable thoughts about my companions and the nature of the game drive. Every few minutes we drew to a halt while telescopic binoculars were trained on distant brown specks invariably and excitedly described as red-throated, lilac-breasted or yellow-vented, before being ticked off as sighting number 343 in a neat birdwatcher's diary. I have no grudge against birds or birdwatchers, but this was not what I had come to Africa for. Meanwhile Richard, an avid bird lover himself, was completely unfazed. I was doing my best to stay calm.

Then a miracle occurred. Just in time for the scheduled stop for sundowners, at a riverside spot overlooking the floodplain, shafts of silvery sunlight broke through the cover of black cloud. As we stood sipping iced drinks and watched grazing herds of zebra, waterbuck and impala, sky and river were undergoing a kaleidoscopic transformation from metallic greys to molten golds and glowing reds. Portly hippopotami, with young ones in tow, were emerging to graze. Elephants, accompanied by calves as baggy and wrinkled as the elders, were making their way purposefully towards the river, while crocodiles, disguised as half-submerged logs, lined the banks.

That evening, dinner was under the stars. The candlelit table, looking good enough for royalty, was a bonus for the crew of a film company who had flown in from Maun that afternoon. Engaged to take photographs for next year's safari catalogue, they had abandoned their search for photographic encounters with the Big Five in evening sunlight. Gesturing towards the star-dusted canopy over our heads, Mothupi assured us that it was an omen promising clear skies for the following day. Confident in his prediction and undeterred by uninvited winged nightlife, bombarding us and our candlelit table, we tucked into roast guinea fowl, exchanged safari experiences and philosophically toasted whatever nature had in store.

The next morning, just as Mothupi promised, the sky was a peerless blue. Neither had he forgotten my mission. He instructed the driver to take us to an area of woodland. Lions, I knew, rested in the shade for most of the day, and this time I was not to be disappointed. Looking remarkably docile, two lionesses were dozing under the low-lying branches of an acacia. Although no more than a few metres away, they treated our presence and the ensuing photographic activity with regal indifference.

On our way back to the river, we had several sightings of elegant, tremulous impala. Poised mid-action, they watched us tentatively before racing away. We paused to photograph a waterbuck, its head and shoulders framed by long grass, then a handsome Cape Buffalo staring intently in our direction. Mothupi warned us, that when feeling threatened, the buffalo's armour-plated Viking headdress could be lethal.

'What's more,' he added, 'buffalo have been responsible for more deaths of humans than any other animal in the park.'

The morning coffee break was held at a perfect spot for viewing game. Closeby, a giraffe with enviable long eyelashes posed for a portrait, before loping into the bush. Before us the clear waters of the meandering river, with its constellations of water lilies, held and released transient images of creatures pausing to drink. A water monitor scuffled through the sand and slipped out of sight. There was no shortage of hippopotami watching us watching them, eyes and ears peeking above the water.

On our last evening game drive, we were taken to the adjoining Moremi Reserve, the first wildlife sanctuary created by an African tribe. Under the guardianship of the widow of Chief Moremi the Third, the Batawana tribe realised the need to preserve this unique habitat for future generations. Today the reserve occupies nearly one third of the Okavango Delta. As we approached the North Gate entry over the long and clattery log-built Khwai River Bridge, baboons and monkeys scattered. At first, the scenic route along the river revealed more pools for wallowing hippos then, as we entered mopane woodland, the track became increasingly sandy and we were dodging sweeping thorny branches. An area of decimated woodland indicated that elephants had passed this way.

A few minutes later, just metres ahead, a lioness with three cubs in tow crossed a sandy area towards some low-lying acacia, where she swiftly took shelter. Known by local people as the 'don't come near me bush', its umbrella-shape and lethal thorns offer privacy and protection. We drew alongside and waited. After a few minutes, we could hear the delightful suckling and gulping of cubs taking their mother's milk. Then the most inquisitive ventured out. Before long there were two, then three. Tails waving, they played like puppies beneath the trailing branches.

Well and truly hooked, we left Khwai River Lodge, with a pledge to return.

Makgadikgadi Pans

Another back to reality night in the prison camp surrounds in Maun before the estimated 576km drive south to Khama Rhino Sanctuary – a route that traced the fringe of the great Makgadikgadi Pans. A relic of one of the biggest inland lakes in Africa, the pans are situated between parallel faults formed by an upwarping of the earth's crust about 2 million years ago. To this day, they sport a strikingly beautiful and unique wildlife setting. While the similarly positioned and adjacent Okavango Delta is quite literally an inland delta in the desert – in the shape of a huge pan, fed by the 'handle' of the Okavango River – the Makgadikgadi Pans form a series of separate depressions surrounded by sandveld and dunes. Both rely on rivers with seasonal fluctuating water levels to keep them supplied, and both have been home to nomadic Bushman for centuries past.

Motopi, Khumago, Rakops, Mopipi and Orapa were just some of the villages marking our journey along the western fringe of the pans, each with a history stretching back to the Middle Stone Age – while the remains of a curved stone wall on the island of Kubu, within the pans, is believed to be connected to the Great Zimbabwe Empire. In the more recent times of the last century, the Makgadikgadi Pans became increasingly important as a route used by white traders. It started when Livingstone announced the existence of Lake Ngami and the Bushmen of the region pointed out permanent water at Gusha Pan on the northern side. Traders, missionaries and explorers flocked to the area. Amongst them were Andersson, the Green brothers and, more importantly for us, a certain James Chapman: traveller and explorer, James Chapman hunted extensively in the region.

Such was the explorer's reputation that a group of baobab trees, named after him, are a 'must see' on every group tour visit to the region. It was on a return visit in 1861 that James Chapman brought the artist Thomas Baines with him. Baines painted the baobab trees – capturing their swollen water-bearing trunks, great heavenward reaching arms and leafy profiles – naming them after Chapman. Thus, this more recent explorer namesake is responsible for putting Richard's father's family name on the map, right in the heart of Africa. We would have liked nothing better than to stand before the great baobab trees with our cameras, but time and distance dictated that we keep heading south to Serowe.

Khama Rhino Sanctuary

One of my favourite wildlife images is the back view of a rhino. There is something about its size and composition, especially when in motion, that is engaging. The front view is pretty compelling too – a reminder of both its strength and its weakness. There is nothing so fierce or single-minded as a charging rhino. It was the chance encounter with the black rhino, on Namibia's Waterberg Plateau, that provided an adrenaline rush in an otherwise uneventful game-drive – a memorable mock charge.

The rhino's dilemma is that its formidable horn that makes it a fierce combatant has also led to its near extinction. By the late 1980s, rhino were all but extinct in Botswana. It is difficult to believe that the terrible slaughter has been, and remains to satisfy man's mythical belief in the aphrodisiac properties of its horn. While the Chinese take the ground powder of the horn to increase their sexual powers, the Yemeni belief in the horn's ferocious sexual powers – its size and shape – led them to use it to form the handles of the obligatory khanjar: a practice adopted throughout Yemen and Oman that contributed to the trade and slaughter of rhinos throughout both countries.

The first attempts to protect Botswana's rhinos were made by taking the drastic and brutal measure of removing their horns. This did not work for two reasons. Without a horn, the female is unable to defend her young against predators, and secondly the horn does grow back again, albeit slowly.

In an effort to save the species, the residents of Serowe decided to protect the few remaining rhino in Botswana in order to allow them to breed in safety. In 1992, they established the Khama Rhino Sanctuary, just 20km northwest of Serowe. By 1993, four rhino from Northern Botswana had been translocated and placed in very large bomas, built by volunteers from the local communities. By June 1995, an electric fence was completed, local people were trained and employed to patrol the reserve, and all rhinos were released from their bomas to roam freely. In 2002, at the time of our visit, the sanctuary was home to twenty *weit* rhino, and one recently introduced black rhino. Other wildlife which have either been translocated or settled naturally include zebras, blue wildebeests, giraffes, leopards and ostriches, as well as varieties of antelopes and small mammals and two hundred and thirty identified species of birds.

I was interested to learn that the name 'white' rhino – derived from the Afrikaans' word *weit* – is misunderstood. *Weit* does not refer to skin colour, but to the shape of the rhino's mouth, a wide letterbox shape designed for efficient grazing. The black rhino's skin is darker, and its more rounded mouth and pointed upper lip are designed for browsing. In fact, both rhinos enjoy wallowing in mud and are more likely to be mud-coloured. Their shared fondness for rubbing against convenient anthills or trees to rid themselves of parasites has reduced vast pyramidal-shaped anthills in the park to rounded mounds and trees to stumps. To prevent further damage, the rangers have erected convenient rhino itching posts on the edge of the pan.

Since we had come specifically to see and take photographs of rhino we headed for the Serowe Pan, a natural waterhole surrounded by nutritious grassland, said to be their favourite stomping ground. In an area of sandveld, we came upon a weit female and her calf grazing near the track. Protected by park wardens, the rhinos are accustomed to safari vehicles, and this pair behaved as if we didn't exist. Engine off, cameras ready and the late afternoon sun shining directly onto the rhino, it was the perfect photo opportunity.

There was one problem. The adult was grazing with her back to us. There is a limit to the number of shots of a rhino's behind, even for a confessed addict, and this one was in no hurry to turn round. On the other hand, we were reliant on the fast slipping sun for good light. The more adventurous calf moved in frequent short staccato bursts that invariably ended under the female to suckle. Finally, our patience was rewarded. Between us, we succeeded in a selection of shots of the magnificent square-lipped female and her offspring.

Our second encounter was with a young male. This time he was close by the track and facing in the right direction, but now the low sun provided a glaring backdrop. Even when we broke the rules by creeping out of and round the back of the vehicle to get close-up shots, details of his prehistoric features were lost in shadow. He made no attempt to retreat, but stared with a soulful expression of uncertainty and 'how do I sit this one out?' Finally, he demonstrated exactly how – he lay in the grass, resting his horn-heavy head on the ground, but with one wary eye on us.

Leaving him to his solitude, we reached the waterhole just as the sky was turning burnt sienna. Zebra and eland were warily approaching to drink, and then the solid form of rhino and the elegant head of a giraffe appeared, silhouetted against darkening sky.

There is a great deal more to the history of Serowe than rhino. One of the largest traditional villages in Africa, it is the birth and burial place of Botswana's first president, the late Sir Seretse Khama – the founding father of Khwai River Lodge. The life-story of this remarkable man is a wonderful real-life fairytale. As a young man and heir to the Ngwato throne, he caused uproar in the family when, in 1948, while studying law in London, he met and married Ruth Williams, an English woman. The consequence of such a breach in tribal custom was that he was exiled and, since his father was dead, his uncle took the throne. Subsequently, various breakdowns in tribal structure occurred, and in 1956 Seretse returned to Serowe with his English wife and began working towards the independence of Botswana, a British Protectorate at that time. Ten years later, this was achieved. Knighted by England's Queen Elizabeth II, Sir Seretse became the country's first President, a position he held until his death in 1980.

Today Ian Khama, Sir Seretse's son, has the title of Chief of the Ngwato, and his English mother holds the title of honoured wife of the late King and mother of the Chief. As no guide was available, we were unable to visit the Royal Cemetery on Thathaganyana Hill, where Sir Seretse's grave is marked by a bronze duiker, the Ngwato totem. A keen conservationist and photographer, his spiritual presence remains integral to Botswana's successful wildlife story in the Okavango Delta. Here at Serowe, the place of his birth and burial, the rhino sanctuary is a wonderful living tribute to his memory.

The Limpopo River

The sandy bed of the 'Great grey-green, greasy Limpopo River, all set about with fever trees'[5] stretched alongside, marking the border with South Africa and our route east to the Pont Drift Border Post. In the dry season, to cross to South Africa at Pont Drift, one literally drives over the bed of the Limpopo River. During the wet season, when the river and its tributaries overflow, visitors have to be airlifted or leave their vehicles at the far side and cross by the rustic cable car. The long last stage of our journey, along yet another bone-shaking gravel road

---

[5] Rudyard Kipling, *Just So Stories*

through the Tuli Block, was crossed by a series of 'drifts' or dry streambeds, feeding into the parched riverbed of the great Limpopo, a wide corridor of sand.

This block, or strip of land, was intended for the railway linking South Africa and Rhodesia in Cecil John Rhodes' ambitious plan for the Cape to Cairo railway. Political manoeuvrings, plus the number of rivers crossing the Tuli Block, thwarted the plan and along with it, Cecil Rhodes' dream. Today the strip remains divided into privately owned farmland. We were heading towards the 90,000 hectare Tuli Game Reserve at the block's eastern end. This was to be our last night in Botswana, and we intended to spend it in luxury at Tuli Safari Lodge.

Dramatic outcrops of rock in an open desert landscape marked our approach to the reserve. The most remarkable of these is undoubtedly the legendary sheer cliffs of Solomon's Wall. This stark basalt dyke once formed a steep-sided dam wall across the *Motloutse* (Large Elephant) River that held back a great lake. The rock wall, resembling a fantastic castle or citadel built from massive stone blocks, was named by an early European visitor, who was reminded of the fabled lost city of Ophir from the myths and legends about King Solomon.

The deep pool that forms below the dyke wall when the Motloutse is in full flood is imbued by local people with yet another legend of a serpent living in a pool. If you walk alone by this pool, the serpent will rise and hypnotise you so that you must continue walking towards it, whereupon it will stick its tongue in your eyes and drag you to the murky bottom. Today, the pool was no more than a damp patch. Nevertheless, eyes fixed firmly ahead, we drove through a gap in the wall to the far side.

This was elephant country. In afternoon's heat, great family gatherings, sheltering shoulder to shoulder beneath the widespread branches of magnificent trees, were reminiscent of scenes from Kipling's *Just So Stories*. Minutes later, the track passed between a female elephant and her calf. Separated from her offspring by our vehicle, the alarmed mother bellowed and rushed towards the Land Cruiser, ears flapping. Making a hasty retreat to a more distant spot, we watched the calf trot across to join the anxious parent.

From wilderness to a wonderland of pristine lawns, streams of running water, flowering shrubs and plants and the thatched reception of Tuli Safari Lodge. Our time in this Garden of Eden was short lived. Not for the first time on our travels, we encountered a BBC film crew. On this occasion, they had taken all available accommodation. Camping was not looked upon favourably and it was too late to cross the border into South Africa. Completely unfazed, the manageress escorted us to an open-sided bar – an impressive design built round the trunk of a six hundred year-old nyala-berry tree – and took out her mobile phone.

Iced drinks in our hands, we waited for our fate to be decided. Minutes later, a sand-splattered 4WD crunched over the gravel and skidded to a halt. A remarkable replica of Richard Briers, in the role of Tom Good from *The Good Life,* emerged.

'Self-sufficient?' he asked unceremoniously, briefly casting his eyes over us and our home on wheels. 'Come on then,' he said, without waiting for a reply, 'follow me. I've an out of the way spot. You can spend the night there.'

He shot off along a deeply rutted sandy track. We followed, dodging two jousting warthogs and skirting another, grovelling on its knees in an attitude of prayer. Lurching and bouncing, we followed our host between great banks of sand until we were trailing alongside a huge promontory of rock. Where it ended, he made a 180 degree turn and stopped abruptly. We juddered to a standstill, bumper to bumper.

'Over there,' he said, pointing to yet another huge nyala-berry tree. 'An elephant retreat, but they seem to have moved on. Look, I've things to do,' he explained, glancing at his watch. 'Have to rush. Keep your hand on the horn if you need me. By the way,' he added, one leg in and one out of the vehicle, 'light a fire. Keeps prowling animals at bay.'

Then he was gone.

We were alone and parked literally on the banks of the great Limpopo River among the sprawling roots of magnificent trees and dangling snake-ropes of lianas reminding me that this was the haunt of Kipling's 'bi-coloured python rock snake'. The legendary fever trees with their yellow-green branches lining the banks were so-named because at one time, it was believed that as a result of their proximity to water where the malaria mosquitoes breed, they were the cause of the disease. In the great dry riverbed small pools of limpid water gleamed in failing light, hinting at diminishing underground supplies needed to keep trees and animals alive until the overdue rains arrived.

By now, the sun was behind the trees and expectations of luxury had plummeted. This was raw reality as distant from the safe 'in the wild' luxury safari lodges as you can get. We were in the wild and alone, beneath the limbs of a tree so huge that you could not see its uppermost branches. 'An elephant retreat,' there was no doubt about that. The ground was a thick carpet of dung. Feeling not unlike Katharine Hepburn in a scene from the *African Queen,* I began shovelling a space clear for our collapsible table and chairs. Meanwhile, Richard had collected a pile of dead wood and dried dung and before long had a fire burning and the kettle on. We had enough provisions to keep hunger at bay.

As darkness settled, a handful of impala filtered through from an adjacent clearing. The lead male, with beautiful lyre-shaped horns perched like a coronet on his elegant head, momentarily mesmerised by the flames of the fire, remained poised in perfect stillness, as if cast in bronze. A scuffling in the branches of the nyala-berry tree drew our attention to a family of night apes foraging over our heads. As tongues of flame sent orange stars shooting towards the night sky, already crazy with stars, we had an unfailing sense that we were being watched by dozens of unseen eyes. We sat facing the fire, backs to the vehicle, searching the darkness. It wasn't the night of luxury we had envisaged, but it was an extraordinary experience of Africa in the raw, touching the very soul of the wilderness we sought.

South Africa

Kruger National Park, December 2nd

Nothing there is beyond hope, nothing that can be sworn impossible, nothing wonderful, since Zeus, father of all the Olympians, made night from mid-day, hiding the light of the shining Sun, and sore fear came upon men.

Thales of Miletus, Greek philosopher

'What will you do if the sky clouds over?' Richard asked a fellow traveller.

'Commit suicide,' was the unflinching reply.

The response may not have been serious, but it does illustrate the intensity of feeling associated with an eclipse, even to this day. Ancient civilisations, including Stonehenge, Babylonia and Egypt, each developed a unique approach to an eclipse. The myths and legends that evolved were associated either with the forces of good or the forces of evil. One strongly held myth, especially in Eastern cultures, is centred on an invisible dragon or demon that devours the sun during an eclipse. The Chinese believed that the forces of evil could be frightened away if they produced a great noise by banging on drums or shooting arrows into the sky. As recently as the last century, the Chinese Imperial Navy fired ceremonial guns during an eclipse to scare off invisible dragons.

Not all cultures feared an eclipse. The Tahitians believed it was an act of love between the sun and the moon. Even to this day, people of the Arctic are said to believe that an eclipse is a sign of divine providence when the sun and the moon temporarily leave their places in the sky to check that things on earth are satisfactory.

Our month-long journey through Namibia and Botswana was at an end. We had driven across the Limpopo River at Pont Drift and made our way to Punda Maria, the most northern camp in South Africa's Kruger National Park. Listed as one of a number of favoured sites from which to view the total solar eclipse of 2002, it was our goal and the last staging post on our journey. We were not alone. Like us, thousands of people were travelling long distances to one of the sites in Southern Africa and Australia.

For months if not years ahead, plans had been laid and books written giving precise details of the timings, weather predictions, guides to photography, accommodation and travel. With only days to go, everything was coming to a head. Local people were as full of expectations as long-distance visitors, and were no different to their ancestors in their belief in the powers of either good or evil associated with the eclipse.

'*Mwari* (God) is passing by – this is a good thing,' stated Chief Magano Nxumalo from the Magona tribe. For his people, the eclipse is a symbol of wealth and goodness. The profits from catering for the needs of the six thousand visitors staying at his village just outside the Punda Maria Gate of Kruger National Park, helped to make his belief come true.

'Everything in our shops has been sold out. This (eclipse) is good for us,' he affirmed.

Others, forbidden by their gods to watch, believed that if they witnessed the eclipse they would be struck by lightning and burnt to ashes. Some saw eclipses as portents of death, famine and pestilence. For many overseas tourists who had travelled great distances to witness the event, it was a once in a lifetime experience.

'It will change your life. It is something you cannot miss out on,' insisted a German visitor.

On the day before the overshadowing of the sun, the skies were a peerless blue, and all that man could do in preparation had been done. Fortunate to have found and secured comfortable thatched lodge accommodation at Punda Maria, we spent the morning touring the nearby Mahonie Loop, to see how the wildlife was preparing for the event. From elephants strolling nonchalantly through bushveld, to grazing impala and a handsome saddle-bill stork watching over his yellow saddle for movement in the Matukwale Dam, they appeared unfazed. Blossoming shrubs and intense green vegetation were evidence that some early summer rain had fallen. The euphoria candelabra was reaching for the heavens, and the stately baobab's bulbous limbs had burst into leafy crown.

Back at the camp, the skies remained intensely blue. Not one wisp of cloud was evident and, according to the experts, clouds only develop with the day's increasing build-up of heat. Therefore, cloud cover was unlikely in early morning – the time of the long awaited event. There was no build-up of cloud, but excitement was brewing. We could hear the drumbeat of the musicians accompanying the first troupe of local dancers welcoming the eclipse. Others perpetuated the belief that the drumming would keep evil away. From the doorway of the lodge, we watched rhythmic dancers moving in the dappled shade of a circular platform built round the trunks of trees. The chanting of women accompanied by drumbeats, handclaps and the mournful trumpet sound emitted from a kudu horn continued until darkness fell. The night sky was brilliant with a galaxy of stars. It was a good sign.

'What have I done to upset the gods?' was the 6 am voice of despair that I woke to. Through open curtains, the sky was completely obscured by a bank of stationary grey cloud. With just over an hour until the start of the one minute, eighteen seconds total solar concealment, it did not bode well. Minutes later, mugs of tea in hand, we stationed ourselves on the nearby brow of the hill – an excellent viewing spot, but for the moment we were gazing at thick cloud. Then a change occurred. It could have been collective wishful thinking, or maybe the forces of good were on our side after all. Slowly but deliberately, a breeze stirred and grew stronger. Over our heads we watched thinning cloud move like veils of mist, and there through the haze, pale as the moon, was the sun. A unified murmur of relief greeted this wan apparition.

A tantalisingly 'now-you-see-it, now-you-don't' performance ensued. An excellent sighting of the moon's 'first bite' out of the sun was followed by obscurity from more passing cloud until it sifted away again. Then, heralded by an increase in 'evening' birdsong, the dramatic and sudden arrival of an eerie deep twilight went hand in hand with an unearthly silence and a noticeable drop in temperature. As the moon's shadow started to slip away from the sun, a brilliant spearhead of light widened to a shaft that travelled swiftly across the sky, flooding it with light. This conceptual moment of first light, coupled with the sensation of the swift passing of the moon's shadow, is the moment that remains lodged firmly in my memory. The celestial wedding was over the celebratory breakfast about to begin.

***

The lure of Africa remained. I was addicted, especially to the Okavango. When we discovered that Orient Express Safaris owned and ran not only Khwai River Lodge, but two further contrasting lodges in the delta, we made arrangements to spend two successive nights at each. While Khwai River Lodge offered both wet and dry safari experiences, as the name suggests, Eagle Island was in a position to offer wet safaris, and Savute Elephant Camp exceedingly dry. This time, the entire trip was going to be of the spoilt five star variety. We salved our consciences by reminding ourselves that we had done it the hard way. Now like butterflies we were going to arrive, dip into and depart from each lodge by winged flight, albeit of the Cessna variety.

Addicted to the Okavango

In an ocean of desert, a great river that never reaches the sea spills tentacles of deepest blue creating islands of green – an extraordinary and temporary oasis filled with mysterious woodland and open savannah – a haven for wildlife.

The Okavango Delta

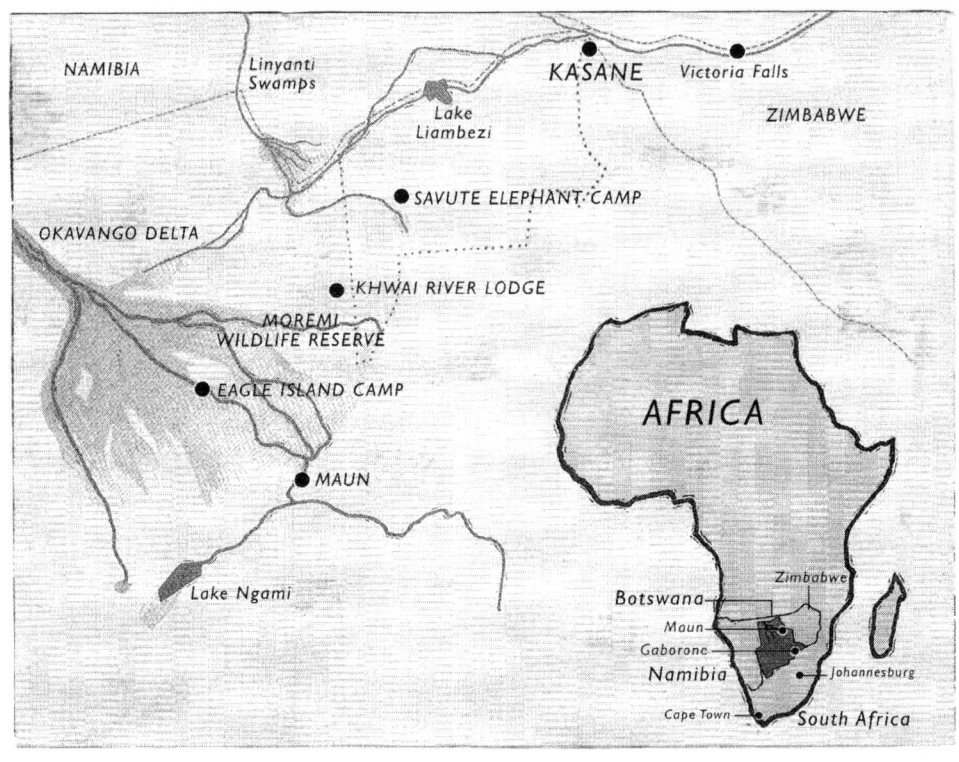

Khwai River Lodge
December 2004

'I was born in a mokoro,' boasted Mothupi with a wide smile, launching into another fascinating story from his life in the bush. The chief guide at Khwai River Lodge, Mothupi added star quality to a safari lodge that already offered the ultimate in luxury in a perfect wilderness setting, overlooking the floodplain of the Khwai River. Knowing that Mothupi was nearing retirement, plus our fascination with learning more about his history and its link with the history of the lodge were pressing reasons for a return trip.

He may not literally have been born in a *mokoro* – dug-out canoe – but Mothupi is a member of the Bayei tribe whose ancestors, in the eighteenth century, fleeing the expansion of the Lozi Empire along the Zambezi River, travelled down connecting waterways from Zambia in canoes and settled in the delta. His progress from near-naked boy hunter to chief guide began when he was recruited as a tracker at Khwai River Hunting Lodge. In 1969, when the lodge was opened by Sir Seretse Khama, it was one of the first hunting lodges in the delta.

Setting up a Hemingway-style hunting lodge was one thing, but inviting celebrity guests to track dangerous game in an unknown wilderness was another. Born into a family that lived primarily by hunting and fishing in and on the banks and islands of the delta, and travelling the snaking waterways in hollowed out canoes, the delta was in Mothupi's blood. Armed with instinctual and practical tracking, hunting and navigating skills, he was in the right place at the right time, and was the obvious choice to be recruited as a tracker.

As time went on, further problems to arise were the distances that visitors – tracking and hunting game – had to cover on foot, and the need for transport to recover the game. The answer: Mothupi must learn to drive. This accomplished, he faced the next step up the ladder to becoming a fully-fledged safari guide and member of staff: he was invited to take his meals in the dining room. He reminisced about the first occasion when, seated alone at a polished table, he wrestled with unfamiliar knives and forks.

'The knife. It was impossible!' he exclaimed. 'It cut nothing and usually ended up on the floor. Not like my hunting knife.'

Now, in addition to his deep knowledge and understanding of the delta, equipped with newly acquired skills plus a flair for conversation, and unfailing humour when recounting tales from the past, he was as invaluable to game viewing safari visitors of today as he was to the visitors of the original hunting lodge. Along with two fellow visitors we started the evening safari by playfully insisting that we would settle for nothing less than a close encounter with a leopard or cheetah.

'Okay,' Mothupi replied, 'but it won't be easy, and this evening, lions may have to do.'

Within minutes, we drew alongside two lions sleeping off the effects of eating more than half a buffalo from a recent kill. One acknowledged our presence by rolling his eyelids, before succumbing to total inertia. The edge of a shady clearing was the perfect place to watch the drama unfold: a hyena emerging from the cooling effects of a mud bath; three contented wart hogs sharing another mudhole, while a ground hornbill, holding a coiled snake in her beak, carried her victim to waiting young. A giraffe with an elegant Modigliani neck eyed us curiously from behind a screen of bushes, before rising inelegantly to its feet and cruising to a safer distance.

'Searching for minerals,' Mothupi explained referring to a lone bull elephant patiently loosening soil with his foot. 'Essential for his diet.'

The serious birdspotters were kept busy as we made our way from bush to the floodplain. A place overlooking the river on the opposite bank, where a gathering of indolent lions were lazily noting the movements of a line of buffalo, was the selected spot for sundowners and stories from the past. While Mothupi added lemon and ice to our drinks, we fired questions about the origins of his tribe in the delta.

He explained that when the Bayei arrived, the River San were already there: 'as far back as anyone can remember.' Villages were widely scattered and, he assured us, there was no animosity. The River San lived on the watersides, hunting and fishing and moving from one part of the river to another, following the movements of game and fish.

'But,' Mothupi insisted, 'they had no canoes. They learnt how to build canoes from my people. Only then did they penetrate and settle further into the swamps. We shared our skills,' he added. 'Fishing nets, strung between canoes, a fence of reeds with tubular basket-like traps, built across water channels, the San learnt from the Bayei; they caught fish by using poison and scooping baskets.'

The resonant honking of a female hippo guarding her young calf, eyes just above the surface of the water, caught our attention and jogged Mothupi's memories of his father's love of hunting and eating hippo meat. He explained that there were two ways of catching hippo, on water or on land. For the Bayei, both methods depended on the use of their ingenious barbed harpoon. When a hippo was ambushed, the hunter thrust the harpoon into its body. As the animal struggled, a wooden shaft, attached by a long rope to the spear, would detach, leaving the spear hooked into the animal's flesh. Led by the rope, the hunters chased the animals in their canoes or on foot, finally killing them with handheld spears.

'On one occasion', Mothupi reminisced, 'the spear came out. One minute we were chasing a hippo, and the next the hippo was chasing us, so fast and furious that the only escape was to scramble up an anthill. We were very frightened and clinging on for a good hour in hot sun, until the hippo lost interest and wandered off.'

The use of deep pits, covered with loosely woven papyrus, along the animals' grazing route, the Bayei learned from the River San. Instead of the upright spear hidden in the pit, the Bayei carefully balanced a lethal harpoon from an overhead branch. When the animal trod on the grass and fell into the pit, the rope, attached to the weapon, was released and the harpoon plunged into the victim's back. To safeguard their kills, Mothupi's family transported them by mokoro, or large papyrus rafts, to an island. Here, safe from other predators, they cooked the meat and feasted. What they couldn't eat, they smoked and dried.

Now the sun was sinking, and it was time to return for candlelit dinner in the open-sided dining area of the lodge. Background music was the resonant grunting of hippos. Emerging from their daytime river-pools, hippos freely wandered under the stilted accommodation and spoiled themselves by grazing on the sweet grass surrounding the lodge.

On our final morning we passed through Khwai village, home of the River San people. 'Obey Your Thirst!', instructed a sign over a shop selling beer. The number of people who did was evident from the ingenious use of empty cans laid sideways on and plastered with anthill clay for the walls of a traditional rondavel house. While Mothupi dealt with the paperwork for entry into the Moremi Reserve, Richard joined forces with a safari companion and set off on foot to cross the celebrated log bridge over Botswana's Khwai River. Following in their wake, we clattered across the swaying carpet of logs, slowing to pick up the guys before they became a snack for the Moremi lions. Then, trundling through mopane woodland, we finally reached the river's floodplain. Here, Mothupi stopped and pointed to a herd of impala; standing perfectly still, they were staring intently in one direction.

'A predator,' he said. 'See they are nervous and watching.'

We set off in the direction of their gaze, and after a few hundred metres, saw a pair of bachelor lions strolling nonchalantly through long grass towards us.

'The lions we saw last evening,' he explained. 'They've been quenching their thirst. Now they're heading back to the remains of their kill. For the moment, the impala are safe.'

Morning coffee was in the shade of an impressive *Kigelia Pinnata* – sausage tree – its branches laden with dangling fruit resembling giant sausages.

'Be careful!' Mothupi warned, stooping to pick up a truncheon-sized pod and demonstrate its weight. 'It's heavy. If one falls on your head, you'll know it! This tree,' he added, becoming more serious, 'this is the tree from which we made our mokoro.'

Remembering his last mokoro, a gift from his grandfather, he became unusually nostalgic. When the Batswana tribe were planning to set up the Moremi Wildlife Reserve, all the villages established within the boundaries had to move. As if he were symbolically burying this stage in his life, Mothupi explained that he had buried his mokoro near his village, beneath the waters of Xaxaba Lagoon. He was determined to return and retrieve it from its resting place.

'I know the spot', he assured us. 'I carved the date on a nearby tree. 1962.'

The most colourful of Mothupi's hunting memories were associated with his uncle. If his father's passion was for hippo meat, his uncle's was for python. On one occasion, when chasing after a python with his uncle, the snake attempted to escape by hiding in a ready-made tunnel. However, the tunnel was several inches too short, and the end of the python's tail protruded. Ordered to grab the tail and pull the snake free while his uncle waited with his knife, Mothupi tugged with all his strength. But a young boy was no match for the powerful and resisting snake. Finally, his uncle's determination to succeed was such that he chopped off the python's tail, took a long sharp stick and, thrusting it into the snake's body, pulled the speared victim until he wrenched it free.

On another occasion, after a particularly vigorous buffalo hunt, gesturing to Mothupi's loins, his uncle asked why he was naked? Abashed, Mothupi realised that in the chase, he had lost the piece of animal skin attached to the baobab twine round his waist.

'It was like this!' he said, demonstrating the size and position of the animal skin with a tissue-wipe and enjoying our sceptical responses. 'Nothing at the back,' he assured us. 'The adults, they had bigger skins – impala – from front to back, but boys, very little.'

Finally, as we left the floodplain and headed for the bush Mothupi stopped. 'There!' he said, directing our gaze until we saw quite clearly the prize we would have otherwise missed: a reclining cheetah, camouflaged in the dappled shade of a fever tree. A poised and deceptively fragile beauty, she appeared to tolerate our presence until we satisfied our lust for shots. It was a splendid end to our visit, and set another jewel sparkling in the crown of Mothupi, a legendary guide.

Eagle Island

From aching desert dryness and mopane woodland to the deep green of riverine plains and shallow lagoons, where tentacles of deepest blue penetrate swampland like ink on blotting paper and snaking rivers create islands of trees. Etched in the sand, a network of animal tracks, laid down beyond the memory of man, criss-cross the vast wilderness.

This was the stunning eagle's eye view of the Okavango Delta seen from the Cessna, taking us from Khwai River Lodge to Xaxaba Lagoon. As the plane lost height, the thatched roofs of Eagle Island Camp, set among a great canopy of trees on the very edge of the lagoon, rushed to meet us. It was difficult to imagine a more isolated and more beautiful wilderness setting. From Cessna to a waiting tractor, we arrived in style, in time for afternoon tea on the waterside terrace beneath a canopy of massive trees – jackalberry, sycamore fig, African mangosteen and knobthorn – overlooking an infinitesimal carpet of water lilies that would have made Monet swoon. All around us, fish eagles, pied kingfishers, cormorants, egrets and dozens more could be seen or heard. Nothing had prepared me for this magical setting.

The evening safari was not on water, as we expected. This was the first day of the cross between wet and dry safaris and miraculously, we had arrived to experience both. It was nearing the end of the hot dry season: the water level of the lagoon was falling, and dry land was emerging from swamp. In a matter of days, the waterways would be too low to navigate and land safaris on the drying-out island would take over. Freddie, the camp manager, had completed a test drive on emerging land, and now we were in the capable hands of Mighty, a local guide, and his 4WD.

Part River San and part Bayei, Mighty grew up on the periphery of the Moremi Reserve. Adept in the land and water skills of both tribes and endowed with a passion for detail and perseverance he possessed all the qualities of a natural guide. Now with high summer temperatures before expected rain, the post-seasonal swamps of soggy grasslands and beds of waterlogged reeds tested his driving skills as he guided the growling engine towards firmer ground.

Huge pyramidal termite mounds – the only mountains on the island – leggy ivory and wild date palm give drama to a landscape dominated by marshlands and swamp. As the floodwaters recede, so the herds move in to feed on new grass. Unused to vehicles, bachelor groups of lechwes, zebras, antelopes and giraffes were skittish and nervous, pausing just long enough to satisfy their curiosity. Females remained out of sight, protecting the newly born or waiting for the arrival of more young. Bull elephants, roaming wooded scrub, eyed us warily to ensure we keep a safe distance.

A nervous black-backed jackal, skirting a field of russet grass, drew our attention to a hyena crouching in the near-centre. Disturbed, the scavenger lifted the horns and half-eaten bloody skull of a buffalo, dragging it to one side as if to escape our watching eyes. Its weight and the distance were too much, but the temptation to eat was stronger than the urge to run. Drooling glutinous saliva from an open mouth, she stared hard at us then continued with her meal. Even from a distance, the sound of teeth crunching bone was disconcerting. We left her to feast on the remains of a recent kill by lions.

Stopping for sundowners under a magnificent baobab tree and next to a pile of buffalo skulls reminded us that we were not the only visitors to this site. One minute it was lighthearted chatter and the tinkle of ice against glass, and the next a deep-throated roar. We froze. Mighty assured us the lions were far away, possibly on another island.

'But,' he warned, 'here, on these islands, lions swim. Look,' he urged, pointing to nearby tracks in the sand. 'Buffalo prints. If we find buffalo, then maybe we'll see lions too.'

The trail of prints and droppings led us towards the Boro Channel, marking the southwestern boundary of the Moremi Reserve, and to a convenient parking spot behind a screen of trees. Within minutes, five huge black buffalo ambled towards us, stopped and stared at the vehicle, assessing the situation more in nervousness than aggression. As soon as they passed, you could sense their relief as they broke into a trot until they reached the safety of bushes.

In growing darkness, we heard again the lions' roar. But now it was time to head back to the safety of the camp. Full headlights and Mighty's powerful spotlight sweeping the darkness, picked out dozens of pairs of lit eyes: a herd of zebra, a cerval cat crouched in the lower branches of a tree, and spring hares, sprinting along the sandy track before us. Back into the swamp, the engine struggled and revived, while all around us, under the cloak of darkness, unseen dramas played deep into the night.

In morning light, we could see all too clearly the heavyweight obstacles we had to overcome on the last water safari of the season. Hippos lorded over the receding waters of the lagoon, making it too dangerous to venture out in a lightweight and easily overturned mokoro. We set off by motorboat, heading towards the one remaining channel deep enough to navigate, to find that a huge male hippo had wedged himself mid-stream. Circled by the twitching ears and watching eyes of resident females and young, Mighty navigated the boat towards the shallows, confusing the macho male. He snorted and noisily submerged to follow.

Swiftly turning the boat, we headed downstream between walls of papyrus reeds, into the vacated narrow channel. It was pure blue and pure green and, at our passing, great clouds of birds peeled against the sky in a never-ending stream. Then, as reeds gave way to open water and marshland, the birds grew in size: flocks of great white egret, contorted question marks – long legs trailing they lifted, dropped and reassembled; storks, herons, geese rose and fell in sequence. We rounded a corner and there before us, like cardboard cutouts, black against the sky, the elegant long-necked silhouettes of cormorants poised on the topmost branches of a dead tree.

Beneath us in reflected sky, great packs of primeval fish trapped in shallow pools struggled to survive: a fish eagle's paradise. Its haunting, evocative cry followed us, soaring high over trees. Closeby, one imperious and snowy-white descended to a nest of reeds, while another plucked at a fleshy kill. The channel narrowed – so thin and shallow and clogged with trailing roots that Mighty struggled to free the engine and pole us between towering walls of reeds, renewing the peel of wings and bringing us within inches of a tiny Malachite kingfisher: brilliant jewel of the reeds.

As the corridor of reeds gave way to open sunlit bays with mounting banks of sand, we entered the Nile crocodile's domain. One, still as stone, lunged his huge tail to one side launching into the water. We bobbed in the wake, watching a line of bubbles move downstream. Another, with slotted pupils in glass eyes and bottom jaw teeth jutting between the flesh of its upper snout, lay in wait on the sandy bank. The pulsing soft throat threatened – touch me if you dare! Suddenly, they were everywhere, playing dead, camouflaged, rust against sand, grey-green and blue against waterlogged reeds, an unnerving display of glazed eyes and clamped teeth.

Closeby in a narrow channel, a badly savaged hippo waited: waited for death. Driven off by a dominant male, his putrefying wounds, too painful to submerge, were cruelly blasted by summer sun: an open invitation to flies and blood-seeking birds. Saddened and helpless, we moved on, wondering how long it would be before the crocodiles moved in.

As marshland grew from its watery hold and the russet landscape opened and spread, the range of birds grew in size and strangeness, as if each had adopted a weird disguise to outwit enemies or give an edge to a survival technique. Each as an individual was a fascinating part of nature's art, but collectively, as they appeared along the banks of the stream, it became an exhibition of winged freaks. An elegant blue crane balanced on a mannequin leg; a stork, with a yellow saddle across its red and black-banded bill, waded past the 'which way am I facing Hammerhead or Messenger of Deat?'. Closeby, a black egret – poised, head beneath his domed wing like a Victorian photographer beneath his umbrella – shared a shrinking pool of stranded fish with a Marabou stork. Hunched and vaguely obscene, he sported pink-bristled cheeks and a sausage-shaped pouch. And this was just the start.

The sheer variety amazed, as one after another each was identified, ticked off, logged and binoculars focused on the next in line. It was impossible not to be swept into the enthusiasm by the immediacy of a display that would have dazzled even the ultimate enthusiast, David Attenborough himself. Meanwhile, across the sweep of drying land, grazing herds of startled red lechwes, waterbuck and impala stared and took off only to stop at a safe distance and stare again. Kaleidoscope scenes swept by – an elephant reaching for figs, another scratching its rump against a tree, an island of baboons – while all around the never ceasing pulse of wings rose into the sky.

Candlelit dinner was on the terrace overlooking the lagoon. We sat under the vast canopy of a jakalberry tree, held in the embrace of a strangler fig. Even the trees are predatory here. Fruit bats were on the move and grunting hippos on the prowl. As we studied a menu that included a choice of ostrich stew or kudu steak, it became clear that we were no less predatory than the rest. Richard opted for ostrich stew, but the reality was too close at hand for me. I considered taking a leaf out of the hippos' book and making a stand for vegetarianism, but weakened at the mouth-watering prospect of butterfish steak. 'Go-away!' called a Grey Lourie. 'G'way! G'way!'

Lords of War at Savute Elephant Camp

After a romantic dinner under the stars in the camp's boma, we gravitated to the viewing deck overlooking the floodlit waterhole, to watch the approach of a herd of breeding elephant. Knee-high calves ran between the legs of elders as, shoulder to shoulder, they broke into a fast walk eager to reach the water. We estimated that there were two large herds, noisily and amicably quenching their thirsts. Then Philip, the camp manager, swung his powerful spotlight across the far sloping bank of the dry Savute channel, catching the fire in dozens of eyes burning in the darkness.
'Lions,' he warned. 'An ambush!'
Slowly and methodically, the low-slung forms crept across the hillside and lay in wait along the well-defined elephant track – a route etched in the depths of memory. This was the route the elephants would take that evening to go into the deep darkness of woodland. This was where the lions were waiting to attack, not a full grown bull or powerful matriarch but a grown elephant with sufficient meat on his bones to feed the oversized pack – for pack it was; a fierce hunting pack with the smell of elephant blood still in their nostrils from the last kill.
That night in our tented camp, we woke to hear deep-throated roars and our blood froze as the 'lords of war' staged not one, but two attacks. Above the threshing and cracking of falling trees, above the lions' chorus of urgent roars, the anguished terror of trumpeting cries tore into the night as the elephants fought to survive the army of teeth and claws and fought to understand.

The following morning, we learned that each year at Savute, as the dry winter months approached, individual lion prides gather together and form a 'super pride', often numbering into the thirties: a formidable force which is capable of taking on the largest living land mammals – elephants. With no instinctual fear of attack, the adult elephants have yet to come to terms with this phenomenon. Although on this occasion the lions were lying in wait, and one could not but believe that the elephants must have been aware of their presence, they did not alter their course, but walked straight into the ambush. Later, the second herd took exactly the same route, and they too suffered an attack. It was as if the elephants believed that all they have to do is trumpet their presence and the lions will slink away, as they do in daylight.

With the promise of a close-encounter with the super-pride, Ruster, our guide, drove to a spot on the periphery of the camp. There before us, looking as tame and harmless as huge contented pets, were the lions, all thirty four of them. Lounging in scattered shade, they occupied the underside of each bush, watching, dozing and lying sprawled on their backs, legs akimbo, as they did their least to survive day's terrible heat. Cubs with glowing amber eyes and soft fur adopted kitten postures and waited. Nearby, an amorous male broke the air of inertia. Driven by deep, heat-defying needs and accommodated by a receptive female, he rose to the occasion, exhausted himself and then flopped beside her again and again.

Ruster pointed overhead to the silhouettes of hooded vultures perched in a skeletal tree. On the ground beneath, four lionesses with rasping tongues and blood-soaked jaws licked the last traces of flesh from the skin of an elephant – their last kill. A tangible reminder of the dark side of the lions of Savute.

The size of the pride, the combined latent energy and the need for huge quantities of meat in a place deserted by water-seeking herds dictated change – change brought about by the forces of nature. The mysterious Savute River's coming and going, governed by tectonic plate movements deep beneath the Kalahari sands, last flowed in the late 1980s. During the dry season, herds of buffalo, antelope, zebra and wildebeest – the traditional 'lunch-on-the-run' menu of lions – migrate north to the Linyanti River and swamps, returning with the seasonal rains. Manmade boreholes along the Savute channel pump sufficient water to dried-up water holes to satisfy the remaining elephant herds, scattered antelope and the prides of lion that have opted to stay.

To survive and adapt to the drought conditions, the lions of Savute began to hunt elephant, unleashing a taste for elephant flesh and the knowledge that one elephant would supply more than enough meat to satisfy the appetite of the entire super pride. Ominously, on the night following the 2002 total eclipse of the sun in Chobe, an ailing elderly elephant, alone and dying, was discovered and eaten by lions. Some believe that this was a catalyst and the start of regular organised hunting of elephant by lions at Savute.

The sheer size of an elephant brought down as a victim of teeth and claws, followed by the long drawn-out tortured death, magnifies the horror. Elephants have yet to learn a strategy of defence against these 'lords of war' who, like the sabre-tooth tiger, have turned to new and desperate killing techniques.

That evening at the camp, we watched *Ultimate Enemies*[6], an incredible film of lion hunting elephant in Savute. At the height of the hunt, a lioness drops from an overhead branch of a tree onto the back of an elephant. The rest of the pack leap onto the victim's sides and legs. The shock, weight and number of attackers

---

[6] D. & B. Joubert, *Ultimate Enemies*

succeed in dragging the elephant to its knees. Miraculously, this elephant breaks free.

There is no doubt about it that Savute offers the ultimate rawness of experience in the wilderness, especially where lions are concerned. Nothing made of flesh and bone is safe when they are on the prowl. Drought conditions have dictated the building of stout fences, reinforced by electric wiring, to protect the camp from powerful water-seeking elephant herds, while hyena-proof gates guard each tented camp. Nothing is safe from lions. One night, the flailing claws of two lionesses, fighting over an impala, ripped the side of a tent. Inside, two terrified guests huddled together for a night without sleep.

Teeth and claws may rule the land, but beaks and claws bring terror from the skies. During the afternoon's oppressive build-up of heat, while I succumbed to the lure of the four-poster in our air-conditioned tent, Richard watched and photographed the hunting techniques of a yellow-billed kite. Doves that came to the waterhole to drink were easy pickings. From a favoured dead tree, the kite disdainfully plucked each victim before feasting. Lighter moments were introduced by troops of vervet monkeys and baboons that, along with a variety of birds, wait their moments on the periphery of the verandah to steal food especially prepared for guests.

One afternoon, while indulging in cake and tea, a vervet monkey dropped like a ball from between the overlapping folds of a sunshade onto my table. Snatching a piece of prized lemon drizzle cake, he bounced back and was gone. By the time he returned for an encore, Richard had joined me. Taken by surprise and threatened by the presence of a male, the monkey bared his teeth. Richard bared his teeth in return. Our uninvited guest left empty handed.

Philip capped this story by telling us of a newly arrived female guest. Sitting quietly, listening to a welcome speech, she was holding an iced drink in her hand. Suddenly the drink was snatched from her grasp. The thief, a vervet monkey, glass in hand, sat on the edge of the verandah nonchalantly sipping, leaving the guest shocked into silence by the speed and boldness of the theft.

Ruster was equally at ease whether tracking game across dried out marshland, sighting and identifying brilliantly plumaged birds, or explaining the practical and medicinal uses of plants and trees. Of these, the devil's thorn, easily identified by its lethal twin horns and delicate mauve blooms, was remarkable and memorable for the immediacy of a 'hands on' demonstration. In the shade of an island of magnificent baobab trees, Ruster added water to the plant's trailing stems and leaves and rubbed them between his fingers. Seconds later, he had a handful of frothy shampoo.

The ridge of sand linking the rocky outcrops of Gubaatsa and Gcoha Hills is a favoured hiding place of the leopard. Late one evening, we glimpsed one on the move. Later, we climbed the slippery blue-grey boulders of Gobabis Hill to a panel of ancient San rock art. This great vertical slab of rock, sheer and pale sand-coloured, was the chosen canvas. The red-ochre outlines of an antelope, the size and shape of tsessebe, an elephant and second antelope, with the impressive long straight horns of an oryx, stood in line one above the other. All three were superimposed on older much faded outlines, including that of a spotted giraffe.

Safe on their island of rock once surrounded by a vast lake, the images now looked over an open treed plain.

It was a place for philosophising. Like Richard, Ruster grew up in Rhodesia (Zimbabwe). Reminded of their homeland, they reminisced about the past, drawing upon memories of Manicaland, the Shona people and their language. *'Nzou!'* they called, simultaneously laughing and pointing to an elephant grazing on the plain below. Ruster confessed his longing to return, but he declared, 'Not while Mugabe remains in power.' Meanwhile, I was focused on finding the safest route for a hands, seat and feet descent over slippery boulders.

Inevitably, we ended our drives in the vicinity of a waterhole – this, after all, is where most of the action takes place. An old bull elephant quietly and methodically digging into the soil of a dried-out pool finally reached soft wet mud, and sprayed the cool liquid onto his heat-parched skin. A battle between two bull elephants provided some lively combatant poses. Finally, in a manic display of male bravado, the larger contender, attempting to intimidate his rival by charging headfirst into a tree, momentarily stunned himself before chasing the upstart across the plain into woodland.

Every photographer's dream was to capture the silhouette of an elephant drinking at the waterhole at sunset. Tonight the sky was red, and the first elephants were arriving. Just to remind us that the battle was not yet over, the lounging forms of lions, scattered in surrounding bush and across well-worn tracks leading to the water, were keeping watch and waiting – waiting, no doubt, for the cover of darkness. A leading matriarch, finding her pathway blocked by recumbent lions, trumpeted alarm, then displeasure and marched on. Reluctantly, the lions slunk a few metres away. The elephant led the herd to surround the water hole, in the dried-out pool. There she kept guard and wasted no time in driving approaching lions away.

As we left Savute, we knew that with the expected rains and the return of migrating herds, the Savute elephants would have a few months of respite. We wanted to believe that in the long-term, there was hope for the elephants, and that it was only a matter of time before they too adapt to the terrible changes overtaking them.

Savute Update, November 2010

It was with some surprise, but great relief, that I learnt from Warren Stone – General Manager of the Orient Express Safaris, Maun, Botswana – that there was no longer a super pride of lions at Savute; in fact, the lion population had been reduced to two small fragmented prides, each consisting of five and six members respectively. Without the number of lions to form a super-pride, hunting elephant – apart from the very young – is no longer practised. Nature has taken control, or has someone been listening to my prayers?

In Transit

It was after the second trip to the Okavango that we knew in our bones it was time to move on. Things were changing at a vast pace in Dubai. As the speed of development continued and increased, the Lower Gulf was becoming overcrowded both on land and at sea. With aspirations already underway of a snow dome, the world's tallest building (Burj Dubai) and a replica of China's Forbidden City, Dubai's reputation as the world's biggest and most ambitious building site continued to grow.

On a more modest level, our villa amidst dunes was now a villa surrounded by high-rise blocks. What is more, just streets away, a new mosque had been built. We have nothing against mosques or prayers, but the magnified metallic level of noise, especially during prolonged Friday prayers, was such that even with doors and windows of the villa closed, it was impossible to think, never mind attempt conversation. Hilarity was added on one occasion when the muezzin's mobile phone went off, competing with the call for prayer.

Our only resource was to head for *Sunset Song* and escape into the Gulf, or make for one of our retreats through wadis into the mountains or desert. However, it was becoming increasingly clear that these too were undergoing profound change. Sailing in the Gulf was ever more congested, and surrounding desert was not only being levelled and built upon at an increasing pace, but every newcomer had a 4x4 and was keen to test 'dune bashing' skills on what was remaining. The magnificent rolling dune landscape that we had traipsed across, leaving nothing but our footprints and had captured on our photographs, had gone forever.

Unspoilt places to take visitors who didn't want to spend their time in five or even seven star (Burj Al Arab) hotels, glitzy shopping centres and restaurants were fast disappearing too. Throughout the desert, tarmac roads were replacing graded roads and tracks through wadis. Updated versions of *Off-Road in the Emirates* left no route, place or even ghaf tree to sit under, unmapped and with such precise detail and directions that there was little for the independent minded explorer to discover for him or her self and nowhere to go to escape the crowds. The border post into Wadi Bih had become a main entry point for illegal immigrants, and was now closed to all except Omani passport holders. Five star hotels appeared in the most unlikely places including Dibba (six), and in the previously inaccessible fishing village – except on foot or by boat – of Tigi, en route to Musandam. Wilfred Thesiger's 'Arabian Nightmare' had become alarmingly true. Time and tide in the Emirates was swift and waited for no man.

The Gulf continued to be dredged and developed at a vast rate. Juxtaposed, next to images of the Pyramids, the Taj Mahal and the Colosseum – the world's largest manmade palm tree island hosting ten thousand villas and apartments – had plans for over sixty luxury hotels before 2007. With a 'little' help from the Dutch dredgers we met on safari in Botswana, the even bigger Palm Jebel Ali was well underway and further along the coast, two hundred and sixty man-made islands were still being coaxed into the shape of the world.

We were the exception rather than the rule. Dubai was attracting five million visitors a year and there were queues of people waiting to get permits for work and become residents. An increasing number of friends and acquaintances, hooked on the air-conditioned five star Emirati lifestyle, were buying property and settling down. Others were staying to complete their working life in the Gulf before returning to their home countries, or to live in the more accommodating climes of Spain or Cyprus. For many, the lifestyle was upmarket, the salaries tax –free, and there were increasing numbers of work opportunities.

For us, as much as we had enjoyed our time in the Gulf, we knew in our hearts it was time not only to move on, but to return home and be closer to our families. Then a timely opportunity: Richard was offered employment at Exeter International Airport in Devon. Though not at the managerial level he was accustomed to, the timing and place satisfied our immediate needs.

We had six weeks to prepare for our exodus. After a near decade in the Gulf, this was insufficient time for making decisions about what to sell and what to take with us, especially for invaluable possessions like the Musso and *Sunset Song*, that were so much a part of our lives. With so many people coming and going in Dubai, the market was overloaded with goods for sale. In the end, we made arrangements to have everything packed, shipped and ready to follow us on our exit. We were more successful in the sale of the remaining boxes of *Images of Arabia*, blank greeting cards, using our photographs. Magrudy's – the Ottakar's of the Middle East – relieved us of the entire collection.

We left the Gulf, but not our connections with it. It transpired that the Sheikh of Sharjah has long and warm affiliations with Exeter University, both as a former student and as a benefactor: he set up and funded an Islamic Department and library. The Sheikh's visits to the university, via Sharjah to Exeter Airport, where Richard was based, kept the bloodline open, so to speak.

Exeter

Weeks after we touched down on English soil, the Ssangyong Musso was delivered, started on the button and looked perfectly at home in the forecourt of our new Exeter home. Then *Sunset Song* arrived and spent a few months recovering in The Retreat – a boatyard in nearby Topsham – an ancient river port on the east bank of the River Exe. Her final home was a mooring on the far and west side of the river, offshore from historic Powderham Castle. The seat of the Courtenay family since 1325, the castle has remained in the same family to this day and is currently home to the 18th Earl of Devon. With Dartmoor, just a stone's throw away, we were surrounded by and engaged in Devon's fascinating past, including that of Starcross Yacht Club.

Just downriver from Powderham, the club lacked the setting, facilities and weather of Dubai Offshore Sailing Club. In fact, it did have a remarkable riverside setting, but with the grave disadvantage of being lodged on a concrete island, with the road from Starcross to Dawlish on one side and a railway on the other. Formed in 1772, Starcross, one of the oldest yacht clubs in Britain, is housed today in Brunel's (converted) former Atmospheric Pumping Station Building, alongside the 'Atmospheric Railway'. The launching place for boats, beneath the tunnel upholding the railway, created an atmospheric learning curve for the spoilt Dubai team.

As latecomers to the club, we were allocated a river mooring way up the undredged, tidal Exe estuary – a far cry from the leisurely English breakfast and walk-on mooring at DOSC. First, we had to get the dinghy from under the clubhouse. There were pairs of doors to unlock, followed by much heaving and manoeuvring of the beast onto a trolley. The tidal launching place beneath the railway tunnel was amidst water, mud and weed, with trains powering overhead, blowing warning whistles on the approach to nearby Starcross Station and railway crossing. For the initiates, it proved something of a stamina test.

The first attempt to launch an inflatable dinghy that had been in storage in Dubai for a number of years ended unceremoniously. Unsuitably clad in shorts and fair weather boating shoes, I was standing under the tunnel on the edge of the incoming tide, holding the rope attached to the recently blown-up dingy that was bouncing like an excited dog on a lead. Meanwhile, Richard was putting the trolley to bed and re-locking the succession of doors, before making his way back to join me. Suddenly, an explosion like a gun going off was followed by a succession of reverberating blasts. Shocked but still standing and unharmed, I decided that it had not been the gunman on the loose that I had feared. Then, as I focused on the dinghy, I became aware that she was slowly but surely growing smaller; in fact, she was shrinking before my eyes. The perished rubber that had survived storage, shipping and inflation, had given up the ghost.

The second attempt was this time in a brand new fibreglass dinghy of the Walker Bay variety. While I had resorted to wearing green wellington boots, Richard remained with trousers rolled and bare feet. We escaped the tunnel, rounded a wooden pier and set off up river to where *Sunset Song* was tugging on her mooring. Some forty windblown, wave-ridden minutes later, we drew alongside and Richard tied the dinghy to the mooring rope.

'Okay. Get on,' was the unceremonious invitation to board.

I could tell he was in captain mode. Then a conciliatory hand was offered to assist me onto the dinghy's lurching side. I looked up to see the side of *Sunset Song* curved over us like the belly of a whale, the sheer side of the stern – the line of tightly knotted ropes.

'You get on,' was my considered response.

From the wallowing vessel, I watched as Richard clambered, Tarzan-style, up the ropes to the far away deck. He then hung a ladder over the side, to tempt me to join him.

Reunited with his beloved *Sunset Song*, he set about inspecting and testing and righting and caressing, from time to time calling on assistance from his caffeine-indulging crew.

Between activities, there was no doubt about the loveliness and naturalness of the setting. To one side were the green hills of the deer park of the estate belonging to Powderham Castle, and across the water, the sun-blessed villages of

Topsham and Lympstone hugged the shoreline. Cormorants preened and rested on vacant buoys. With a majestic whooshing of wings, two swans crossed within feet of our bows. The evocative cries of curlew, and glimpses and sounds of so many more visiting and resident birds, pealed from the skies.

We allotted the mooring top marks as a picnic stop, but sailing remained a different story. The Exe provided a twice daily tidal challenge we had yet to test with *Sunset Song*. This day was no more than a trial run, to and fro in the dinghy, to get the feel of our new surrounds. There were bigger challenges ahead. On our return to the club, the tide was out. Well, before we reached the tunnel, the dinghy became stranded on tidal mud. Stepping out, I felt my boots slowly and steadily sinking, taking me with them. Attempting to move, I left one mud-filled boot behind.

'Stay where you are. Don't move!' came an urgent command.

I had no problem obeying. I wasn't going anywhere but down. Wading calf-deep in soft mud and weed, Richard came plodding to my rescue. With much squelching and struggling, we rescued the boot and got ourselves and the dinghy to dry land. Sluicing the vessel and our limbs from a nearby hose, we put her to rest and then, dreaming of bacon sandwiches and a gallon of tea, made for home.

There was one problem. We had no bacon. Taking the second instead of the first exit off the Countess Wear[7] roundabout onto the Topsham Road, we made a detour to a local store. While I was locating lean rashers, Richard had gravitated towards wine-stacked shelves. It was when I was preparing to purchase my goods, I became aware that the entire shop had grown still and silent. Fellow shoppers and keepers alike were watching us with wary eyes. In his own world, Richard was calling out to ask which wine I preferred.

'Jacob's Creek – remind us of Dubai, or Cabernet Sauvignon? Both maybe,' he concluded, joining me at the till.

Back at the Musso, I reassessed our mud-splashed, windblown selves, then caught sight of myself in the wing mirror. A dishevelled hairstyle provided the final touch. While most of the hair that had been pulled back and tied had escaped and was projecting in various directions, remaining remnants were sticking in the air like radio antennae – details that had escaped my escort's eye. The cracked window of the nearby fish and chip shop reminded me that this was a neighbourhood where vandalism had recently occurred. Not surprisingly, our unkempt appearance had caused a degree of suspicion and, quite probably, fear that we were about to rob the till.

Devon's Beating Heart

Sailing apart, Exeter was our home and our heartland. We watched yachts, like toys with full-blown sails, bowled out to sea by winds and tide from the mouth of the Exe; explored the ancient smuggling ports of Topsham and Lympstone, on the river's eastern edge, and from the west bank looked across the deer park to the

---

[7] Roundabout named after a weir constructed across the River Exe in 1286, on the instruction of Isabella de Fortibus, Countess of Devon

silver mirror of the Exe from Powderham Castle. Beneath the stone canopies of the west front of Exeter's beautiful cathedral, we gazed at sculptured reliefs of ancient kings, whose lovely and expressive faces looked back on us as they have looked on passers by for over five hundred years. We explored villages of thatched cottages and roadside coaching inns strung along narrow, winding lanes, but it wasn't until we ventured onto the wilderness of Dartmoor that we were fully conscious of the heartbeat of Devon.

A narrow road meandered across the moor roughly from east to west. On either side, highland peaks capped by granite boulders rose to over 600 metres in places. Like a giant's playground, outlines of tumbled rocks, pushed up through sedimentary layers millenniums ago, hug the skyline reminding us of the *inselbergs* of Namibia and *kopjes* of Botswana. Taking the name Tor from the Celtic word for tower, the Dartmoor outcrops are a magnet for travellers; abandoning vehicles by the roadside and watched by scraggy sheep, they trudge across moorland to climb to the summit of these mammoth boulders, forming antlike silhouettes against sky.

Our focus was the remains of ancient settlements of Neolithic ancestors. The route we chose wound between the dramatic tors of Hay, Rippon and Corndon, then downhill to an old stone bridge at Dartmeet – literally, the meeting point of the tributaries of the great River Dart. Devon's two great moors, Exmoor and Dartmoor are the birthplace of its rivers; they rise in clear springs in the marshes, funnel and wind their way over moorland, through farmland and forest, between folds in the hills to the sea and the coastal towns to which they give their names: Exe, Teign, Plym, and Dart.

Minutes later, we crossed a second bridge in the direction of Merrivale, a wide-open valley guarded by great tors, and strewn with granite boulders. According to our map, the area was littered with the remains of ancient settlements, but after scanning the wide expanse of moorland, we were at a loss where to begin and decided to a ask directions from a fellow traveller parked nearby. His response, in a strong Welsh accent, reminded us that tribal hostilities in the British Isles were alive and well. The very mention of a stone circle set our Celtic traveller onto a diatribe of accusations of wrongs the English had perpetrated against the Welsh.

'You don't believe that Stonehenge is English?' he challenged.

His rhetoric continued for several minutes, highlighting a list of English claims, all of which he proclaimed were not only false, but were unjustly taken from the Welsh. Loath to prolong the engagement with revelations of my part Norman background, I was tugging on Richard's sleeve and edging away in the direction of King's Tor from where, in all probability and with a buzzard's eye-view, we would be able to make out where the ancient circles lay. Our compatriot's voice followed.

'You call these hills? They're mounds, not hills. If you want to see real hills, visit the Brecon Beacons. Go to Wales.'

Hills or mere mounds, the moorland and its granite tors provided settlers with defensive homelands from which they could see enemies approaching from afar, as well as materials to build walls for villages: safe 'pounds' of thatched roundhouses.

We set off across a fairly level plain of rough grassland dotted with boulders, and came unexpectedly upon a standing stone. A lone sentry, some six feet in height, it remained where it had been planted centuries ago. Our route continued across marshy ground and over a startlingly clear stream, before the climb up a staggered slope to great boulders of granite, marking the windswept summit of King's Tor. The reward was a magnificent view across moorland to the quintessentially English patchwork of fields and surrounding forest, once royal hunting grounds. In the very distance, the waters of the English Channel shone like tinfoil. Overhead, billowing cloud filled the sky.

Dramatic changes of weather are intrinsic to Dartmoor. On good days, cloud formed by sea air that cools as it rises over the moor rolls in and billows overhead, then just as suddenly parts, flooding the land with golden light. Cloud shadows streak across the landscape. On darker days, when the sun is obscured by cloud, mists cling to the valley sides and an air of mystery surrounds the moors, reviving legends about the Prince of Darkness, who rides from the forest accompanied by his red-eyed flame-spitting hounds. Said to have originated in the demonisation of wolves that once roamed the moors, the legend is kept alive by place names such as 'Devil's Bridge' and 'Hound Tor'. This dramatic atmosphere has inspired artists, poets and writers over the centuries – most notably perhaps Sir Arthur Conan Doyle's tale of Sherlock Holmes, *The Hound of the Baskervilles.*

It was on our descent that Richard suddenly stopped and pointed to a double row of standing stones. Stretching some fifty metres in an approximate east-west alignment, they formed a ceremonial passageway, marked at the halfway point by a rosette of stones: a tantalising enigma hinting at ritualistic rites of passage: birth, marriage, death, or religious cult? The only other visitor, a ruminating bullock, paused and strolled nonchalantly by. There was no standing on ceremony here. Nearby, the remains of a hut circle and a stone circle completed what was left of this settlement, just one of many on the moorland, holding the mysteries of the people who, it is believed, lived here as long ago as 1900 BC.

Next on our 'not to be missed' list was a Neolithic burial chamber – said to have been erected by three spinsters one morning before breakfast and dubbed 'Spinsters' Rock' added to the interest. The fact that the legend of the spinsters refers to woollen spinners and not to single women, allows for more plausible, mythological explanations of its origin. In 1848, a certain Samuel Rowe suggested that the legend of the three spinsters is linked with the Norns, three Fatal Sisters of Norse mythology who weave the destiny of the world. In turn, the Norns have also been likened to the 'Fates' of Greek mythology – in this case represented by the three standing stones supporting the great granite capping stone. The burial chamber, along with stone circles, rows of standing stones and single megaliths on Dartmoor, suggest teamwork and communal activities as part of the lives of the Neolithic people who lived here – an organised way of life they shared with Neolithic people worldwide.

Like a gigantic mushroom, its head balanced on three upright stones, the megalith reached to over six feet in height. The design and size intrigued as much as the legends surrounding it. Dating at some time from between 3500 and 2500 BC, the chamber is said to contain many burials and to have once been covered by a long earthen mound. Standing in the middle of a field, on a working farm with chickens scratching and clucking closeby, did not detract from its solemn and imposing presence.

Our final roadside encounter was with a monastic stone cross. Resembling the shape of a headless, portly monk, it is one of number marking routes across the moor, or boundaries of land, once belonging to abbeys and monasteries. Hewn from a granite boulder, the bulbous shaft stood some seven feet tall: a symbol of both suffering and salvation, and a potent reminder of our lives as a journey in the footsteps of the monks who lived and prayed here.

We had visited and attended services at Dartmoor's long-serving Buckfast Abbey. The liturgy and plainchant led by the monks evoked a moving and tangible sense of the present reaching out to and touching the past. The long and complex history of the abbey includes its foundation in 1018, then established and run by Cistercian monks from 1147 to 1539. Destroyed under the Dissolution of the Monasteries, the abbey was rebuilt and taken over by French Benedictines in 1882. Today, its reputation extends to include vineyards and the production of palatable Buckfast Wine.

All this delving into history was thirst-inducing and called for a visit to Widecombe-in-the-Moor – a village known, to those of us of a certain age, by the rhyme in which 'Old Uncle Tom Cobley and all' ride to Widecombe Fair on the back of a grey mare belonging to Tom Pearce. This scene, depicted on a board outside the local primary school, marks the start of Widecombe village. A tearoom offering traditional Devonshire afternoon tea, served with scones piled with thick cream and jam, also came with picture postcard views across the village green. Before us, the sunlit tower of the cathedral was framed by autumnal trees.

Looking beyond the cathedral and beyond Dartmoor, we had set our sights on a land whose standing stones, monasteries and ancient tribes promised to surpass those of any other. Ethiopia was on the horizon.

*****   *****   *****

When in *The Decline and Fall of the Roman Empire,* Edward Gibbon wrote that Ethiopians 'slept near a thousand years, forgetful of the world by whom they were forgotten', he was not to know that some two hundred years later, 'forgotten' tribes were just awakening in Ethiopia's deep south. In 1974, extreme drought conditions in the remote Lower Omo Valley, where the Mursi tribe lived in virtual isolation, caused them to migrate to neighbouring highlands; it was this movement that took them into contact with other tribes in a world unknown to them and by whom they were unknown.

The more recent discovery by the world at large of the existence of the Southern Omo tribes is believed to have given birth not only to an upsurge in group tours, but to an aggressive form of photo-tourism in the Omo region. Responsibility for this has been attributed to newspaper articles, magazine features and tour company literature adopting and using such emotive language as 'remote', 'warriors' and 'wilderness' to lure travellers and tourists into the region. Add to this a series of TV documentaries, followed by two BBC 'Tribe' programmes with Bruce Parry in Southern Omo. Ethiopia's 'little visited' deep south and its 'untouched tribes' were being broadcast across screens worldwide.

Our interest in the past, and the opportunity to visit a land that was so in touch with its 'living past', was overriding our fear of losing the sense of space and independence we sought when travelling. We knew we were not going to be lone travellers. Nevertheless, we hoped to catch some glimpses of this previously 'forgotten world' of ancient tribes, as well as that of Ethiopia's deep religious heritage.

On expeditions through Oman, we had encountered historical trails connecting Ethiopia with Yemen and Oman. Now, more immediate footprints, linking Ethiopia with twentieth century Devon were before us.

Ethiopia

Ethiopia is old beyond imagination, dating back to the very beginning of mankind. It is the land of the Queen of Sheba, a place of legendary rulers, fabulous kingdoms and ancient mysteries… of island and cliff-side monasteries, of rock-cut churches, of forgotten tribes…

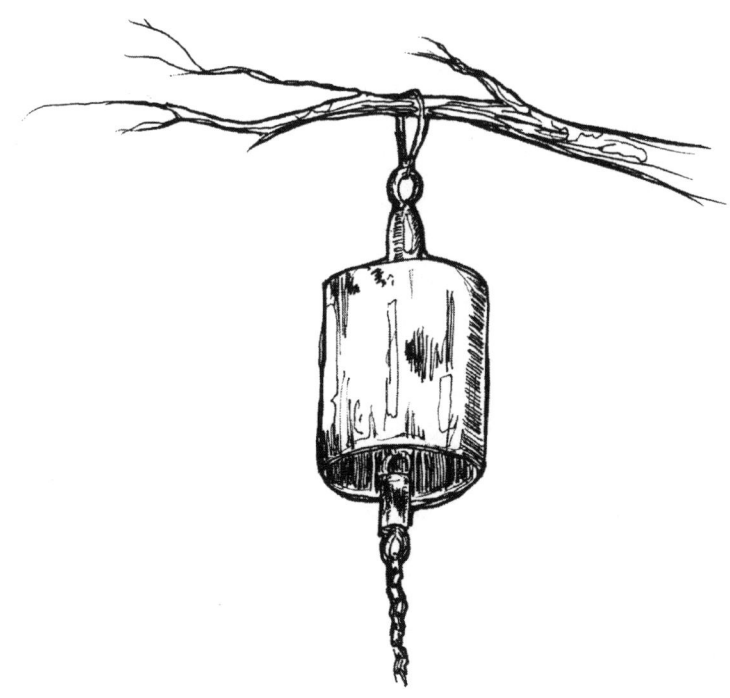

Footprints and Shadows

Addis Ababa 1972

In 1972, when the emperor, Haile Selassie was still holding onto his throne, two young British adventure-seekers from Devon set out to explore this largely forgotten and little known land. In addition to Ethiopia's rich and fascinating religious heritage, they were intrigued on two further counts: first, the knowledge that Haile Selassie, while in exile in England (1936-1941) during the Italian occupation of his country, visited and spent time at Hope Cove in their native Devon. The cove's lovely and solitary south coast position offered the shelter and hope to Haile Selassie and his family that it once offered to ships sheltering from storms at sea. The second was Evelyn Waugh's satirical fiction of an inept foreign correspondent in Abyssinia, *Scoop*, based on Waugh's own journalistic experience when sent to cover Benito Mussolini's invasion of Abyssinia (now Ethiopia).

In the 1970s, Africa as a whole entered its two darkest decades. The epoch of independence that followed colonial withdrawal had not fulfilled its promises of peace and prosperity. Power struggles resulted in opponents exploiting tribal and ethnic conflicts, military might and corruption. Immediately the Allied troops drove Italy from his country in 1941, Haile Selassie returned to his throne. His reign was not a happy one. Ethiopia too was experiencing the wave of discontent that was sweeping through Africa. The medieval monarchy was facing a rising tide of imperial resistance.

This was the world the travellers found themselves in. Arrival in Addis Ababa came with a 'box full of surprises': mounting discontent against the monarchy and a medieval feudal system imposed on a nation of mixed warring tribes, all armed with AK-47 rifles and road communications limited to one tar road through Addis Ababa.

It was when the adventurers hired a battered Volkswagen Beetle to take them on their journey of exploration that they were given two warnings: firstly, it was not safe to travel between dusk and dawn, as the roads were controlled by *shifta*: armed, swift-footed prowling bandits who rob unsuspecting travellers of everything; secondly, in the event that they should encounter His Highness on the road, they must stop and prostrate themselves.

Six weeks later, when they returned the VW to the car hire company in Addis Ababa, they were greeted with amazement:

'We thought you were dead. We heard that two Europeans had been murdered. We thought it was you!'

That they were alive was pretty amazing. The very act of *faranji* (foreigner) travelling unescorted and indiscriminately throughout the country was viewed with deep suspicion. Stopped and questioned by the police instead of being subservient and respectful, Peter, the more outspoken of the two, was non-committal, even churlish in his response. Arrest followed. He was locked into one of a room of cells resembling iron cages, reminiscent of a zoo and filled with local people. Meanwhile, his companion David set forth on a mission to find a lawyer for his defence. When the time came for 'justice to be dispensed', a judge in Western-style clothes and brandishing a fly whisk, aided by a male jury sporting a variety of fuzzy Afro hair-styles and dressed in an assortment of animal skins and drapes, finally agreed to his release.

The second adventure occurred when the two were confronted by a collection of vehicles parked haphazardly at the roadside. As they brought the VW to a standstill, it became apparent that drivers and passengers were on their knees alongside their vehicles, facing the road: behinds in the air, heads and hands on the ground. Seconds later, an increasing ululating murmur heralded the arrival of a grandiose imperial motorcade. As it swept past, seated at the rear in a stretched black limousine was none other than the emperor, Haile Selassie. That police escorts as well as other road users – fully occupied prostrating themselves – failed to notice that the late arrivals were not complying, was their salvation. Surviving arrest and imprisonment on this occasion would not have been so straightforward.

Just two years later, in 1974, the same drought that had driven the Mursi tribe from their isolated existence *In Search of Cool Ground*[8], hastened the demise of the emperor. Haile Selassie was deposed, arrested by the military at his palace and in a terrible irony driven to a prison cell, in mockery of a grandiose imperial motorcade, in the back of a Volkswagen Beetle. 3,000 years of Solomonic rule ended in August 1975, when the deposed emperor was asphyxiated by his successor, Colonel Mengistu Maryam. Mengistu's ruthless and duplicitous Marxist-backed rule climaxed with the launching of a Red Terror campaign to suppress all political opponents. This ended in 1990 when, just months after the disintegration of the Soviet Union, his weakening army, driven from Tigray and Eritrea, was over-powered by the Ethiopian People's Revolutionary Democratic Movement (EPRDM). In 1991, Mengistu fled the country, escaping to safety in Zimbabwe - another twist in our lives. The Road to Democracy (1991-1995) was followed by the Ethiopian-Eritrean Wars (1998-2000). Although a formal peace settlement was signed in 2001, discontent and skirmishes between government troops and armed factions continued.

In 2005, from our base in Devon, we spent the better part of a year planning a visit to Ethiopia. Security warnings of war on the borders with Eritrea, the shooting of innocent protestors, following the May 2005 elections, further riots and bomb explosions in Addis Ababa, as well as reports of banditry in the far south, kept us hesitant. Finally, throwing caution to the wind, in 2006 we took the plunge.

---

[8] David Turton, *Disappearing World Series* – Granada Television, 1985

Addis Ababa, Debre Libanos
February 2006

Drumming, chanting and rythmic handclapping was the dawn chorus that woke us from confused, jet-lagged sleep. Then I remembered. We were in Addis Ababa and staying at the 1950s Ghion Hotel. As if to confirm its age and let us know that we were not the only occupants of the dark shuttered room, an impressive row of bed bug bites running up the inside of my arm was claiming my attention. Meanwhile Richard, who obviously didn't taste as good, was bite free and investigating the noise.

'It's not a riot,' he cheerfully informed me as he pulled back the shutters. 'Looks like a wedding.'

After a delay in Alexandria, our flight from Heathrow arrived at Bole Airport at 3 am, European time[9]. Transferred by shuttle bus to the hotel, we arrived to find we had been allocated a room in an annex complex, across the lawns from the main hotel building. First impressions of dark brown cupboards, dark brown furnishings, dim light bulbs, mosquitoes, a giant sized cockroach and the stench of sewage were not promising.

Named after the Ghion River (The Blue Nile), the source of which Ethiopians call Ghion, the hotel was purportedly an upmarket government place to stay in Addis Ababa. Disturbed sleep didn't help, and it was obvious that the disturbance was set to continue.

Hastily dressing and arming ourselves with cameras, we emerged into brilliant sunlight to capture some of the highlights of the celebrations taking place in the hotel's extensive sunlit gardens. As one glitzy Western-style wedding party disappeared into a waiting row of Rolls Royce limousines, bedecked with white ribbons, another arrived to wend its way through gardens festooned with blooms of jacaranda and bougainvillea to a favoured spot in front of the fountain for the celebrated pose. Brides, grooms, attendants, musicians and guests were as splendidly turned out as Western royalty.

This was a side of Ethiopia not featured in world news, the wealthy Westernised elite. Just three days' drive away or a couple of hours flight was the world of ancient tribal villages we had come to see. It was to be a journey back in time.

Advised against the dangers of independent travel in the Lower Omo region, we had made arrangements to join a small group to travel with the company Explore. We hadn't completely forsaken independence. Arriving early, with two days at our disposal before the start of the trip, we located Galaxy Express, the local Avis car hire company, planned a destination and hired a car, plus a driver to get a taster of Ethiopia's rich religious heritage.

---

[9] Ethiopians measure time in 12 hour cycles starting at 06.00 and 18.00; their seven o'clock is our one o'clock. Fortunately for us, most companies dealing with Europeans have adopted their time

'Two, maybe three hour north of Addis,' the manager assured us when we told him of our wish to visit the monastery of Debre Libanos. 'Tar road, mostly. The driver, he know it,' he added.

Debre Libanos had several things in its favour. Unlike a number of Ethiopia's monasteries built on precipitous cliff-sides, volcanoes and volcanic islands, Debre Libanos appeared to be easily accessible. A holy site founded in the thirteenth century by Tekle Haymanot – a revered saint and priest, credited for spreading Christianity throughout the northern highlands and the restoration of the Solomonic line of kings – it is closely associated with the late Emperor and, to this day, remains a place of pilgrimage for Orthodox Christians.

With an out-of action air conditioner and no seatbelt clips in the ageing Honda Accord, we left the shanty suburbs of Addis Ababa and followed a road that wound its way through and round the Entoto Mountains that encircle the capital. Free of the suburbs, the hillsides were clothed with row upon row of eucalyptus trees. Imported to regenerate de-forested slopes of juniper, the fast growing and hardy eucalyptus provide essential supplies of wood. In fact, the entire route was marked by a steady stream of plodding people, who spend days walking to and from markets and collecting firewood and water. There is very little public transport, and they can't afford it anyway. We were soon to discover that the disturbing sight of women and young girls, laden like beasts of burden, with great bundles of wood tied to their backs – very often accompanied by men walking alongside unencumbered, and holding the traditional *dula* or staff behind their shoulders – was endemic throughout Ethiopia.

Further into the countryside, family compounds of thatched rondavel houses nestled among folds of hills. Eye-catching pyramidal haystacks and neat-layered mounds of cow dung, used for fuelling fires, stood in carefully swept courtyards. The route continued through undulating hills, punctuated by shack-like settlements, to Chanco, a street of concrete shops and shanty attachments known as 'the city' by local people. Leaving 'the city' behind, the landscape opened to a wide plateau surrounded by rugged mountains.

Finally, the driver turned off the tar road onto a gravel track running parallel to the gorge of the Gur River. At the far end, in a clearing at the base of a 700 metre high canyon, stood the last in a succession of reconstructed versions of the original medieval monastery. Built under the patronage of Haile Selassie in the 1950s, the monastery's white dome, bearing a beautiful gold filigree cross - held sway over the rectangular walls of the main building that stands guard over Tekle Haymanot's tomb. Close up, colourful images of angels standing on either side of the saintly figure of the late Emperor receiving a crown competed for my attention with those of saints and lions in the stained glass windows.

The importance of the symbol of the lion in Ethiopia cannot be underestimated. Within Judaism, the Biblical Judah – the original name of the Tribe of Judah – was traditionally symbolised by a lion. In Christian tradition, the Lion of Judah, representing Christ, is confirmed in the Book of Revelations 5.5 (New Testament) by one of the elders:

'Weep not: behold, the Lion of the tribe of Judah, the Root of David hath prevailed to open the book, and to loose the seven seals thereof.' Added to this is

Ethiopia's claim in the fourteenth century treatise, *Kebre Negest*: a claim of descent from a retinue of Israelites who returned with the Queen of Sheba from her visit to King Solomon in Jerusalem, by whom she is said to have conceived the Solomonic dynasty's founder, Menelik I. Both Jewish and Christian traditions have it that these immigrants were mostly of the tribes of Dan and Judah, hence the *Ge'ez* – ancient ecclesiastical – motto, 'The Lion of the Tribe of Judah has conquered.'

With these deeply-rooted thoughts in mind, we located a guide, paid our entry fee and waited for him to unlock the door. Moving from bright sunlight into semi-darkness, it took some moments to adjust to the sense of space and emptiness. There were no rows of seats to fill the inner sanctum, as is now customary in most Western churches. The Ethiopian Orthodox services require room for swaying deacons and ornate accompanying processions. Once again, our eyes were drawn to the stained glass windows. Lit from the outside, the compelling faces of saints and lions came to life. In one, a solemn faced lion stands before the two equally solemn faced figures of King Solomon and the Queen of Sheba.

Stained glass windows apart, if the interior of the church wasn't that impressive, its history was. Destroyed by Muslims in the Muslim Christian wars, no trace of the ancient monastery remains. Since the saint's time, it remained the principal monastery of the Showa region, and one of the largest and most important centres of Christianity in the country. It was here in 1520 that the Emperor Lebna Dengel formally received the first Portuguese mission to Ethiopia. Father Francisco Alvares, one of the missionaries, had been sent overland by King John of Portugal. His quest was to explore the land of Prester John, the fabled Christian prince of the East, believed to have once ruled a wealthy kingdom in Ethiopia. Today, with five religious schools within its premises, the monastery has regained something of its former reputation.

As we stood before Tekle Haymanot's tomb, the guide informed us, with perfect solemnity, that the saint who had been blessed with six wings spent seven years standing on one leg and praying. What is more, he survived on seed fed to him by a bird before the unused leg withered and fell off. Not sure how to respond, we maintained a respectful silence. Few places in the world can compare with the myths and legends surrounding Ethiopia, made all the more intriguing by the intricate weavings of fact and legend that no one has been able to disentangle. That the saint dedicated his life to prayer and the spread of Christianity remains undisputed.

Undoubtedly, it was the legends, history and atmosphere surrounding the monastery that made the visit to Debre Libanos so memorable. Sinners, we learnt, as well as saints, played their part. Today, more than anything, the monastery is a solemn memorial to the monks and deacons murdered by Fascists. Following an attempt on the life of the Italian Viceroy Graziani, the monastery, suspected as a centre for rebel activity, was singled out for reprisal. On the 20th of May 1937, during Tekle Haymanot's feast day celebration, Fascist troops descended on the monastery, seized two hundred and ninety seven monks and shot them, before slaughtering more than a hundred young deacons. Graziani telegraphed Mussolini: 'The monastery is closed – definitively.' It wasn't and it isn't. Neither was it the end of the massacre. At least four hundred lay people who had attended the celebration for the saint were transported to the village of Engecha, lined up alongside two ready-made trenches, and mown down by machine gun fire. A sobering history.

It was when we were leaving the saint's tomb and the church that our guide pointed out two somewhat faded canopies, one on either side of the aisle, each crowning a throne once used by Haile Selassie and his wife. A poignant reminder of a man who, during his fifty four year reign, achieved so much for his country and yet miserably failed his people. As the head of the then only independent African country, he led Ethiopia into the League of Nations, survived in exile in England the Italian invasion, and defeat, to be restored to power in 1941. Post-war Ethiopia under Selassie was one of the founding countries of the United Nations, and a prime instigator of the Organisation of African Unity. His failings were equally impressive.

His medieval empire entrenched the status of the nobility and landowners, offered high salaries to self-seeking politicians and lacked an infrastructure comparable to even the undeveloped countries surrounding it. Finally, as the country was slipping into famine, he was caught on film feeding fresh meat to Tafara, his Abyssinian lion. This not only highlights his terrible lack of understanding and empathy with his people, but presents a tragic paradox: the last Abyssinian emperor – the Lion of Judah – feeding the last Abyssinian lion, the symbol of his 'divine' kingship.

While Richard defied rising temperatures and set off to climb the hill behind the monastery, leading to the cave where Tekle Haymanot prayed, my more practical mission was to find a toilet. Eventually I succeeded in tracking down a security guard. Armed with a Kalashnikov and a key, he led me to the small concrete block, housing a row of cubicles that I had previously detected by smell but had been unable to gain access to. Inside was a horror story. Although not open to the general public, it was obvious that previous visitors had no idea what the hole in the centre of the floor of each cubicle was for, and that the place was rarely, if ever, cleaned. It was an early lesson: toilet facilities were a problem throughout the country, and one of the major downsides to travel in Ethiopia. The bush was a far better option.

Finally, while awaiting Richard's return, I parked myself on a bank in the shade of trees, where a gathering of bulbuls made me utterly nostalgic for our oasis garden in Dubai. Not attempting the climb had turned out to be the right decision. Richard had been hoping to take photographs of paintings of the saint and his withered leg's winged transportation to heaven, but he wasn't allowed inside the cave. Suffering from heat fatigue and plagued by flies, his nondescript photos of the cave entrance were no compensation for the discomfort and disappointment he suffered.

A spot overlooking the river, shaded by huge sycamore fig trees and just off the track leading to the main road, was the place chosen for a picnic stop. We were congratulating ourselves on finding a secluded place – virtually impossible in Ethiopia – when an old man appeared. His timing couldn't have been better. I had just discovered that the lunchbox variety of doorstep sandwiches, supplied by the hotel, had been fried. Both Richard and the driver were tucking in without complaint, but I couldn't face cold fried sandwiches. The old man was less fussy, and wasted no time in making off with my offering.

That evening, at a bar in the hotel specialising in local food, we opted for the native *injera*. A fair amount of bad press has been given to this oversized pancake. Made from the cereal *teff,* it is served with a variety of vegetables and meat, and dipped in *wat,* a spicy sauce. I was eager to try it out. While waiting for our food and sipping *tej*, the potent but oversweet mead made from local honey, a waitress arrived with a bowl of water and towels for the traditional washing of hands before eating. The meal was to be a 'hands-on' experience, dispensing with cutlery.

Finally, a mushroom shaped woven table, some two feet in diameter and just the right size for the pancake, was put before us. Unlike the story told of an American who thought the *injera* was a tablecloth, I was familiar with the custom of eating Arabic bread in the Emirates and ready to use my right hand, as etiquette demands, to tear off pieces and wrap the food into bite-size parcels. The procedure wasn't difficult and, at first, it didn't taste too bad. Then, as the novelty wore thin, reality took hold. Whereas the texture and taste of Arabic bread is most palatable, *injera* was everything I had heard and read: cold, flabby and bland. I wasn't having much success with food that day but at least, on this occasion, I tried.

Mount Zikwala Maryam

We had one more day of independence, before the start of a fourteen day trip south through the Rift Valley to the tribal lands of the Lower Omo region, and one day at the end. There was insufficient time to visit Lalibela's magnificent rock-cut churches or the island monasteries of Lake Tana. After examining maps and guidebooks, we decided on the monastery of Zikwala. Although built on the side of an extinct volcano, the foot of the volcano, if not the monastery, was less than an hour's drive from Addis Ababa.

From a romantic viewpoint alone, Zikwala monastery was well worth a visit. It was almost certainly the source of the Abyssinian mountain marked as 'Xiquala' on Fra Mauro's 1459 *Map of the World.* An unknown hermit or traveller from the region must have made his way to the island monastery in Venice where Fra Mauro lived. His tale of the mountain's existence, assisted the monk, who relied on tales of travellers, explorers and pilgrims, to create his dream of a map representing the full breadth of Creation.

Once again, the manager of Galaxy Express obliged us with a driver and the Honda Accord, and we set off on the road south and east through the city. It didn't take long to discover the truth of the author John Graham's pragmatic statement that few roads in Addis Ababa are as congested as Debre Zeyit.[10] In spite of the capital's fairytale setting, close to hot springs and framed by the

---

[10] John Graham, *Ethiopia, Off The Beaten Trail*

Entoto Mountains, we were fast learning that the city remains a growing compacted urban sprawl, surrounding and spreading out from the palace of the former Emperor.

The route through shanty suburbs was in heavy traffic competing for road space with donkeys and people, between a tumble of roughly built concrete shops and lean-to shacks, marked by the occasional modern business enterprise. Added to this is the sad reality of the city's reputation as a centre for beggars and hawkers clamouring for attention, as well as the saddening spectacle of ragged children, polio cripples and amputee war veterans. Before us, a crippled man was attempting to cross the road on elbows and knees. Progress frequently slowed to a standstill. Without air-conditioning, the level of discomfort increased. It was a choice between inhaling diesel fumes and red dust with the windows down, or overheating with them up. We wavered between the two.

We were heading for Debre Zeyit, the 'Mount of Olives' – the Christian name given by Haile Selassie in the 1960s – which, despite having been officially replaced by the Oromo name of *Bishoftu* (watery land) continues to be used. Its remarkable location, at the near epicentre of the most easily accessible crater-lake field in Africa, is overshadowed by its past. The entire area is remembered as the site of Ahmed Gragn's Muslim victory in 1529, which resulted in the looting of churches and monasteries and the destruction of several settlements.

Lake Hora, the largest of six crater lakes on the plains surrounding Mount Zikwala, known for thickly wooded slopes and teeming with birds, was our chosen lunchtime destination. Within minutes of our arrival, a giant fig became the focus of Richard's binoculars. Weaver birds, a white browed robin and red-headed barbets were just some of the winged inhabitants he was pointing out. The lakeside too was alive with hamerkop, snake birds, cormorants, paradise flycatchers and so many more, such as we had not seen since our visit to Eagle Island in the Okavango.

Dominating the skyline and rising more than 600 feet behind Lake Hora, the holy mountain is blessed with the church and Zikwala Maryam Monastery. What is more, the monastery overlooks its own 2km crater lake sacred to Orthodox Ethiopians, who claim that it glows at night. Tradition states that Abbo, an Egyptian priest, who arrived in Ethiopia at the time of twelfth century reign of King Lalibela, founded the monastery. Like Saint Francis, the saint had a reputation for befriending animals, but his friendship is said to have gone as far as living with lions and hyenas. We were keen to see the frescoes, depicting scenes from his life, in the extant twentieth century church.

However, neither the driver nor travellers were prepared for the steepness of the ascent, nor the state of the heavily potholed road. After a growling and slithering attempt to tackle the start of the 10km track to the monastery, the Honda Accord jolted and shuddered to a standstill. We weren't going anywhere. It was all hands to the rescue.

'Even the Musso would struggle here,' Richard declared philosophically, instructing the driver to turn about.

Without the time or inclination to continue on foot in climbing temperatures, we were giving up on monasteries and investing in tribes.

Back at Galaxy Express, the manager, Mekonnen Mengesha, was interested to learn of our planned trip into the Omo Valley.

'The whole world is coming to see the Mursi,' he announced. 'It's the lip-plates. Americans fly into Addis, stay at the Hilton, fly to Jinka in the south, do the last bit by 4x4, then fly back. They're not interested in days on the road to get there. They come to see and photograph only the most exotic people. Come with me!' he instructed, leading us from the reception area to his office.

Turning on his computer, he set it up to display on-screen images of two women and two men from the Mursi tribe, both in full regalia. The women wore full-sized lip plates, their usual cowskin short skirts and bare tops covered by cotton wraps; the men, heavily embellished in strings of cowrie shells and warthog tusks hanging about their ears, were armed with spears and covered in white chalk markings.

'Taken before they left for Japan,' the manager explained. 'I brought them to Addis, arranged passports and flights. They were on stage and TV in Japan.'

He was smiling and pleased with his initiative.

'Good for business,' he added.

When I asked him if the Japanese would come to Ethiopia if the women were to stop wearing lip-plates, his confident reply was,

'They won't stop. If they do, they won't get husbands.'

That the Mursi were paid for taking part in this expedition goes without question. Nevertheless, the reverberations of culture shock and readjustment resulting from the quantum leap into an alien world and back suffered by the group must have been considerable. It also completely undermined tour company claims of encounters with 'untouched tribes'.

We left with heavy hearts. Hoping to beat the floodgate of tourists, we had arrived on the heels of the BBC filming of the second 'Tribe' series in southern Ethiopia, with Bruce Parry, before it had been televised. Like travellers before us, we had been lured by travel literature promising encounters with 'a dazzling number of Africa's lost people', in a 'little visited' region. The evidence against this was growing. All we could do now was wait and see.

Through the Great Rift Valley

Lakes Ziway, Abiata & Langano

Over breakfast on the following morning, we met up with Amy, our tour leader, and fellow travellers. After brief introductions, we were directed into one of three Land Cruisers and set off once more along the slow-moving Debre Zeyit road. With the suburbs of Addis Ababa behind us, a gentle undulating landscape of cultivated fields dotted with sycamore fig – reminiscent of Devon countryside dotted with giant oak – swept into the distance. Signs of intensive farming – strawberries, roses and tomatoes – marked our progress south and into Oromia, the territory of the Oromo people, the largest ethnic group in Ethiopia. Originally from the Kenyan border – taking advantage of Ahmed Gragn's *jihad* against the Christian Empire – the Oromo migrated north through the Rift Valley in the early sixteenth century.

The first in a series of organised paying upfront photo stops was a visit to an Oromo family where men and women were leading long-horned cattle over harvested corn to separate the grain from the husks. An idyllic and natural scene of agricultural charm, it was a gentle introduction to Ethiopia's diversity of Rift Valley tribes. Then, as we headed south towards Lake Ziway, the northernmost of the Rift Valley lakes, the landscape too promised similar diversity. Reminiscent now of southern Oman, wide plains dotted with acacia, strolling camels and giant-sized anthills, unfolded before us.

Fish eagles, kingfishers, mildly obscene maribou storks, white pelicans, sacred ibis and so many more varieties of birds that even the proclaimed non-birder among us became hooked. Standing on the shores of Lake Ziway was a further introduction to Ethiopia's amazing bird life, as well as a reminder of the lake's associations with the country's incredible monastic past. Of the five volcanic islands, at least three are home to island monasteries.

According to legend, Zay Christians, driven out of the Rift Valley by Muslim invaders, escaped with a wealth of illustrated *Ge'ez* – ancient ecclesiastical - manuscripts to the volcanic islands in Lake Ziway. Here they built monasteries and led an isolated existence on their island strongholds until 1886, when the Emperor Menelik conquered the Ziway area and the liberated islanders were free to return to the lakeshore. We could see the outline of *Debre Tsion* (Mount Zion), the largest island. Standing on the highest peak is the monastery of Maryam Tsion; the oldest active monastery in southern Ethiopia, it is also believed to have been the sanctuary for the Ark of the Covenant before it was considered safe to take it to Axum. That the Zay people of Ziway speak a Tigrigna-language, distinct from the locally spoken Oromifa, plus the large number of *Ge'ez* manuscripts stored in the monastery, adds considerable substance this belief.

On a more down to earth level, it was over a coffee break on the shores of Lake Ziway that we became acquainted with our fellow travellers. With ages ranging from the mid-forties to an elder approaching octogenarian status, they were all well-travelled and equipped with a range of professional work experience including diplomatic, photographic, teaching, nursing, accountancy, banking and 'last but not least' a millionaire – that is, until he filed for divorce. David, the millionaire, seemed as preoccupied with leaving his wine cellar in the care of a housekeeper with a passion for quality wine, as with what lay ahead. As a group, we appeared to be bonded by a not unhealthy cynicism towards the promise of encounters with 'untouched tribes', as well as by a difference in age and experience with Amy, the tour leader. What Amy lacked in years, she was already making up for in a confident and authoritarian manner. Our quest was about to begin.

The journey continued through a national park, culminating in a viewing point on a narrow strip of hilly land separating Lakes Abiata and Shala. It was at this point that Amy decided that it would benefit everyone to continue the journey on foot to the shores of Lake Shala. Instructed to leave the vehicles, we were preoccupied with finding sun hats and donning suitable footwear. Temperatures were verging on 40 degrees, there was no shade, and we soon discovered that the supposed track had been swallowed by knee-high savannah grassland. This was an unwelcome wake-up call for the majority of the group who had arrived in the early hours of that morning after an overnight flight from Heathrow and below zero temperatures. It was also of some considerable concern to the elder, John, who had a heart problem and walked with a stick. After some firm insistence, John was allowed to reboard and travel in one of the Land Cruisers. Mutterings about lack of common sense and choice could be heard among less than happy walkers.

Despite the evocative African savannah landscape of blond grass decorated by the occasional flat-headed acacia, suggestive of the presence of giraffe, elephant and more, wildlife sightings were limited to penned ostrich on a farm and wading flamingos in the wetlands as we approached the shore. Back in the Land Cruisers, we were more than happy when the endless sandy track petered out and we drew to a halt at the entrance to a stylish bamboo lodge, overlooking yet another Rift Valley lake. Set against the backdrop of the Arsi Mountains, Lake Langano was a perfect mirror of evocative black and white images in evening light. Swallows swooping over men up to their waists in water, cutting reeds and a row of cormorants perched on rocks, contemplating near perfect reflections, competed for the prizewinning evening photo-shoot before dinner in the open-sided rondavel restaurant-cum-bar. Richard won hands down: two swallows against the evening sky added that final touch of class to his picture of silhouetted reed cutters.

The magic of quiet that descended when the generator was switched off also heralded thick darkness in our bush chalet. Candlelight and a bed swathed in mosquito netting provided the challenge of avoiding either strangulation or fire when attempting to get out of and back into bed. Candle out, fingers in ears to block out the sounds of prowling night predators, I fell into the world of unbroken sleep to be awoken at dawn by an amazing cacophony of competing bird calls.

The Guge Highlands, Chencha, Arba Minch

A puncture on the track from the lodge, where the only other traffic competing for space were herdsmen and their cattle raising great clouds of dust, resulted in the sudden appearance of curious people from local houses. They gathered, silent and watching, until we disappeared in our own dustcloud. We were heading for Shashemene. This meeting place and busy stopover for lorries and trucks – marking a crossroad connecting north and south, east and west – is probably better known to the world at large as 'Jamaica'. Once a popular Rastafarian stronghold, Shashemene was formed by a group of Jamaican devotees of Haile Selassie. Today it is the place where, after the exodus of Mengistu, stragglers of admirers returned, hoping that the new government would reinstate them to the former privileged position granted to them by the emperor.

Singled out by Amy as a place of interest and convenient for a coffee stop, it didn't take long to discover that it was dusty, noisy and crowded; then Dario, the lead driver, warned us to watch out for pick pockets and petty thieves. With some misgivings about the choice of venue and what could lay in store, we headed south once more through a landscape of savannah and semi-desert, marked by a mix of eucalyptus and acacia trees. As the going became more rugged, the roadsides became increasingly busy with processions of people, especially women and donkeys, laden with wood, plastic water carriers and bags of grain, walking to and from local markets.

Eye-catching images covered the walls of thatched, rondavel houses of the Wolayta people: pastoral scenes depicting life-size individuals engaged in farming activities were downstaged by the disturbing image of a pistol-toting male in European clothes. The only villagers about were older men, overeager to pose and make money from being photographed. One elder, dressed in a worn European-style T-shirt and below the knee trousers, had acquired a length of material usually worn as a sarong. Unsure what to do with the drape, he finally hung it over one shoulder and hoped for the best. It worked. His photo was taken and money exchanged hands.

Plantations of bananas and ground peanuts and fields of cotton lining the route alongside the Rift Valley lake of Abaya gave way to dry African bush, decorated with thorny shrubs and sky-reaching anthills. Then the track narrowed and the gradient increased signalling our exit from the Rift Valley into the Guge Mountains. As the trail wound round-forested mountain folds, we passed a number of women. Bent under heavy loads of wood they were making their way to their highland homes.

'1600 metres in 22km,' Dario boasted, as the growling engine juddered, threatening to cut out.

The rough switchback climb through forested slopes of Cyprus conifers continued to mark our progress into chilly, mist-clad heights. Finally the engine gave up and we ground to a halt on a near vertical slope, alongside an impressive drop to the Rift Valley below.

'Rocks, get rocks!' Dario demanded.

Obediently tumbling out, we scattered in search of obstacles to lodge behind the wheels. Mission accomplished, we left the drivers to investigate the troubled engine and were at leisure to admire the view to the great expanse of Lake Abaya. One minute we were alone, absorbed in the scene before us, and then, as one turbaned head followed by several more appeared over the mountainside, our focus changed. A group of smiling, laden women were slowly but surely heading towards us.

Set some 2,900m in the Guge Mountains is the small highland town of Chencha, the home of the Dorze people. Although they speak an Omotic tongue similar to a number of tribes in the Lower Omo Valley, the Dorze are thought to have occupied their present position for at least five hundred years. Renowned cotton weavers, their distinctive tall, beehive-shaped dwellings are not seen anywhere else in Africa. Dressed in colourful turbans and layers of tops, long skirts and shawls and looking as surprised as we were, the women approached us tentatively with open hands.

In common with tribes in the entire Omo region, it appeared that they too assumed, or hoped, that visitors were there to hand out money or other gifts, but they were gentle in nature and without the insistence that can be so trying. Before long, we were joined by more women and girls from the village, and a full-scale scenario of exchanging money for photographs was taking place.

Once we reached the village, we drew alongside a family compound. Inside a ten foot screen of bamboo fencing, a domed dwelling framed by a plantation of *enset* - false banana - stood before us. The elongated dome, thatched and insulated from a combination of enset and grass, gave the tall bee-hived shaped house the appearance of a mammoth.

'Elephant's trunk and eyes,' Dario enlightened me, as if reading my thoughts.

Then it made sense. He was pointing to a narrow front section of the dome where, starting between two small-lidded windows (the eyes), from near the top of the roof, a long curved section (the trunk), dropped to hang over the front entrance. Standing at about the same height as a two-storey house, it was remarkable, both for the originality of design and as a poignant reminder of the long extinct wild elephants that once roamed these forested hills.

Dario had made a number of trips into the Omo region. He was good company and, through his interaction with local people, was fast acquiring first-hand detail about the tribes not found in guidebooks or in guide literature. It was becoming increasingly apparent that he was a true bonus on the trip.

Following on the heels of our companions, we made our way under the lidded entrance porch into the family home. Like the homes of a number of African tribes, the interior is centred round an open fire, as necessary for warmth in the mountaintop altitude, as it was for keeping insects at bay. Different areas of the spacious interior were set aside for living, cooking and livestock, with raised platforms along the sides for sleeping. Ongoing activities that we were encouraged to watch and photograph included the making of bread from the pith of the outer stem and leaves of enset, and the weaving of colourful cotton scarves and lengths of cloth. Speaking excellent English, the eldest son provided a commentary throughout our visit. Like so many of the educated young men we were to meet, his ambition was to be a tour guide.

The visit was most interesting and we felt privileged to be invited into this family home. If there was a downside, it was the set up nature which had all the hallmarks of a growing tourist industry that purportedly doesn't exist: the mother kneeling in the yard, bent over her breadmaking throughout our visit; the grandmother, sitting in an outer room, winding thread onto a reel; a younger brother operating the loom in the courtyard; the commentary throughout. It made sense, but the frustration came from knowing that normal family and village life were on hold and would resume as soon as we were gone.

On our descent, we stopped to exchange greetings with further groups of women and young girls on the long steep climb back to their village. Despite bearing the weight of bundles of wood and other cumbersome loads, their lovely faces wore welcoming smiles. The spontaneous roadside meetings and opportunities to take unposed photographs were gratifying. A memento of my visit, a deep pink and blue cotton scarf, continues to be admired whenever I wear it. I take great pleasure in making it known that it was handwoven by the Dorze people of Ethiopia.

Leaving the Guge Mountains, we headed for an overnight hotel in Arba Minch. We were excited on two counts: the hotel was new and Arba Minch, a small and non-descript Ethiopian town, is known for a spectacular location. Set at around 1300 metres in the foothills of the Rift Valley wall, it overlooks a mountain ridge separating the lakes of Chamo and Abaya. Blessed with mountains rising to over 4000 metres to the west and stunning views to the lakes in every other direction, it is said to even outshine the position of Moshi on the foot slopes of
Kilimanjaro. It didn't take long to discover that the hotel boasted no views, and its newness was such that it was unfinished. However, the rooms were clean and furnished with comfortable beds, covered with intact mosquito nets. We were delighted to discover hot water taps, then less delighted to find there was no hot water. Considering that Arba Minch, which translates as Forty Springs, is blessed with hot water from the Rift Valley, it was surprising – a luxury to be enjoyed by future visitors, we decided.

Trials & Triumphs in the Omo Region

Karat Konso, Key Afar, Jinka

Karat Konso, a kind of frontier town and gateway to the Omo region, boasted a solitary but vital petrol station, a dusty sprawl of concrete shops and houses and a scattering of basic stopover hotels. Here the road split. Taking the right-hand fork, our small convoy headed west. Almost immediately, what had been a graded road disintegrated into a rough track, sending us bouncing and trundling though desert scrub and bush, then into mountainous terrain and the traditional heartland of a good number of tribes including the Konso, Derase, Ari, Banna and Tsemai. A cultural diversity of people that, until drought and the onslaught of tourism, lived in isolated communities, even from near neighbours. One minute our Land

Cruisers were the only evidence of life, and the next, a succession of youngsters appeared from surrounding bush, racing to keep up, hands outstretched.

'Give me money!' was the cry that followed in our wake.

Key Afar, a multicultural meeting place at the weekly market, was our first scheduled stop. As our vehicle slowed, we were greeted by dozens of outstretched hands and, once again, a succession of voices demanding 'Give me money!' The pestering was non-stop, whether it was money for photos, would-be guides, or just plain demands for cash. Dario explained that the youngsters learn to speak English at the local school and use it to seek money from tourists to pay for books, biros and footballs. In some instances, attempts at politeness – 'Hello. What's your name?' – preceded the demand, 'Give me money!' My attempt to break free and photograph a woman carrying a bowl of mangos on her head, was interrupted by further constant demands for money.

The intimidating scenario was something that neither the travel company, nor Amy as tour leader, had prepared us for. A fellow traveller, Dan, came up with the idea that it was a possible consequence of famine relief. Ethiopia and famine had been central on the world stage for some time, and somehow the giving of aid had become attached to the tourist industry. The consequence was that you not only paid for the trip, visits to tribal villages and for each and every photograph, but on-the-spot cash handouts were also expected.

Dan's sentiment was endorsed by Tony Wheeler, the co-founder of the *Lonely Planet* series. After making a circuit of the 'Historical Route' around northern Ethiopia, he came to the conclusion that:

> The knee-jerk Ethiopia-equals-famine image generated by decades of foreign aid has created the idea that every foreign visitor is there to distribute largesse.

– Wanderlust Travel Magazine, 2005

There was no doubt about it – we had entered high hassle territory, where 'distributing largesse' was high on the agenda.

And so it continued, following on our heels as our journey progressed. At a roadside coffee stop, people from local houses asking for money were outshone by two teenage girls. Although the women in this region were fully clothed, the two girls were topless, a strategy to ensure cameras clicked and money exchanged hands. Finally, a new graded road took us to Jinka, the largest settlement in the south and the 'Gateway to the Omo Region'. With its air-landing strip, shops, petrol station, bank, hospital and boarding school that accommodates children from surrounding villages, as well as a growing plethora of small hotels, Jinka is the hub and most important settlement in the south.

With high temperatures and high hassle behind us, it was a relief to escape and spend the night at the basic but adequate Goah Hotel. Once again, concrete rooms were furnished with beds and intact mosquito nets, but this time we had the sheer luxury of an ensuite with hot water. There was only one shortcoming – the electricity went off without warning, heralding a night of preparing for bed, followed by a morning of getting up in the dark.

Breakfast provided a chance meeting with a local tour operator. Andualem Gebrekirstos, from the Ari tribe, grew up in a village next door to the Mursi and spoke their language. Andualem was quite open about the damage that the upsurge in paying upfront photo-tourism was doing to local people, and that it had the potential for damaging genuine forms of tourism. He stressed the growing problem in tribal villages of only selected people getting their photos taken and ending up with fistfuls of money – good looking girls, those wearing tribal costumes and very old people were favourites. He was also concerned that begging and pestering were out of control.

'Future hope,' he stressed, 'lies in education. Fifty percent now attend school, but more boys than girls.'

The group was waiting to leave. I bade farewell to Andualem, but not before exchanging email contacts.

'Let me know, how your visit to the Mursi is,' he called after me as I turned to wave.

Bile Village

A long, hot 40km drive through rugged terrain. Then a distraction. Heading in the opposite direction, first one 4x4, then another rumbled by. And so it continued. As our journey progressed, I counted a total of fifteen vehicles. Slowly but surely it dawned on us that there was only one attraction on this track: the 4x4s, with their cargos of camera-wielding tourists, were leaving the very Mursi village that we were approaching.

'Untouched and little visited?' I muttered to Richard. 'Dream on!'

Suddenly, from out of the bush stepped a man and teenage boy – both naked and armed with AK-47s. Like audaciously painted statues of Greek gods, they posed alongside the track then disappeared to reappear at intervals in similar poses until we reached the village. We drew to a halt beneath a group of trees, and emerged to find a welcome committee of young women, lip plates hanging, sporting head adornments embellished by an overload of cowrie shells and innovative arrangements of metal and plastic that was nothing short of the bush equivalent of Ascot.

A token handful of painted men, warthog tusks dangling about their ears and AK-47s over their shoulders, were outshone by the naked man and boy who were now posing alongside them. Spots applied to form a belt round the waist, dropping to a gun-holster effect, left nothing to the imagination. A girl had dabbed large spots over her breasts and it was the standard design on clay lip plates being offered for sale. The design, said to imitate the spots on a guinea-fowl – a favourite with the Mursi – had been put to effective use.

Mesmerised by the scene before me, I was then diverted by the sight of the back end of Amy as she disappeared on hands and knees into one of the *tukul* (thatched huts). Armed with loose sheets of paper with a handwritten list of words from various tribes and their meaning in English, she was intent on engaging in 'cultural exchange'. That only two of the words – *achelli* (hello) and *dorri* (house) – were Mursi had not detered her.

Meanwhile, strict orders not to take photographs until given the word had created a volatile situation for those of us who remained outside. In heat defying temperatures, we were attempting to share the scant shade of a solitary thorn tree with a growing mass of Mursi, while engaging in a more lively form of cultural exchange.

Greetings of: 'Hello!' and 'What is your name?' were responded to by insistent reminders from the Mursi, 'Photo!' 'Birr!' 'Photo!'

Counter responses of 'Wait!' and 'Later!' were duly repeated by the Mursi with some relish. Then, arm pulling encouragement, pleading and demanding took over. Meanwhile, a hand was tugging to remove my shirt. Fear of encouraging a 'shirt-lifting' trend stopped me from parting with it. At one point, I caught a girl with her fingers in one of my pockets. Our eyes met, and we both laughed. At that instant, and for one lovely moment, it was as if our inner selves met, erasing differences of race and experience.

On the wider front, it was only when the clicks and whirrs were in progress and money changing hands that the time-bomb atmosphere dissolved. The most poignant image was a young girl, whose lips were untouched, standing side by side with a girl whose lip had been recently cut and plugged. She was holding a leaf, presumably with medicinal properties, against the wound.

Over a period of several months, this girl will suffer considerable pain, caused by inserting larger and larger plugs until the wound reaches the agreed lip plate size of up to 15cm. In this way, the maximum amount of bride-wealth will be paid to her family by her future husband. In common with a number of African tribes, cattle are a symbol of wealth to the Mursi, and their most precious possession. The longstanding custom of matching the plate size to the amount of bride-wealth paid in cattle, ensures that the practice of cutting the girls' lips continues.

I took a series of shots of the most demanding girls. Some held the heavy lip plate in position with a hand or the top front teeth – the four front bottom teeth have been pulled out to make room for the plate – others left the heavy plate hanging. Smiling is not an easy option when wearing a lip-plate, and the absence of any sense of pleasure was most apparent. Each girl held an empty earthenware pot on her head to top the display. At one point, while guiding two sarong draped, heavily painted men into position, warthog tusks dangling about their ears, I found myself looking down the barrel of an AK-47 and wondering if the safety-catch was on.

Immediately the photoshoot ended and crisp notes were handed over – we had been warned that old ones are unacceptable – warthog tusks were removed, pots dumped and lip plates left dangling. Then, just as natural interchanges began to take place, a new set of 4x4s arrived and, like an audience at the end of a show, we filed out to make room for the new arrivals. The Mursi were on stage once more.

As we left the village and trundled to a picnic stop, I was still attempting to come to terms with the remarkable yet crazy encounters with the Mursi, when some men from the village, including the naked 'Greek gods', appeared from the trees and settled down to share our food. Now my head was spinning. That morning, reports of cattle raiding and tribal gun fights in the area had made our safety, and therefore our visit, uncertain, yet here we were, sitting in the bush sharing a picnic lunch with armed, naked and painted men from that very tribe.

En route to the next overnight camp, my mind was replaying images from the morning's scenario: images of those women on the sidelines who were not demanding attention and not attracting photographers. Young mothers, bottom lips hanging like bits of perished rubber, holding infants they were unable to kiss and looking utterly miserable. A poignant reminder, not only of the discomfort from wearing the lip plate, but that it is only a matter of time until the stretched lip can no longer support the heavy clay plate. This was evident from the number of young women using a hand or the top front teeth to hold the plate in position.

It was not only the suffering and discomfort that were so disconcerting. The impairment of speech and of the facility of eating and drinking were overshadowed by the sheer loss of sensual pleasure from a pair of lips. This was brought home by the sight of older women in the tribe. They remained in the background away from the photo frenzy, their stretched, useless lip had been cut off, leaving them sadly deformed. Finally, the image of the girl with intact lips posing beside the girl with her lip newly cut stayed with me. I counted a further five girls of marriageable age whose lips had not been cut. There were so many unanswered questions. I knew I would have to wait until I contacted Andualem to get reliable answers.

At this stage of the trip it had become apparent that any disappointment we shared over our visit could not be blamed on the tribes; they were responding to the need for cash in the market economy and commercial world they had been catapulted into. It was increasingly clear that the most serious misconception given by the media and tour company literature is that the Mursi remain isolated in a remote wilderness, visited by the occasional anthropologist or intrepid traveller. Some thirty years ago, this may have been true, as the Mursi were isolated pastoral nomads, but today, they are in the process of becoming settled agriculturalists and maybe, when the onslaught of tourists with cameras declines, like their highland neighbours they will carve out a new ethnic identity for themselves. That they are remarkable, engaging and enterprising people was unmistakeable.

In an exchange of emails, Andualem Gebrekirstos shed further light on some of the positive changes taking place in Mursi culture.

Money for Photographs

When I visited the Mursi, nine years ago (1997) no one asked for money for photos. People gave gifts of soap or razor blades. The kids feared us and used to run away.

Lip plates
Girls can refuse to have their lips cut, but if they do, they face pressure from the family and society. A girl's family will gain thirty to forty cattle when she gets married. The bigger the plate, the bigger the gift to her family.
A Mursi woman must wear the plate when she serves her husband his food.
It is the men who make the decisions.

Education
There is no regular school for the Mursi, but there is a missionary school near Maki, a Mursi village. I saw about forty five boys and ten girls at this school. There is also a mobile elementary school at Haile Wahu, about 34km from the village you visited, with thirty three boys and thirteen girls. They read Amharic and some English. Some will attend the government boarding school in Jinka. It is about 65km.

Reasons why some of the girls in the Mursi village were not wearing lip plates
One couple are Christians and have refused to have the wife's lip cut.
The other girls, married to Mursi men, have not had their lips cut because they are from other tribes – Surma, Dizi and Kuyego. The men pay only one or two cows to the chief for these non-Mursi wives.

Andualem Gebrekirstos

Mago National Park

Buffalo Camp

Howls of baboons and colobus monkeys, backed by a deep throated chorus of frogs, were the competing early morning calls as we emerged from tents at Buffalo Camp. Once known for a thousand strong buffalo herds, today's diminishing numbers have been seriously depleted through poaching. Similarly reduced, elephant numbers are now estimated at around two hundred, while surviving waterbuck, bushbuck, hartebeest, kudu and the tiny Guenther's dik-dik are said to remain hidden in thick bush.

Along with Omo National Park, Mago forms the nearest thing in Ethiopia to the savannah reserves of East Africa. Dissected by the Mago River, most of the park lies on the hot and steamy Rift Valley floor at an altitude below 500m, while the northern sector rises to an escarpment, reaching 2,528m at Mount Mago. Like us, the majority of visitors are here not to see remaining wildlife, but because of the proximity to the villages of tribes who live in the Southern Omo region. A late arrival and early departure at the camp allowed no time for exploring the African wilderness surroundings.

On the road, sporadic sightings of waterbuck petered out as bush savannah gave way to a landscape of sand and desert scrub. Dust-devils and high-rise termite mounds preceded us along a track through deep, loose sand, reminding us once again of the Kalahari sands on the way to Botswana's Tsodilo Hills. Over our heads, circling keen-eyed vultures were on the look out for wildlife snacks. We were heading for a campsite located on the banks of the Omo River, the centre stage for making contact with a number of tribes who have inhabited the region as far back as memory takes them.

As our journey progressed, it was obvious that, quite literally, the road to mass tourism is being laid. At one point, on a deeply rutted track through bush, we stopped to allow the bird enthusiasts to watch and photograph an eagle hovering overhead, when a convoy of 4x4s arrived and remained stuck behind our vehicles. A traffic pile-up in the bush. The only way to move was head to tail. All too soon, this will not be a problem. Alongside the 'offroad' track, a wide, gravel all-weather road is in the process of cutting straight through the bush, across age-old cattle trails and – in one instance – through the very heart of a village. On the move once more, newly constructed concrete bridges took us over streambeds and across wadis with flying ease.

A coffee-cum-photo stop at a point overlooking the Omo River turned out to be a gathering place of individuals from local tribes. We were eagerly awaited by a mix of people, all heavily painted and in tribal costumes. Especially notable were half naked men, Kalashnikovs casually slung over shoulders; on some, the gun barrels faced to the back, on others to the front, or the guns were propped across shoulders, pointing at various angles. A Karo woman with short curly hair, a beaded headband and a 3-4 inch nail through the flesh below her bottom lip – demonstrating the latest jewellery trend or a grim determination to get attention –

had quickly become the focus of cameras. I retreated to a nearby hillock to get some distant shots of Richard bargaining and exchanging money with portrait hunters, before joining the ensemble and taking a selection of obligatory paying upfront shots.

Murelle Camp, Kolcho

Set in an area of dense acacia woodland alongside the Omo River, the region once boasted a wealth of wildlife, including the full range of big cats, elephant, antelope and buffalo. Today, apart from patrolling baboons, if you take a stroll by the river, you may see the odd crocodile snoozing on the banks. While on a quest for exotic birds, Richard all but tripped over one. You may also see the occasional buffalo or gazelle disappearing into the bush. Supplies of AK- 47s – 'from Russia with love' – have seen to the rapid demise of more exciting wildlife, not to mention members of warring tribes.

Meanwhile, some of our fellow travellers were finding the paying upfront for photos so trying that they were dispensing with cameras altogether; others were spending an increasing amount of time focused on the wide variety of birds. While taking a stroll by the river on the lookout for birds, John was diverted by the rustic scene of long-horned cattle grazing in the shade of a tree. While attempting to focus his camera, a local man, resting unseen nearby, suddenly raised his head and his AK-47, and called to another, also brandishing an AK-47, who ran to the would-be photographer, demanding payment. Intimidation worked. The visitor, who hadn't got as far as taking the shot, obediently paid up. Another lesson had been learnt. Birds don't charge, but cattle, or their owners, do.

As afternoon waned, convoy after convoy of 4x4s arrived. Forget the melting pot of tribes: the camp was fast becoming a melting pot for global tourism. The little visited wilderness was getting pretty busy. Visitors from Germany, Holland, France, Belgium and distant Canada were settling in. Some had landed at the nearby Jinka airstrip, thus avoiding the three day drive from Addis Ababa. Fortunately, there was no shortage of accommodation or land. While some visitors disappeared into luxury lodges, others set up camp between distant trees and quiet returned.

Just five years previously, when the safari expedition leader, Tim Lapage visited southern Omo, although photo frenzies were taking place in some villages, he learnt that no more than one thousand tourists had passed through Mago Park in the previous year, and he met only a handful of Spanish tourists during his entire stay. In the past few years, things have changed dramatically. So much so that the number of visiting tourists in 2006, could well be in the region of one thousand a month.

The track snaked uphill through lengthening shadows, leading to a collection of rush-woven cylindrical shaped houses; standing on stilts, some three feet off the ground ensured that the inhabitants were safe from snakes and predators. Perched on a slope near the edge of a high plateau, the Karo village of Kolcho looked down on the Omo River. Its remarkable setting provided an excellent vantage point for sighting approaching visitors and enemies alike, but we didn't have long to admire the view. Within seconds of our arrival, we were surrounded by women and girls dressed in goatskin skirts, plastic beads around their necks and hair woven into bulbous knots, dyed red with ochre. A tribal dance was on the agenda.

Using white body chalk, a group of sarong-clad men had decorated their faces and torsos with heavy stripes and the inter-tribal favoured guinea fowl spotted design. They gathered and conferred, preparing to entertain the visitors. Then, arms about each other, they stood in a line. Opposite, and some distance apart, several women joined hands, facing the men. Moving and swaying from side to side, to the accompaniment of rhythmic hand clapping and chanting, the dancers gravitated towards and away from each other, until the men finally climaxed with some impressive jumping on the spot.

'Mating dance,' Dario explained. 'Men and women move forwards and backwards, towards and away, then pair off and disappear into the bush.'

We disappeared down the track, rhythmic chanting still in our heads.

Like the Hamer to whom they are related, the Karo people have high cheekbones, light features, easy smiles and are comfortable with tourists. It wasn't until they were in jumping mode that I noticed one of the men was wearing the clay hair bun, said to denote his success in killing a human or wild animal that year. Killing either man or beast was a sign of his success as a warrior. Incongruities like this continued to intrigue and disconcert; the strange *pot pourri* of deep-seated traditions still practised, even brutal ones – tribal rivalries and killings, alongside set-up performances, celebrating these very customs for tourists with cameras.

It was a stern reminder that the prism through which we view life depends so much on where we were born and brought up, the circumstances that have influenced how we feel about and view life – an understanding, so clearly expounded by Tim Lapage:

It is a world that can be in no way related to our western values or attitudes, where a child born to an unmarried girl is left to die under a bush with its mouth full of earth, where sex is a harsh and brutal short affair, and life is by the Kalashnikov. Here the wild intensity of the tribal dance is a regular occurrence; intertwined with alcohol and waving automatic rifles it is always their most frequent and intense statement of freedom.

– *Independent Safari*, 2001

As the 4WD bounced over the rutted track, I couldn't help but wonder about the identity or nature of the person or wild animal that the guy sporting a head-bun had killed that year, and we were only into the second month.

The three hour (50 km) bone jarring drive to the next campsite in rocketing temperatures was a killer. Several of the group had suffered with 'off' days, and now it was my turn. I felt nauseous and wiped out. Miraculously, the site was impressive in every way. Set under huge shade-shedding trees, a row of walk-in tents, ready furnished with beds, was home for the next three days. Once the terrible trapped heat was released by rolling back huge canvas flaps to allow a passage of air through mosquito net curtains, the spacious tent was a great place to recover from days travelling off-road. While I collapsed in horizontal mode, Richard was preoccupied setting up a drinking water cooling system. First, he wrapped bottles of warm water in wet cloths, then tied them to the tent frame and left them hanging.

'Latent heat,' was his explanation. 'It's the only refrigeration on offer.'

Later we discovered the ultimate luxury – a row of primitive wooden huts enclosing basic but operational showers and toilets. I slept on and off all afternoon; not even the enticing smell of fresh pizza being lifted from an underground oven tempted me to rise for the evening meal.

I was sorry to miss the food, but not the after dinner ritual. Amy had adopted this time to give us a 'briefing' for the following day. That was fine, but she was in the habit of getting carried away and reading aloud pages of information, from hand written notes that were far from brief. A great deal of this was superfluous, or could be read at our leisure from our own selection of books. There was, of course, no electricity. This was overcome by a trendy headtorch: constant head movements from the notes to our faces caused the light to flash to and fro in a most disturbing manner for the entire duration of her discourse. It was the last thing we wanted or needed after a long hot day, when we were looking forward to unwinding and relaxing over a glass or two of wine.

On this particular evening, Richard was able to absent himself to administer to my needs, which included bringing me a bowl of soup. What is more, his latent heat cooling system worked. I had cool, refreshing water to drink.

Woken at 4 am by baboons, frogs and colobus monkeys, we assembled in readiness for a trip to another Karo village, this time to witness the traditional bull-bleeding ceremony. As we suspected, the event had been set up and paid for in an advance. By the time we arrived, the selected victim, a melancholy white bull, was already in place, and was being held in position by several men. One man kept his hand in the bull's open mouth, forcing its neck down and forward to enable a second man to pierce with an arrow, the swollen artery in the beast's extended neck. A third man was on hand with a gourd to catch the flow of blood. Once the vessel was full, the bull was released and the contents stirred. After scooping and eating handfuls of coagulated blood, the taster wiped deep red globules from his lips before handing the bowl to a friend to drink the remaining liquid.

Practised by a number of pastoral tribes in Africa, the primary purpose of the bleeding is to provide nourishment from drinking the blood, as well as the milk of cattle, as part of the diet. It had a been good photo opportunity, but there was a strange low-key feeling as we left the village and followed the track back to the campsite. Then somebody raised the question hanging over us: how many times would a bleeding for tourists take place that week? Sadly, we decided, too many.

In spite of assurances to the contrary, it was becoming increasingly clear that in the dry season, no tribe in the Omo region is inaccessible, whether by 4x4, boat or on foot, and that adventure-seeking tourists have taken full advantage of this. The result of the sudden increase in organised tours has been the swift development of a strictly commercial relationship between highland tribes and tour group organisers. In itself, it is understandable. It is the speed at which it is taking place that could backfire on the very people it is benefitting.

Back at the camp we were relieved to be offered an afternoon of rest; me once again in horizontal mode in the tent and Richard with his binoculars trained on visiting vultures.

Turmi

Our journey continued across the Omo plains, through the extensive territory of the Hamer people to Turmi. Our first encounters with the Hamer had taken place at Mago Park, where a number of them were employed. It was soon apparent that they spoke good English and were friendly and at ease with visitors. Boys, keen to act as paid guides, took every opportunity to make money. Socially mobile, they were fast becoming businessmen. Laundry costs had apparently doubled from a year ago. 5 Birr (50p), the payment for a pair of hand-laundered trousers, had risen to 10 Birr (£1). There was no shortage of demand for their labour.

Regional markets in the Lower Omo region have been the meeting place of tribes who travel long distances on foot to barter goods for many years. That tourism has added another dimension to market forces has ensured that many of the tribes now have ready cash and purchasing power. I was slowly discovering that the practice of exchanging money for photographs, so often blamed on tourists with cameras, is in fact controlled by the tribes who dictate payment, both for visiting their villages and for taking photographs. Local women, quick to recognise the economic benefits of this trend, have wasted no time in using it to their advantage.

A visit to the market in Turmi was on the cards. Located at a major trading hub on the Konso-Jinka circuit, it is the most important market in the region. It was at this location, during the recent BBC 'Tribe' visit to the Omo region, that Bruce Parry found it was no longer possible to maintain the impression that he was an intrepid traveller visiting 'unknown' tribes. Parry and the film crew were outnumbered by other travellers. It was just as busy today. Not surprisingly, it was also high hassle territory.

The greatest frustration was not so much the demand for photographs, as the demands from would-be guides who refuse to leave your side, insist on giving information you don't want, and become aggressive if payment for this information is not forthcoming. Young boys in particular were persistent in offering their services. It was a market and, we reasoned, it should have been possible to wander round freely, engaging spontaneously with traders. As soon as we made it clear to one pair of insistent followers that we wished to be left alone, another was on our heels.

Hamer women are strikingly good looking and they know it. Neither have they been slow in learning to use their looks to their commercial advantage. Thought to have roots in Ancient Egypt, the women are easily distinguished by their goatskin skirts, cowrie shell necklaces and, to indicate their status in the tribe, extravagant displays of copper and iron bangles on the arms and legs. Up to three heavy iron torques welded round the necks of married women, unnervingly suggestive of slavery, are said to denote the wealth and prestige of their husbands.

Another distinguishing feature of the women are the ochre-coloured plaits woven into their hair. As soon as visitors appeared, pairs of strategically positioned girls launched into action, with one rubbing the traditional mixture of animal fat and red-ochre into the roots and plaits of the other's hair, attracting a bevy of tourists with cameras. The girls were quick to point out that payment for each photograph must be doubled to accommodate both participants in the action. Others were ready and waiting to take up suggestive poses, showing off their figures to the best advantage, with considerable success. Plump thighs and waists suggested that efforts to make money from being photographed have not left them starving. In this region, many of the youngsters went to school and the majority of the women wore T-shirts, but not the Hamer women.

Hamer men are known for some pretty distinctive tribal practices too – notably wife-beating, which can only be stopped if considered too brutal: a practice, reminiscent of medieval England, when a man could beat his wife as long as he didn't maim or kill her. Wife-beating by Hamer men is second only to the frenzied whipping of the naked backs of female relatives, of the male initiate, at the Bull Jumping ceremony, the most important event in Hamer society. Evidence of this can clearly be seen by the deep scars across the women's backs. When Tim Lapage witnessed this event, he described how 'the tail of the whip wraps cruelly around their [the women's] back, savagely tearing at the flesh', and 'their ugly bleeding gashes are quite shocking.'

That both men and women drink heavily before this event is not surprising.

The ceremony itself is the culmination of a three day long initiation rite for the young men of the tribe approaching manhood. On the afternoon of the third day, up to thirty bulls are lined up in a row. The stark naked initiate has to leap onto the back of the first bull, then from each to the next, before turning round and repeating the rite of passage three times. Bruce Parry was filmed participating in this highly energised event – just one of the ways in which he attempted to become a member of the Hamer tribe on his second visit to the Omo Region.

Omorate, People of the Delta

The Land Cruisers bowled and bounced along the track, occasionally overtaking armed, bone-thin men, herding cattle or goats in a world so filled with red dust that the sky was no longer visible. Minute particles of sand filled the air, covering vehicles and travellers alike – sticking to damp skin, clothes, hair, eyelashes, each and every orifice. We were heading for a Dassanech village, set on the eastern bank of the Omo River. Nomadic pastoralists, forced to flee their homes during the expansionist wars of Turkana in the eighteenth century, the Dassanech settled in the southernmost part of Ethiopia round the delta of the Omo River leading into Lake Turkana, in the Kenyan Rift Valley, adding agriculture and fishing to their lifestyles.

At Omorate, the nearest settlement to the Kenyan border, we were obliged to stop and hand in our passports before approaching the village. There was an unpleasant feel to the place. In part, this came from the sense of an abandoned city still hanging over it from a failed agricultural programme when the Derg (Marxist Military Committee), together with the North Koreans, initiated an irrigated cotton industry. 40,000 acres were cleared and farmed before the economics of transporting the massive cotton crop over 550 miles of tortuous Ethiopian roads brought the project to a standstill. The town of Omorate grew around this project, and has been returning to the desert ever since.

Of more immediate concern was a group of Mafia like men, possibly leftover workers from the failed project, who were demanding money intended for the elders of the village we were visiting.

Not long after our escape through a haze of heat and dust – whipped into the air by a hot dry wind – we passed through a rickety fence surrounding a compound, which housed a collection of domed woven huts, covered in animal skins. Like the legs of gigantic insects, long-legged poles held platforms to support supplies of sorghum, stored inside bundles of dried grass high off the ground, safe from rats and flooding. Everything looked temporary, easy to dismantle and move on. Before we had time to emerge from the vehicles, we were surrounded by villagers, and the familiar photographic scenario was in full swing.

Once we succeeded in disentangling ourselves, we followed in the wake of a bevy of small children, vying to escort us through fields of sorghum and tobacco lining the banks of the river. En route, we passed a series of open-sided shelters housing hand operated corn grinders and, on the periphery of the village, a row of now defunct windmills, once used to power machines for the same purpose. Both were gifts from the people of Denmark to the Dassanech. It was also apparent that a system of irrigation in the fields lining the riverbank, had once existed. The problem for the Dassanech, as for other people in Ethiopia who receive outside aid in the form of machinery, is that as soon as the item breaks down, there are no spare parts and no expertise to mend and maintain it.

The Dassanech have a history of adapting to the inhospitable and changing conditions they face in order to survive. In times of drought, when they lose their cattle, goats and livelihood through disease, drought or raid by neighbouring tribes, they deal with this by switching to cultivating crops of sorghum and tobacco on the shores of Lake Turkana. Failing this, the people become *Dies,* or poor people, and turn to Lake Turkana for their livelihood; here they hunt fish or crocodile and occasionally, hippopotamus. Ideally, being *Dies* is temporary, and in time, they can become Dassanech again.

Although well into the dry season, the river was in full flow. A young girl, wearing a knee length leather skirt, was filling a plastic bottle with water. Her skirt is a sign that she is now a woman in Dassanech culture: she had been circumcised. This remains one of the most disturbing aspects of Dassanech life. A girl is subjected to the brutality of FGM at ten to twelve years of age. Severe complications and suffering during teenage marriage and childbirth are ongoing results. Without it, a Dassanech girl cannot marry and the father won't receive a bride price in cattle for his daughter. As well as meat, milk, leather for clothing and mattresses, cattle provide status in the tribe and the bride-wealth that allows a man to marry. It is this that makes the Dimi, the celebration of his daughter's circumcision, the biggest ceremony in a man's life.

Distracted by laughing voices, I turned to see a line of children following Amy along the water's edge, in a fun version of the conger eel. Rising from a bed of reeds, a Goliath heron made a dignified skyward retreat. Joining a handful of stragglers, threading a passage through a waist-high field of tobacco towards the village, I made my way towards the waiting Land Cruisers.

Shortly after retrieving our passports at Omorate, we stopped for lunch at a 'rest house' that turned out to be bottom of the pile for flies, cockroaches, dirt and all-round squalor – and this was in daylight. Mind you, we were covered in red dust and looked so down-at-heel that any respectable place would have refused us entry. Maybe it was the heat and the dust, but a low key feel followed the visit. In spite of a great deal of outside aid, time, money and equipment invested to help the Dassanech become part of the market economy, there was an absence of a positive sense of change and of moving on, both in their farming practices and their lives.

It was a relief to arrive at the tree shaded park, and particularly satisfying to stand under the shower and watch pale flesh emerge as layers of red dust disappeared down the plughole. Later, in recovery mode, through the tent's mosquito-netted open doorway, I watch two vultures circle over a nearby tree and pink Sabi Star of Africa blooms deepen against bruised evening sky.

Karat Konso

The following day, in an area where several tribal boundaries merge, we head for the rustic settlement of the Arbore People. The cosmopolitan feel to the place has been explained by the Arbore tradition of intermarrying with other ethnic groups. Another tradition, linking their ancestral ties with the Konso people, is their role of acting as middlemen in trade between Konso highlanders and tribes from surrounding lowlands. A further encouraging result of this intertribal communication has been a movement, led by the Arbore, to put an end to tribal fighting over land.

We passed a number of women from various tribes as they trudged along the track, wood strapped to their backs and carrying gourds or plastic containers of water, before arriving at the village: a collection of circular thatched houses with rooftops twisting to ragged points, each surrounded by a bush-like barricade. At first the place seemed deserted, then one by one, people emerged from a shaded area behind the houses.

It didn't take long for noticeably vociferous villagers to swing into action on the money for photos front.

Elders wearing brightly coloured head coverings and shawls were both demanding and photogenic. The women's love of jewellery was obvious from the layers of brightly coloured beads and aluminium necklaces, as well as wide collars studded with cowrie shells round their necks. Black scarves loosely covering their heads or shoulders suggested some Islamic dress-code influence from neighbouring Borena people. But that was as far as it went. Bare breasts seemed strangely at odds with covered heads. It occurred to us that the scarves could be a throwback to a concession to former Arab slave traders. Converts to Islam were not taken as slaves, and the Arbore people have a reputation for having benefitted from trading in slaves and ivory in the past.

Ethiopia's slave trade was a lucrative one. From the sixteenth to the nineteenth century, the country's main source of foreign revenue was from slaves. At the height of the trade it is estimated that 25,000 Ethiopian slaves were sold every year to markets across the world. The walled Muslim city of Harar in northeastern Ethiopia was a commercial centre, where the taking and trading in slaves was big business. In 1855, the British explorer Richard Burton became the first European to visit this Islamic city. In an edited account of his visit he is most unflattering about the place:

... strewed with gigantic rubbish heaps upon which repose one-eyed mangy dogs; rulers: petty princes, who have a habit of killing all those who are suspected of aspiring to the throne; and the people: of whom many are disfigured by scrofula and other diseases.

Among other vices practised in the city, he tells us that Harar was a halfway house for slaves and that Abyssinians and Amharas (Ethiopians) were the most valued:

... the worst are kept for domestic purposes; the best are driven by Western Arabs or the subjects of the Imam of Muskat, in exchange for rice and dates.
– *First Footsteps in Africa*

That the Imam of Muscat is mentioned was a potent reminder of the dhow yards of Sur, south of Muscat, and the dhow's longstanding trading importance – on the aptly named Trade Winds – in gold and slaves from the east coast of Africa to Oman.

In 1876, the French poet Rimbaud became the first white man to travel into the Ogaden region of Ethiopia. He also visited and lived in Harar, and is reputed to have run guns to King Menelik of Showa. It is rumoured that he too may have been involved in slave trafficking. In spite of his popularity with local chiefs and royalty and his interest in Abyssinian culture, the loneliness he suffered is poignantly expressed in his memorable plea, 'What am I doing here?'

Today, the Arbore have not only moved on and forward but such is their success that a recent documentary about their making peace with tribal enemies in Southern Ethiopia captivated audiences in the capital, Addis Ababa.

Our journey was taking us in a loop towards Karat Konso and back into the heartlands and villages of the Tsemai, Ari and Konso tribes. Not long after the tar road had given way to a furrowed track, we climbed a small hill and stopped at a viewing point, overlooking the neat stone terraced hillside of the Konso people. To one side, a couple of typical thatched village houses, and to the other, an empty wilderness of scrubby desert. Suddenly, from out of nowhere, we were surrounded by children and adults with outstretched hands chanting,
'You! You! You! Photo! Birr!'
Minutes later, when passing a Konso village, a celebrating and inebriated crowd of men literally swarmed around and onto our vehicle singing, chanting and banging sticks together. Uncertain of the mood or intention, we could only look out from our cage as Dario slowly nudged his way through the huge, dark,

enervating wave. Suddenly, I came to. From the back seat of the vehicle, without lifting my camera, I took a series of shots. From that moment, in order to achieve any degree of photographic spontaneity, I was shooting from inside the vehicle, without using the viewfinder and keeping the camera low. I was learning to shoot from the hip.

When the track into the southern highlands descended and cut through open bush, the mere sound of the engine acted as a magnet. Children shot like bullets from the undergrowth, scrambling to reach us. Hands outstretched, they ran like deer to keep up, until they dropped exhausted by the wayside to be replaced by new contenders. Slowing down to cross a streambed invited ambush. Once again, we were plunged headlong into a region where a 4x4 and a white face attracts a forest of outstretched hands and sends painted child buskers into frenzied somersaults, or leaping into action with exaggerated performances of the traditional jumping dance.

Further along the track, we stopped to photograph lozenge-shaped beehives hanging from an acacia tree, when an old man appeared from nowhere. People have a habit of appearing from nowhere in the bush. First he requested my sunglasses and somehow must have acquired them, for I never saw them again; then he attempted to swap his grubby turban for my sunhat but this time he didn't succeed. Finally, we did escape. On the ascent once more, we were approaching the neat terraced hillsides of the Konso people. Women and girls wearing two tiered gathered skirts – the shorter top tier hanging over the skirt proper – tramped along the dusty roadside, heavy loads strapped to their backs.

Settled agriculturalists, the Konso have made good use of the barren hillsides, building row upon row of beautifully buttressed stone walls to protect their crops from flash floods, cattle and intruders. Originally from the East and speaking a Cushitic language, their reputation for wanting to keep to themselves is reinforced by their fortress-like settlements – staggered up the hillside and surrounded by stone-built walls. Whether or not it was intentional, the similarity in design between the heavily layered houses to the design of women's overlapping skirts was striking.

By decree and design, our entry into the settlement was on hands and knees through a low tunnel – the only way into the compound and a useful deterrent to intruders. Crawling from darkness into bright sunlight, I scrambled to my feet to be greeted by a gathering of women and children. Dressed in the traditional skirts, some of the women were bare breasted, while others were wearing adopted Western-style T-shirts. Children, dressed in a mismatch of Western-style clothes, swarmed around us. A long, winding procession close on our heels, we followed one of the villagers trekking through steep and narrow passages that separate family homes within the compound. Finally, we arrived at the community house: a grand thatched and open-sided meeting-place, where everyone gathers for celebrations and community events.

I was anxious to see the carved wooden sculptures, the famous *waga*, erected by the Konso people when a warrior dies. This unique design used for a Konso hero, distinguishable by the phallic ornamental *khalasha* worn on the warrior's forehead, is dying out. Sadly, widespread theft and sale of the much coveted remaining gravestones has resulted in a great loss to the community. However, *waga* were not on the agenda. Amy had other plans; she was keen to introduce the travellers to a local shanty bar. Taking one look at the shack serving as a bar, in unusual, uncooperative mode, Richard put his foot down. He had no intention of drinking in a 'run-down, fly-infested hovel'. Similarly minded, I too declined.

As we sat and waited in one of the Land Cruisers, regretting our lack of independence, a small boy came to the window with a hand-made miniature version of a *waga* – not exactly what we had hoped for, but it was genuine craftwork and a memento. Minutes later we were joined by fellow traveller, Pete, who wasted no time in assuring us that our decision had been the right one.

'Went purely out of curiosity,' he insisted. 'Most sleazy place I've ever set foot in.'

There was another surprise in store. The overnight stop was a 'hotel' in Karat Konso; a row of concrete rooms, naked light bulbs and no water except in buckets, and squalid beds with filthy sheets and pillows. We stripped and sprayed the beds, used sleeping bags for bedding and towels for pillows. Just to add to the discomfort, a noisy late-night bar prevented sleep until the small hours.

Singing Wells, a Crater Lake and Hot Springs

Borena, El Sod, Wondo Genet

A deep sandy track led through a landscape dotted with flat-headed acacias and blooms as delicate and white as bridal veils. Strolling camels and strangely shaped termite mounds, ranging from tall, thin and phallic to slumped sculptured figures, stretched to the horizon. We were in the territory of the pastoralist Borena people, and heading for one of the celebrated wells where they water their cattle. For more than two millennia, the Borena have eked out an existence from the bleak landscape, shifting to seasonal breeding grounds and using communal wells, set out according to the traditional *gada* system.

Although linguistically and ethnically the Borena are regarded as a southern branch of the Oromo nation, their semi-nomadic lifestyle has more in common with the desert nomads of Kenya. It was when Abyssinian highlanders made inroads into the northern part of their territory that many Borena families were forced to migrate southwards. They subsisted by cattle raiding and attacking agriculturist settlements in northern Kenya, acquiring a reputation as fearsome warriors. Today, within Ethiopia, the Borena's reputation is one of a peace-loving and gracious people.

We stopped for a picnic lunch at a cliffside viewing point. Below and before us on a wide plain, a long line of assembled cattle and a scattering of camels patiently waited their turn to reach the well and quench their thirsts. This vital ritual for the animals belonging to each clan takes place every two to three days. Meanwhile, I noticed a Borena woman standing guard over a cow under a nearby acacia tree. Suddenly, it dawned on me that the cow was giving birth. Just minutes later, the young calf was standing and being licked clean by its parent.

Navigating a downhill route to the plain, Dario led our small convoy to a parking place at the base of the cliff face. Here we abandoned the vehicles and followed on the heels of a guide, who took us to the entrance of a narrow sandstone passageway that wound its way to a trough near the well-head. Walking just ahead of us was a Borena elder; wearing Western-style shorts, a lightweight weatherproof jacket, sandals and a wrap-around turban, he was guiding his cattle to drink.

Climbing to a narrow ledge alongside the water trough, we looked down on the stairway leading to the level of water in the well. Using the steps as a ladder, a line of a dozen or so men, dressed in boxer shorts, formed a chanting human chain tossing buckets of water from one to the other, from the water level at the bottom to the trough at the well-head, then back to be refilled in a non-stop circular belt of movement. This strenuous work was made easier by the men singing and chanting to encourage each other in the task. Hence the singing wells.

I felt honoured to be present at this unique tribal event that was not deliberately set up for tourists, but part of the daily life of the proud and colourful Borena people. Although we had paid for the privilege of a visit, there was no dressing-up for the camera, and no demands for money. It was truly inspirational. In addition to the splendid scene at the well, the colourful dress, shawl and beads of a woman supervising her cattle and the unarmed casually dressed men were remarkable contrasts to the near-naked, heavily armed tribal people we had been visiting in the southern Omo region.

Nevertheless, in common with neighbouring Omo and Kenyan tribes, the Borena do retain an age-old tradition – they measure their wealth and worth in terms of the size of their herd of cattle. The people depend on their cattle, not just for their livelihood but for prestige. It is said that a Borena man holds his cattle in such high esteem that he asks his neighbour about his cattle before enquiring about his wives and family.

Magado Drought

Just months after our visit, it was with great sadness that I read of the effects of one of the worse droughts in living memory to hit the Borena. After six months of rainless heat, of the two thousand cattle owned by Borena families in Magado, just two remained. The older men were so devastated by the loss that first one, then several others, hanged themselves from skeletal acacia trees surrounding the village. The men took their lives because to them the shame of losing their cattle was too great.

Plans to persuade the Borena to abandon a lifetime tradition and sell their cows at home and abroad are underway. In fact, USAID, a US government project, swung into action at the height of the drought by setting up a small-scale slaughterhouse to kill severely weakened animals. The meat was dried and sold to provide savings for the owners to buy new animals once conditions improved. Once again, it is about change and moving forward.

Our journey too moved on. This time, we followed a gravel road to a small village lying near the rim of the saline crater lake of El Sod. Known locally as the House of Salt, the deep crater is famous for its lake of black salt. Standing on the edge and looking down on inky blackness some 200 metres below, the lake appeared both starkly beautiful and somewhat menacing. Heat was still up, so only the ultra fit or foolhardy were considering to trek the zigzag path to the crater floor, passing donkeys laden with blocks of raw salt on their way to the top. The villagers make money from tourists by charging them to trek to the lake, and a group of clamorous youngsters was close on our indecisive heels. Feeling neither ultra fit nor, at that moment, foolhardy, both Richard and I decided to limit our activities to trekking round the outer rim and photographing the lake from afar.

'I told you to wait!' Amy's authoritative tones rang out. She was admonishing John, who was attempting to make a head start on what promised to be an arduous trek for a near octogenarian. Satisfied that we had made the right decision, we set off towards a viewing-point, only to discover that we too were playing Pied Piper to a gathering throng of children.

Tremors of relief from weary travellers at the first sighting of a straight tar road for more than ten days as we approached Yabello were superseded by Dario's relief and anticipation of filling up with fuel at a new fully fledged petrol station. His excitement didn't last. Fuel supplies had run out. Dropping us at the local motel, he set off in search of black market supplies. Listed as basic, we were expecting the worst, only to be pleasantly surprised. Set up and run by an enterprising young man from Addis Ababa, the simple ground floor building offered neatly painted rooms, furnished with comfortable, clean beds and covered by intact mosquito nets, plus the sheer luxury of an ensuite where everything worked.

For the bird lovers, a touch of five star quality was added by the motel's position, close to an area of acacia scrub. Sightings included white-tailed swallows, Streseman's bush crows, white-headed buffalo weavers and the 'Go-away' grey lowrie, last seen and heard in the Okavango Delta.

Dilla, Shashemene, Wondo Genet

On the tar road once more, heading for the hot-springs resort of Wondo Genet, we began the long drive north through a landscape transformed from bush and anthill savannah to tropical orchards. Plantations of coffee, papaya and mangoes give way to *enset* (false bananas), pineapples, sugar cane and Mexican apples. Village houses within compounds and shaded by trees, lines of washing, power lines and evidence of community organisation not seen for days took shape. It was like driving through time.

Dilla, the administrative capital of the Gedea zone and an important agricultural centre, set amongst the fertile green valleys of the Eastern Rift Valley Escarpment, is an important centre for rock engravings and a wealth of medieval *stelae* (obelisks) marking twelfth century graves. That Dilla was the venue for lunch in a modern, impeccably clean restaurant came as a pleasant surprise. Over fruit drinks, *injera* and spaghetti, we were hoping that a visit to one of the stelae fields was on the cards. Of the two largest, the Tututi stelae are said to be phallic in design, while those at Tutu Fela are of the engraved anthropomorphic (human) kind. Either would satisfy.

All too soon, we discovered that once again, Amy had other plans. The route we were following was taking us back through Shashemene, and she had organised a visit to the Rastafarian Black Lion Museum: a set-up which celebrates the community's Jamaican Rastafarian roots. At this point, fellow traveller Madge admitted to being a fan of Bob Marley, and pointed out that when the BBC were filming the 'Pole to Pole' series in Ethiopia, the team had visited Shashemene with the intention of including the Rasta community on film with Michael Palin. However, neither the team nor Michael Palin had been able to persuade the Rastas to take part. It seemed that hard times had now driven the devotees to join the Ethiopian cash for visits scenario.

Speedy mindset adjustments from ancient stelae to ageing Rastas were followed by a further briefing from Madge. She reminded us of the Rastafarian belief that Haile Selassie claimed to be the direct descendant of the Israelite Tribe of Judah through the lineage of King David and Solomon, and as such, he is believed to be the Lion of Judah mentioned in the Book of Revelation. This new faith, adopted by his Rastafari followers from Jamaica, accorded the Emperor divine status and led to them adopting the name Rastafari from Ras Teferi (Tafari), that of the emperor before he was crowned. Such was the strength of belief that all were expected to prostrate themselves in the Emperor's presence – even at the roadside, as witnessed by the two young travellers from Devon in 1972.

Thus prepared, we were taken into a dark Victorian-style room to meet Robinson, an ageing Rastafarian with greying plaited locks. After briefly describing his Jamaican/Indian roots and his devotion to the late Emperor, he played a video of himself talking about the commune. Jotted notes include: Rastafarian devotees of Haile Selassie given 500 hectares of land to set up a commune in Shashemene. The arrangement ended when the Derg took power and the Emperor was murdered. Devotees left for New York, promptly returning when the present government took over. They are waiting and hoping for the restoration of the Ethiopian monarchy and reinstatement to their former favoured position.

'But', Robinson concluded, 'Things have changed. The government is corrupt, and bribes and residency fees have to be paid.'

Developments were not looking good for the Rastafarian community in Shashemene.

A detour to Lake Awassa, the smallest of the Ethiopian Rift Valley Lakes, was another step into the past. We stood for a while, absorbing the stunning mountainous backdrop and watching men fishing from traditional reed boats. Binoculars and cameras were soon trained on a shoreline dense with vegetation and teeming with birds. Then Awassa city took us forward in time: a main wide street, lined with modern buildings, culminating in a gold domed mosque. Its reputation as a centre for learning and education included housing the Headquarters of the Forestry Commission. It was a brief respite before backtracking along a dust-hazy track filled with donkey-drawn carts and the depressing sight of women and young girls trudging along the roadside, laden like beasts of burden. Finally, we were approaching the resort of Wondo Genet for a night of comfort among forested hills.

Established as a recreation site for the royal family in 1964, the resort was bequeathed its present name, meaning 'Place of Heaven', by Haile Selassie. Situated near hot springs and surrounded by forest, it is said to more than live up to its name. Whether it is the curative properties of the hot springs and swimming-pool, abundant bird life, shaded hills for hikers or just a place to chill out for weekenders from Addis Ababa, the resort attracts a constant stream of visitors. Emperor Haile Selassie was so enamoured that he had a private lodge built in the grounds. With all the hallmarks of a Hemingway hunting lodge, including worn out bearskin rugs on the floors, it has now been integrated into the hotel.

The only downside to Wondo Genet appeared to be its susceptibility to earth movements, the most recent being an earthquake in 1983. Although its magnitude was not determined – after all, it is Ethiopia – its severity was such that the frightened inhabitants gathered in the Orthodox church below the hotel to sing and pray for an entire night and day.

In fact, Wondo Genet did have another downside. Where there are visitors there is money, and where there is money there are people who want a share. The entrance drive to the hotel was thronging with hawkers and guides, offering everything from pineapples and papayas to car washes, horse and cart rides or guided walks – anything that could warrant a cash handout.

Through the crowd I noticed a woman and her two young daughters, all bearing heavy loads on their backs and making their way downhill. Purely from the point of view of using the image to support the need for change, I asked the mother if I could take a photo. As soon as the shutter clicked and I was preparing to make a payment, two men stepped forward, demanding that I give the money to them and insisting that they would pay the women. I quickly handed the notes to the woman. It was saddening to watch the mother and her daughters attempting to run to escape the predators, despite their heavy burdens.

After extricating ourselves from the crowd, we were escorted to an ageing semi-detached bungalow. A distinguished looking colobus monkey, its black face contrasting with white wimple-like surrounds, was on guard near the entrance. Despite its years and lack of upkeep, the bungalow offered a quiet and cool resting and recovery place. While my priority was a shower, Richard's was bird watching: parrots, hornbills, barbets, flycatchers, tree pipits and more kept his attention until darkness fell. Washed and spruced-up for dinner in the space-age dining room, complete with a roof sporting pyramidal and cone-shaped glass modules, we hardly knew the place, recognised ourselves or our fellow travellers.

Return to Addis Ababa

The final 260km to Addis Ababa took us from the Rift Valley to the undulating landscape of the plateau. Once again, harvested fields, dotted with the occasional sycamore fig, were reminiscent of English summer fields, dotted with giant-sized oaks. It was the steady stream of people walking along the roadside that was the reminder that it was indeed Ethiopia. As we neared the capital, shanty settlements and traffic increased until, at times, we ground to a standstill. Back at the Ghion Hotel, we discovered that we had been upgraded to the main building. Antiquated quilted walls and an equally antiquated ensuite revealed its age, but everything appeared clean and everything worked, including the less than modern TV and telephone.

A Rock Cut Church and Ancient Stelae

Adadi Maryam, Tiya Stelae

A bell hanging from a tree and a Coptic cross standing on a grass covered mound at ground level were the only signs of the presence of a church. Like Lalibela's architectural wonder of eleven rock-hewn churches, the church of Adadi Maryam, although smaller and more roughly hewn, is a subterranean semi-monolith, encircled by a tunnel leading to monastic cells.

Of the various accounts of the origin of Ethiopia's remarkable rock-hewn churches, the most memorable is the legend that tells us that the twelfth century King Lalibela was transported to heaven by an angel and shown a city of rock-cut churches which he was ordered to replicate. King Lalibela was allotted a time span to complete the work. When his masons failed to meet the deadline, angels descended from heaven to complete the task. That the churches were hewn out of rock below ground level, have survived Islamic attempts to destroy them, and to this day remain as places of Christian worship, is something of a miracle.

Just a few hours drive to the south of Addis Ababa, Adadi Maryam, the southernmost extant rock-hewn church in Ethiopia, was accessible on the last day of our visit. Our arrival couldn't have been better timed. It was Sunday, a service was in progress and we were invited to attend. A flight of worn stone steps took us way back in time and to the start of a passageway leading to the hollowed interior that forms the main body of the church.

Removing our shoes, we followed the guide to the inner enclave where a priest, dressed in a shimmering pink robe and wearing a gold crown – not unlike one of the magi from a nativity scene – was addressing his congregation of women and children. As the service progressed, even without the chanting and drumbeats of swaying deacons and attendants that accompany more imposing celebrations, the intonation of the ancient ecclesiastical language of *Ge'ez* was deeply moving.

Scholars date the church sometime between the twelfth and fourteenth centuries, while local tradition holds that it was built on the orders of King Lalibela when on a visit to nearby Mount Zikwala in AD 1106. Whatever the origin, the history of Adadi Maryam is said to include discovery and violent attack in the 1520s by the Arab leader from Harar, Ahmed Gragn. The priests were killed or fled, and although the attackers could not destroy the church, it fell into disuse until it was miraculously discovered by local hunters and reopened during the reign of Menelik II (1889-1913). It has remained in active use until this day. Its survival and the opportunity we had to share with local people an ancient Christian service, practised from the time of the apostles and unchanged for some two thousand years, was both unreal and tremendously special.

Then an unrealised dream. We were about to cross a medieval boundary between Christian and pagan Ethiopia. Just 30km down the road was the ancient stelae field of Tiya, the most northern of a belt of mysterious engraved stelae that stretches across southern Ethiopia, through Dilla to Negele Borena. In spite of recent research and extensive work by French archaeologists, remarkably little is known about either the origin or the markings engraved on the Tiya stelae. Like the much older and larger stelae of Axum, thought to be the only comparable constructions in sub-Sahara Africa, the Tiya stelae are believed to predate the arrival of local Christianity and to have been erected as grave markers.

Interestingly, that Ethiopia's southern stelae belt passes through the heart of the modern territory of Gurage, whose language is closely affiliated to Tigrigna, the language spoken at Axum, raises the possibility that they could be a forgotten offshoot of the pre-Christian stelae building tradition at Axum. Another theory states that some of the stelae have links with the decorated gravestones erected by the migrating Oromo people, whose ancestors may have displaced the original stelae-erecting society. The site promised to be as complex as it was fascinating.

There was no on-site guide and no on-site information, but we were fortunate to have Dario as our driver and guide. Familiar with the place and the set up, he left us with a flask of coffee in the shade of a tree, and set off to locate the local man in charge. Within minutes, we were standing before a wooden gate leading into an overgrown field. The gate was unlocked and we were on our own. Before us, rows and clusters of gravestones were scattered across an extensive area of overgrown blond grass. Fringed by spindly thorn trees and cordoned off by a three foot wire fence, it was about as informal as you can get for a UNESCO World Heritage Site.

Bathed in sunshine, stillness and silence, I followed a rough pathway that took me towards and alongside a row of two dozen or more upright stones. Standing guard over mass graves and ranging roughly between three to six feet in height and of a cylindrical or phallic design, they are thought to date back some two thousand years, to the ninth century. Their incredible age, plus their smooth, rounded and slightly stooping posture, gave them the appearance of gentle guardians of long forgotten people.

Just a few metres away, I caught up with Richard. Camera poised, he was standing before a single stone, some two metres in height. Of a rectangular shape and bearing carefully engraved swords and abstract symbols, it was one of a number of stelae on the site, believed to be from the twelfth century. On this particular stone, two swords, each, marked with a cross and pointing towards the ground, were positioned over and above a row of three swords pointing skywards. The central of these was also marked with a cross. Beneath the swords, two circles hovered over what appeared to be a pair of leaves rising from a stem.

The meaning behind the engravings on these more recent flattened stelae remains uncertain. One theory has it that the swords could either represent the number of people killed by a warrior, or mark the place of rest of those killed in battle. The circles and twin leaves could on the one hand symbolise human features or the sun and the moon over a traditional headrest. Whether or not the carved form of a cross on three of the swords relates to the twelfth century arrival of Christianity at Adadi Maryam posed yet another conundrum.

Finally, one gravestone in particular stood out in both structure and clarity of meaning; the engraved form of a female lying on her back, arms resting on either side of unmistakable breasts, paralleled a tradition said to be practised by the Konso people – that of burying wives at the side of a hero. This is a theory that adds some authenticity to the oral tradition of the Konso, a tradition that suggests their migration to their present homeland from the eastern Rift Valley Escarpment.

Mute, mysterious and haunting, the stones of Tiya stood before us – silent witnesses to a forgotten world – a 'grave' contrast to Adadi Maryam, where the sense of the living past was very much alive.

Both the rock-cut church and the stelae field added definitive layers to Ethiopia's enigmatically complex history: a place like no other, where the sophisticated Westernised elite of the capital live in a society a world and time away from a complex and living past. We had no more than brushed the surface, yet we left with a sense of the great movement and change that is taking place; change from within, as well as through contact with the outside world; change that will bring hope for the future of the rich, colourful diversity of ethno-linguistic people that remain as utterly fascinating as they are unique. There was no doubt about it – the wonder of Ethiopia outshone the downsides of our visit.

The Gambia

2007

The bicentenary of British attempts to stop slave trafficking in The Gambia gave priority status to the smallest country in Africa

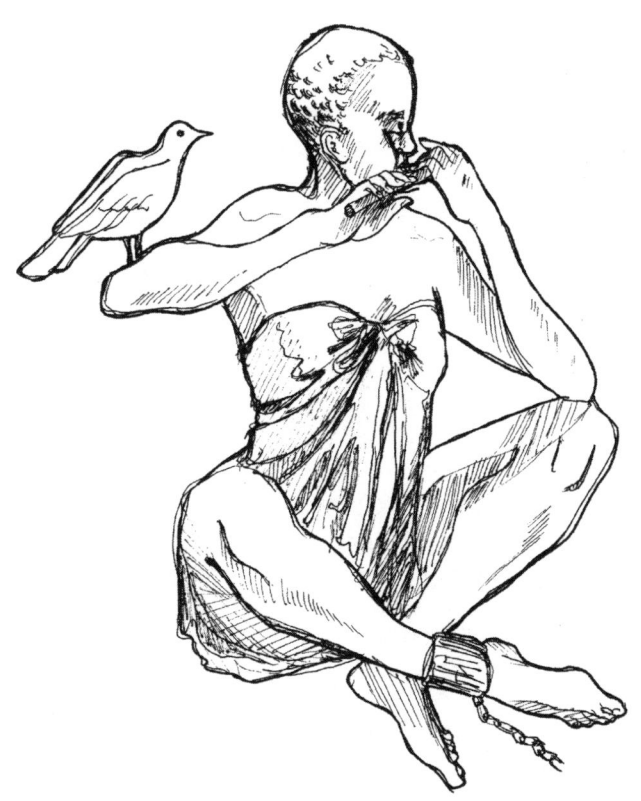

Banjul
March 2007

Heat and a ground floor room backing onto the main highway into Banjul ensured a sleepless night. Hardly the quiet room we had requested at the Palm Grove Hotel. The following morning, resettled on the second and top floor of a wing projecting towards tidal mudflats and lagoons, with the added bonuses of a fan and a small balcony overlooking a tree favoured by our much loved bulbuls, we were content.

Accommodation sorted, we arrived for breakfast and were welcomed into the dining room, not by the rhythmic beat of African drums, but the crackling vocal tones of a rendition of 'My Old Man's A Dustman'. Economically viable package tours have made the Gambia a place to come for winter sun; amorous encounters, notably of 'mature' women with young local men, appeared to be the main attraction. This trend, started by the Swedes in the 1970s, was taken up by the Dutch, and finally a new breed of sun-seeking Brits. Quite what 'My Old Man's A Dustman' had to do with this or any other aspect of life in the Gambia we couldn't surmise.

Although we had taken advantage of package-tour costs for flights and a base from which to operate, once we arrived we had made arrangements to travel independently; on this occasion, it was to the island of Jinack on the north bank of the Gambia River's estuarine mouth. In addition to the opportunity to see and photograph forts built by the British some two hundred years ago to stop the trafficking in slaves, it was the novelty of crossing the river and escaping to stay in an African-style hut on a coastal island, with the promise of leopard tracts in the sand, that had acted as a lure.

Jinack Island

Leaving fellow holiday makers preparing for a week recumbent round the pool by day and nights in local disco bars, we settled ourselves in the hotel's reception area to await the arrival of our host. Within minutes we were greeted by Foday Fawally, the owner and manager of Jinack's Madiyana Camp, escorted to his upmarket Range Rover, and driven along the Banjul Highway to a bridge over Oyster Creek – a waterway that separates the city and island of *Banjul* (Bamboo) from the mainland – en route to the estuary.

Independence Arch, notable as much for its size as its incongruous appearance, was worth a photo stop. Built to commemorate the successful July 1994 military coup that took President Yahya Jammeh to power, the 35m high structure sports a triangular roof over a balcony, providing views across the city. Sheltered by the arch, a life-size sculpture of a soldier cradling a young child remains as a symbol of the military giving new life to the Gambia. Foday assured us that the arch was also a reminder of the president's power and prestige.

'Drivers have to stay alert,' he warned. 'If you don't get off the road when the President and his entourage appear, you'll be arrested!'

This was a circumstance experienced by the Dutch author, Cees Noteboom (*Nomad's Hotel*). When visiting Banjul, on his way to return a rented bicycle, he noticed a commotion ahead and saw a policeman waving his arms. He knew what he had to do, but his attempts to get off the road were delayed by large potholes. As he struggled to avoid them, he saw a black Mercedes sweep by. He is too slow. It is the president and he is arrested.

For us, reality took hold at the port, as much a dumping ground for clapped out vehicles and the skeletons of abandoned boats as it was for the coming and going of fishing boats. It was shambolic. At its widest point, the River Gambia reaches 8km, and the nearby working ferry crossing, taking from one and a half to two hours, is reputed to be notorious for long queues and long delays. So much so that the crossing from Banjul on the south bank to Barra on the north bank is said to be as frustrating for locals and visitors as it is for Senegalese travellers attempting to leave and enter their divided land.

It is all rather complex, and came about in 1807. The British wanted to end the trade in slaves and the French, who had colonised Senegal, didn't. To enable them to succeed, Britain bought the island of Banjul, at the southern tip of the Gambia River's mouth, from a local chief in 1816. Renamed Bathurst, after the Earl of Bathurst, who had approved its occupation and development, it was also a staging post for an additional large fort, built to protect trading interests and to deny access to the river by slave traders. Four years later, the River Gambia was declared a British Protectorate. In 1826, Fort Bullen was built at the mouth of the Barra River opposite Bathurst. This defence of British interests was further endorsed by an upriver fort at Georgetown (Janjangbureh), the highest shipping point for large boats on the river, and the main staging post for *slatees* (local slave merchants). Along with the French, tribal chiefs and kings, who had grown wealthy trading slaves with the Europeans, local slave traders were not happy at the prospect of the end of this lucrative form of trade.

While waiting for Foday's *pirogue* (wood and reed boat) through a deluge of circling gulls, we watch fishermen coming in with their catches, while just beyond, the Banjul ferry was setting off on its river crossing. Then we are off. Shaded from the sun by an overhead bamboo screen, the chugging engine takes us across the river towards Barra and the remains of Fort Bullen. Its walls, linking four rounded towers, gleamed white in late morning sun. With cannons trained on open water, it was in a prime position to launch attacks on illegal slave ships.

As we head north and west across choppy waves, Foday explains that Jinack is separated from the mainland by a *bolon* (creek), and this is what gives it its island status. Together with a stretch of adjacent mainland, Jinack forms 49km of Niumi National Park.

'In theory, the park is protected,' Foday continued, before pausing to fill and light his pipe. His voice rose from a cloud of smoke. 'In practice, only one man is responsible. In other words, protection is impossible.'

Meanwhile, the on-duty boatman was navigating the pirogue towards and alongside a wooden walkway.

'Welcome to Madiyana,' Foday said, offering his hand to help me disembark, and gesturing towards an open-sided rondavel restaurant and bar.

It was a delightful shady retreat and idyllic place for lunch that we were more than ready for. Solomon, the elderly cook, learnt his gourmet skills by working with a French chef in Senegal. It showed. Pasta served with a tangy meat sauce and salad was as simple as it was tasty.

Tropical afternoons are for siestas. We retreated to our African-style chalet with woven reed walls and a thatched roof. Shutters, mosquito netting over the bed and resident agama lizards helped to keep unwanted insects at bay. Birds calling over the sound of waves collapsing and retreating on the beach was the music playing as we drifted towards sleep. Life doesn't come much better.

An awakening shower – a tub of water and a jug – in a bamboo-sided washroom open to the skies. By late afternoon we were ready to be escorted on a trek through woodland savannah and dry bush, past a saline lake to a Mandinka village on the island's far side.

Fig and cashew nut trees, colourful fruit hanging, lined the final stages of the route, while rice paddies, dry until the rains in June, and – rumour has it – lucrative crops of marijuana clothed low-lying land on the outskirts of the village. Sadly, although the island is a designated national park, Foday's warning about lack of protection was all too true. Amado, our Mandinka guide, explained that there is no one to prevent villagers letting cattle roam where they will, or local boys from hunting monkeys, genets, civet cats – any wildlife – with packs of dogs. Owls too are targets, especially in rural areas, where they are regarded with superstitious dread.

'Local people believe they are transformed wizards or witches and their call announces a death. If an owl is seen in daylight, it is stoned to death,' Amado finished dramatically.

The village itself – a mismatch of traditional thatched rondavel houses and concrete rectangular buildings with ironclad roofing – boasted a nursery and primary school. Before long, we were surrounded by a growing band of clamorous children. Diving into the local shop to buy sweets, Richard took on the role of Pied Piper until rescued by Amado. Families were busy cooking over cradled open fires. Each and every woman appeared to have a baby strapped to her back. One female, holding a bowl of couscous in one hand and a mobile phone in the other, was caught between two worlds. Only the solemn imam sat apart, fingering his prayer beads, hoping for fat donations for a new mosque.

With Foday's story of catching the eyes of a leopard in the light of his torch fresh in our minds, we started back in failing light, eyes searching low-lying dappled shade and overhead boughs just made for draping feline limbs. Before long I had the feeling that it was we who were being watched. Leopards are the native big cat in the Gambia, and although recent sightings are rare, rumour has it that their tracks can be found just about everywhere on the island. With nothing more to boast of than the twittering of bulbuls and a green pigeon's contented notes, we arrived at the bar in time for sundowners and I made a plan. Even if the last of Jinack's leopards were keeping out of sight, I set my sights on finding and photographing leopard paw prints in the sand.

In the cool light of dawn, we set off on a walk to the border with Senegal, a mile or so along the coast. While Richard was preoccupied photographing some of the more obliging five hundred and sixty known varieties of birds, I was in competition with the incoming tide, attempting to capture an intriguing range of prints in the sand. Varying in pad and claw size, a number of tracks led to and from low-lying shrubs and tamarisk bushes that stretched to infinity along the white sands of the beach; identification would have to wait. Finally, reaching a lagoon that marked the boundary with Senegal, we settled in the hollow of a nearby dune to watch a gathering of pelicans, cormorants, herons and varieties of wading birds sharing the pleasures of their watery kingdom. With leisurely pursuits in mind: reading in a hammock for me and fishing for Richard, we started back for another afternoon in paradise.

The President's Patch

Sindola Camp

Bypassing prostrate tattooed, overweight and overexposed bodies grilling white flesh in the sun, we strolled the walkways of the gardens of the Palm Grove Hotel. A selection of carved wooden totems – not dissimilar in style to the sombre faced *Moai* (stone statues) on Easter Island – was the focus of our cameras. We were passing time, waiting for a lift to Sindola Camp, a luxury retreat on the doorstep of the President's country mansion, amidst his tribal lands.

Morning drifted into afternoon before the driver finally arrived at the locally known and joked about GMT – Gambia Maybe Time – and escorted us to an ancient black Peugeot for the start of a journey through shanty suburbs, punctuated by impressive new villas. Open fronted shops spilled goods onto the pavements while randomly built, half-finished houses crowded the roadside. Before long, black tarmac gave way to a red sandstone graded road, littered with potholes of increasing bomb-crater sizes. To help prevent my head from hitting the roof and my feet and ankles from jarring against the metal floor, I resorted to clinging with both hands onto the one remaining overhead handgrip. Seatbelts were non-operational and suspension ineffectual.

Heat and concentration on life preserving techniques all but prevented enjoying the change of scenery as we trundled and lurched along the rutted track, through great forests of mango trees and heady rhun palms running parallel to the course of the Gambia River. Thickly coated with layers of red dust billowing from the road, the foliage showed no hint of green. Further inland, clusters of traditional thatched mud-brick village houses replaced concrete shanty settlements with corrugated iron roofs. Africa in the raw was taking shape. A sense of nearing the wilderness increased when two warthogs trotted across the road, narrowly missing death-on-impact from our racetrack driver. Long horned cattle wandered under mango trees in village compounds; women prepared food and pumped water from wells while men passed the hot hours sleeping or playing draughts in the shade; vultures circled overhead. Further inland, away from the river, the vegetation became brown and arid. It was March and the start of the dry season.

Finally, we were approaching an island of green – an oasis in an otherwise sun-scorched landscape: Sindola Safari Camp, a place where the president's visitors and upmarket travellers chill out. Set amidst lawns framed by neatly trimmed casuarina hedges, our air conditioned thatched rondavel was surrounded by vibrant flowering shrubs and trees – mango and banana, date palm and hibiscus, avocado and lemon, coconut and oil palm – a true and unexpected Eden for birds and humans alike. After a 'welcome' hibiscus drink, we headed for a cool dip in the pool. We were not the only visitors. Visiting swallows, swooping and rising in perfect symmetry were quenching their thirsts.

A pool of waterlilies, fringed by the vibrant pinks and reds of hibiscus and bougainvillea blooms, was the setting for sundowners alongside the open-sided dining room. At the entrance we are stopped in our tracks by a remarkable life-size statue of a slave girl. With the remains of a fetter clamped to her ankle, she sits cross-legged, playing a flute while a dove, perched on her shoulder, completes the poignant image of peace and forgiveness.

For a time, we have the place to ourselves and then voices announce the arrival of a body of British males. We soon discover that they are from Universal Concern and are here to check on various farming projects set in motion on earlier trips. The emphasis is to help local people develop efficient farming practices, both for their own needs and for the production of crops for sale to hotels to replace current imports. The links to Devon continued. One of the team, a Professor John Wibberley, was from Shaldon, just down the road from Exeter.

The timing of our visit was such that we were invited to share the after dinner entertainment put on in honour of our fellow guests: a traditional dance, performed by the local Jola people from President Jammeh's tribal village. A speedy reference to my Bradt guide reveals that the Jola are said to have migrated from Egypt, bringing with them palm seeds, cotton and rice. Apart from large-scale rice cultivation, they are known for collecting honey, palm wine tapping, fishing and collecting oysters. An industrious people, they measure their wealth by the amount of rice they possess as opposed to the neighbouring Fulani, whose wealth is measured by the number of cattle they own.

Escorted by fellow guests to take our seats before the open-air stage, we learn that favours from the president to the people from his tribal village include cut-price rice plus 24 hours of electricity and running water – privileges not enjoyed by others from surrounding villages.

Meanwhile, Jola men were providing the background rhythm of drum beats while women dancers (*kanali*), dressed in full-length brightly coloured robes with matching turbans tied on their heads, formed a semi-circle, clapping together pieces of wood and chanting; then one by one the women took centre stage. 'Fertility dance' was my neighbour's explanation for a performance, where boldness of presentation was matched and magnified by the women's ample forms. Accompanied by rhythmic drumming, the lead woman, legs bent at the knees, moved forward in stilted jumping movements that became increasingly energetic and frenzied until, with a final, almost defiant leg-kick high into the air, she ended her routine. This was immediately followed by a fellow contender, who competed with the energy and provocative nature of the previous display.

Hoping for some close up shots, I left my seat and was moving along the darkened side of the arena, close to a fringe of bushes when, from behind, two hands gripped me by the waist before moving swiftly down over my hips. I spun round to see a heavily built, laughing Jola woman move off into the darkness. Anger displaced shock as I returned to my seat. Then an increase in drumbeats and a disguised figure spinning across the stage took my attention.

Dressed from head to foot in an outfit made from layers of dried grass with a wooden pole projecting from the top, the figure resembled a whirling haystack. With a jolt of memory, I realised that this was the *kankurang* man. Complete with his rod of justice, he was the figure of authority in the village, and his dance was to celebrate circumcision, the brutal form of FMG still carried out on young girls by some tribes in the Gambia. The hidden identity of the dancer, known as *cumpo* (secret), plus the speed of his twisting movements, increasing like those of a whirling dervish, contrived to inspire wonder and fear in the watchers. His message to youngsters was that even if something appears frightening, there is no need to be afraid.

That night, in the air conditioned confines of our thatched rondavel, drumbeats from the nearby Jola village, throbbing in the darkness, revived memories of the women's energised dancing, the audacity of the groping Jola woman, and the *kankurang's* empty message of nothing to fear. We agreed that it had been an unsettling evening.

'Try to remember, love. This is Africa, not Devon,' Richard reminded me. 'Best stay close, especially in the dark.'

As the drumbeats subsided, soothed by the sound of Richard's steady breathing, my mind, like my eyelids, grew heavy.

Rising to brilliant sunlight in birdsong tropical gardens, we dodge sprinklers dispensing rainbows to the sky, pearls to the grass. The morning was spent reclining by the pool in the shade of a sweet smelling frangipani visited by colourful birds, and provided time for dipping into the Scottish explorer, Mungo Park's account of his travels through the Gambia.

After last evening's performance, I was especially interested in his account of a masquerade. In 1805, at the near start of his second journey through the Gambia, Park stopped overnight at a Mandinka village where he saw a masquerade garment made from the bark of trees. He learnt that *'Mumbo Jumbo'* - a grotesque idol, said to have been worshipped by some African tribes – is a role adopted by a village male. Disguised in the masquerade habit, he appears before the celebrating village in order to dispense justice to an offending wife. The unsuspecting victim is picked on, stripped naked, tied to a pole and beaten with the rod of justice – a sobering and chilling reminder of the origins and practice of today's figurative use of the term 'Mumbo Jumbo': an object of senseless veneration or meaningless ritual.

Then there were the *Jaloff* people, described by Mungo Park as, 'an active, warlike and powerful race excelling in the production of cotton cloth'[11] – said to stand-out for clinging to former beliefs, traditions and practices. Were they, I wondered, related to the Jola people? They had brought cotton with them, had a reputation for clinging to traditions and there was something threatening in their behaviour.

Closing the journal, I realised that Richard had disappeared with his binoculars. It was time to clear my mind. A cold swim should do it. Then lunch, followed by a siesta, in preparation for a change of scene – a visit to the President's nearby safari park.

Kanilai Game Reserve, adjoining the grounds of the President's weekend mansion – once an area of Guinea Savannah and open farmland – has been transformed into a nature park covering thirty five kilometres of savannah bush, peppered with baobab and cottonwood trees. As afternoon's shadows lengthened, with promised sightings of honey badgers in mind, we set off for a local safari experience on the very doorstep of the camp.

Sadly, it didn't take long to realise that the park has severe shortcomings. Although some species of wildlife have been introduced from South Africa, there was little more to be seen through scrub and waist high savannah grass than a long distance view of a handful of zebra and a startled duiker that disappeared as quickly as it appeared. The highlight of the trip was a visit to a fenced off pool, home to Nile crocodiles. Watched over by lordly vultures, the resident crocs were snoozing on the banks, waiting for the delivery of their evening meal. There was something about the languor of these crocodiles waiting to be fed that reminded me of the weirdest story of encounters between man and beast that I have ever heard.

While travelling on the Nile, Ebu Ceddullah, a venerable Sheikh, related a tale of an amorous liaison he had with a crocodile to the author Evliya Celebi. After being fed with fish heads for several days the crocodile 'strode out of the water, raised her tail and lay on her back.' Recalling that Arabs have sex with crocodiles 'the Sheikh girded his loins and went to it.' [12] It is a long story but ends with the death of the crocodile and its transformation into the daughter of the Sheikh of the Kunuz Arabs, who had been bewitched. The explanation given, why men of this region have sex with crocodiles is that they believe it will cure them of gonorrhoea, from which they suffer. The final disturbing twist – those Arabs who will not commit this act have sex instead with Ethiopian slave girls.

Meanwhile, our solemn faced local guide informed us that two other crocs, who had escaped to take up residence in a natural pool in the park, were busy feasting off remaining wildlife that go there to drink. Not surprisingly, there was not a honey badger to be seen.

In fact, the President keeps the prized wildlife, including lions, wild dogs and ostriches in caged enclosures on the periphery of the camp. Rumour has it that four giraffes, originally kept in the grounds of his walled townhouse in Banjul,

---

[11] Mungo Park, *Travels into the Interior of Africa*
[12] Evliya Celebi, *An Ottoman Traveller: Selections from the 'Book of Travels'*

escaped and met untimely deaths. Approaching the exit of the reserve, the final image of baboons chained to baobab trees confirmed that the President's park has a long way to go to reach traditional safari standards.

We left the Gambia with a promise to return after the summer rains and with the contact details of Mark Thompson, a British man who organises and runs inland river trips: the opportunity to explore the reaches of Hidden Gambia was before us.

Hidden Gambia

Janjangbureh, Mungo Park Memorial
November 2007

Poolside drinks in a garden filled with flowering trees and shrubs, visited by dozens of colourful birds. This was the welcome we received at Safari Gardens Hotel. An eco-friendly and friendly small hotel, catering for independent travellers, it is just one of a growing number run by enterprising Brits who have made the Gambia their home and set up camp away from the growing plethora of package tour hotels. Among these is Mark Thomson. With a supply of riverboats and up-river staging posts, Mark was about to make our return to The Gambia and dreamed-of travels into Hidden Gambia possible. Meanwhile, our overnight chalet, equipped with a mosquito-netted bed and fan, was doing its utmost to keep insects, heat and humidity at bay.

The following morning was the start of a journey of some two hundred miles, as the crow flies, up the mighty meandering Gambia River to Bird Safari Camp on MacCarthy Island. Georgetown, the island's former capital, was an important British administrative centre and trading post in the days of slave trading. Today the settlement, a sleepy, laid-back place, has resumed its former name of Janjangbureh, given by the brother and sister Janjang and Bureh who are said to have discovered it.

With insufficient time to travel up the meandering waterway entirely by riverboat, Mark had arranged and planned an alternating road and river journey. Stage one by road followed the river east to Bintang Bolon, a traditional mangrove staging post for river traffic on one of the many *bolons* (creeks) that wind their way through low lying mangroves towards the river. Accompanied by George, a local Mandinka birdman, who was sitting up-front alongside the driver, we occupied the second row of seats in a people carrier which lurched and bounced for what seemed interminable hours through clouds of red dust, along a potholed road. Open windows – the only air conditioning on offer – did little to combat tropical heat. Three mind bending hours later, we turned onto an overgrown sandy track leading to the venue for the first overnight stop.

Feeling like a misused rag doll, I followed Richard along a gravel path to a gateway topped by carved vultures, leading to a bar-cum-restaurant: open-sided, but with a thatched roof and fronted by a stilted platform over mangrove swamps, it overlooked the bolon. We had arrived on the heels of a Dutch couple. I felt my jaw dropping when I learnt that they had cycled for seven and half hours along the unmade road from Banjul. We recovered from our offroad experience by relaxing with iced drinks in our hands, absorbing the splendid waterfront view to where tomorrow's transport, a boat dubbed the *Safari Queen*, was bobbing on her mooring. The energetic Dutch travellers recovered by plunging into the bolon for a cooling off swim.

A network of creaking, stilted walkways, oysters clinging to the legs, over tidal mudflats led to one of six wooden thatched rondavel huts. Our lodging for the night offered a bed with a single sheet, two small hard cushions, serving as pillows, and an 'over the river' ensuite housing a shower and loo. An ageing wooden balcony did not encourage casual use. There was no doubt about it that the huts had seen better days. It was, however, a place of splendid isolation, with nothing more than the cry of a bird or the sound of moving water to disturb the compelling silence.

A glass of red wine in hand and freshly caught fish on the menu for dinner, under a star dusted dome of sky, ended the day. Armed with maps and books, we traced the route to the final object of our trip: an obelisk set up to mark the place where the Scottish explorer, Mungo Park, started his first journey in 1795, and then in 1805, his second and fatal journey to trace the course and exit of the Niger.

It was from the account of his travels I had been intrigued to learn the origin of the word *bintang (bentang)*. Mungo Park explains that each African settlement had a large stage called a *bentang* which answered the purpose of a public hall or townhouse. It was here that all public affairs were transacted and trials conducted, and as Park tells us, 'the lazy and indolent met to smoke their pipes and hear the news of the day'.[13]

An honest and lovely description, making sense of the origin of a platform on the edge of the bolon, such as the very one we were sitting on.

Further downstream, the ruins of a Portuguese trading post confirmed the bolon's long-term use for river traffic. It was as far back as 1455 that the explorer Alvise Cadamosto, tempted by alleged gold findings, arrived in Senegambia. Geographically well suited, on the trading route to India, riverside trading posts were soon established. In fact, Gambia owes its name to the Portuguese word *cambio,* meaning exchange.

Just then, the only traffic were local fishermen passing silently and swiftly in dug-out canoes, and the fading outline of the *Safari Queen* bobbing on darkening waves. Torchlight guided us over the loose struts of the walkways to find a bat circling our rustic room. Once Richard had granted our visitor his freedom and we had settled for the night, we were serenaded by the whining shrill of mosquitoes. Applying liberal amounts of Deet, heads propped on cushions, we closed our eyes and hoped for the best.

Sunrise was swift. A huge red disk mirrored in the still waters of the bolon. As it rose, it dragged its reflection into an elongated pose then exploded, filling both water and sky with brilliant light. Over breakfast on the bintang, we learned of a

---

[13] Mungo Park, *Travels into the Interior of Africa*

year long expedition undertaken by the adventurous Dutch couple. They had explored nine African countries from Algeria to Kenya by 4x4, making our month long journey through Namibia and Botswana look pretty tame. We were particularly interested to hear of their response to a visit to the Mursi in Ethiopia. The scene of demanding commercialism so appalled them that they got straight back into their vehicle and left. Their current plan was to cycle south into Senegal, then in a circular route, taking them back to Banjul. I was impressed, but we were more than happy to be setting off with Mark and the birdman in the *Safari Queen*. Complete with a canopy, she offered shade and comfort for the next stage of our travels.

Before our upriver journey to Mark's far-flung camp on MacCarthy Island, our plan was to make a downriver detour. The diversion, at our request, was to see and photograph James Island, a small mid-stream rocky outcrop that, to this day, holds the ruins of a British fort among a group of baobab trees. Ideally placed to provide strategic defence for English interests along the river, James Island was originally used as a staging post for the shipment of slaves.

The island was originally named 'St Andrew Island' after a Portuguese sailor who was buried there in 1456. Then in 1651 the first fort was built by servants of the Duke of Courland; this was seized ten years later by a group of 'Royal Adventurers of England', who renamed it James Island, after James, Duke of York. A hectic period of attack and capture by the French and counter attacks by the English followed. Finally, in the hands of the British, after the British abolition of slavery, it was ideally placed and used to intercept French and Portuguese slave ships.

Captured slave traders were hanged and the slaves freed. A number of them are said to have settled on MacCarthy Island. Just opposite James Island on the north bank of the river is the former French trading post of Albreda and the nearby Juffureh village with its 'Roots' connections. Abandoned by traders, the buildings fell into disuse, leaving stories to be kept alive and handed down by local *griots* (storytellers), making Albreda a popular venue for group tours.

Not long after reaching the main river, we realised that the downstream struggle against strong tidal currents, to reach James Island – now a faint silhouette on bruised sky – was going to take too much of the day. After conferring with Mark, we agreed to abandon the plan. Heading back upstream, Mark pointed to Kerewan on the map, our next staging post. Kerewan, Kinteh Kunda, Salikene, Tendaba, Baro Kunda, Kau-ur – evocative names recalling an intriguing past. Temperatures were high and the river was growing increasingly wide. Chugging mid-stream between distant forested banks reminded me of the story told that the borders of the Gambia – following the twists and curves of the river – were demarcated by a British gunboat that sailed upstream firing its guns both north and south. The border was set where the shells landed.

We were now moving freely with the tide. The birdman shared his binoculars: osprey, heron, kingfishers, egret and an Abyssinian Roller obliged. Two river dolphins made a cursory appearance and were gone. Then once again, we were alone on this great river, with its clothed mangrove sides stretching to distant horizons; a sense of the immense size of Africa unfurled; a sense of watching unseen eyes, a sense of contentment.

Finally, chugging up a bolon to Kerewan, we abandoned the *Safari Queen* and the river for a 4WD and a new tar road. Just one month since the rains, but already the Panchang Wetlands were drying out and Sudan savannah, decorated by huge baobab trees, dominated the landscape. Under a billowing cloud of dust, a local family was separating peanuts from their husks: a reminder of the trade in peanuts set up by the British to boost the flagging post slave-trade economy. As distances between traditional mud and thatch villages increased, the deserted road crossed low-lying wetlands, diminishing bolons twisted towards the river and wading birds drew binoculars.

We passed a man on a bicycle and a small boy driving cattle, and then the world was ours once more until we arrived at Farafenni. This sizeable settlement at a meeting place with the road to Senegal was thronging with people, busy at a colourful roadside market. Parked at the roadside while Mark disappeared on an errand, we quickly became the centre of attraction. Curious onlookers crowded the vehicle, and long limbs reached through open windows:

'What's your name? Water?'

'What's your name? Water?' we were asked again and again, as we passed plastic bottles and wilted in humid heat.

Kuntaur, looking like a splendid replica of the African Queen, the *Lady Hippo* and crew were waiting our arrival. Puttering along the creek towards the river, past the roofless but stately remains of a former European residence-cum-trading station, was a reminder that it was in this region that Mungo Park spent five months learning the language and customs of local tribes before setting off on his first journey to explore the Niger.

Spread before us, the silver sheen of the river loops and divides – Pasari Island, Deer Islands, Bird Island. Then Mark was pointing to further forested outlines.

'Baboon Islands, home to rehabilitated chimps,' he explained.

A boat was out, with two men hurling fruit into trees. Suddenly the forested islands were alive with excited cries. An adult male chimpanzee had taken up residence on a branch over the water; barking and calling and shaking the tree, he was making sure we knew who was boss. Chimps of every size appeared, catching and eating the spoils. A visit to Badi Mayo, the headquarters of this remarkable reserve, was planned for our return journey. Lordly hippos, guarding the islands, viewed our passing with twitching ears and unblinking, steadfast eyes.

The air cooled and the falling sun coloured ruffled cloud and water salmon pink. On the upper deck of the *Lady Hippo*, we open a bottle of red wine, fill teacups, and toast the near end of our journey. As darkness swallows the river, we chug to a standstill alongside the mooring at Bird Safari Camp. Lamplight beckons from the open-sided reception-cum-dining area where we join a fellow visitor for the dish of the day: spiced chicken followed by banana flambé.

Our dining companion, a lone birder, confessed to reaching the 200 mark, the birdwatcher's danger zone in the Gambia. He welcomed the arrival of the accompanying Mandinka birdman with open arms. It was the time of year when male birds lose their colourful mating plumage for duller tones of brown and grey, making identification without expert eyes, all but impossible. The birder still had three hundred and sixty varieties to go. The strain was showing in his gaunt expression and the far away look in his eyes.

With an oil lamp in hand, we bade him a restful night and made for the comfort of our people friendly and recently sprayed – mosquito unfriendly – thatched rondavel lodge. The wistful haunting cry of an owl – there are seven varieties at large – drifted over us as we drifted towards sleep.

Janjangbureh, once notorious as the former assembly point for the sale of slaves, was just a short trip by 4WD from the camp. With Mark as our expedition leader, and birder and birdman in tow, we explored the main street of the settlement where the ruins of once stately buildings, said to have been used by former slave traders, overlook the river. While the remains of a deserted riverside building looked authentic, the underground floor of a new warehouse, feted as a place where slaves were once imprisoned, did not. Out of curiosity, I allowed myself to be taken on a brief tour. An old man showed me glinting chains, attached to newly plastered patches on the walls, and pointed to small openings.

'Here slaves get food,' he said.

I gave him the expected donation but, doubting the authenticity, refrained from adding my name to the wealth of signatures in his well-thumbed book.

It is to Janjangbureh that visitors, seeking to find the place where their antecedents were once held and sold, make pilgrimages. By doing so, they endeavour to live with, if not bury the past. Information on two boards at the side of the street helps to dispel misinformation, if not prevent malpractice – primarily that the warehouse was built in 1904 and slavery was abolished by the British in 1807. Oral tradition from the sixteenth and seventeenth centuries maintains that the island was an ideal resting place for ships and boats and that, prior to the abolition movement, Europeans and Luso-African traders used the site as a camping and assembly point for slaves waiting for shipment.

Mungo Park, who travelled with a slave caravan on his return to the Gambia in 1797, after his first expedition, confirms this. He tells us that if no ship was available, the slaves were distributed among local villages until a ship arrived or until sold to black traders. Fettered in pairs, they worked on the land of local people until a buyer was found. News and views apart, it is an historic site that must continue to create mixed feelings in those who visit, in an attempt to come to terms with the past.

With some exciting sightings under their belts, birder and birdman joined us and a handful of locals, with bikes and goats and chickens, just as JANJANBURAY, the local ferry, prepared to leave for the mainland. A driver and his 4WD were ready and waiting to take us from the landing stage to a Mandinka village, where Mark hoped we could find a local person willing to guide us to the deserted memorial. The unmade potholed road was testing for the joints and not conducive to the use of binoculars for the birdmen. Suffice to say, it was a rough two hour ride in climbing temperatures, with virtually no other traffic and diminishing sightings of rustic settlements.

Finally we stopped at the village of Karantaba Tabokoto. Now George, the Mandinka birdman, came unto his own. Within minutes he hired the owner of a motorbike to ride ahead and guide us a further 2km to the neighbouring village of Karantaba Tenda. There, from among a straggle of villagers, he found an elder who knew the whereabouts of the memorial.

Wearing an Omani-style crocheted skullcap and white *dishdasha,* the Mandingo elder was eager to be our guide. Climbing niftily into the front of the vehicle, he directed the driver towards an overgrown track. As we bounced and jolted through shoulder high blond grass, between thorny shrubs and umbrella acacia, it became increasingly clear that visitors to the site were rare. To indicate a change of direction, the ancient lifted his hand in the air. At one point, we waved to a group of smiling Mandingo women resting in the shade of an acacia tree alongside the river.

Then in the distance, the outline of an obelisk melted into a haze of blue. As we approached, a concrete plinth, reaching to some 30 metres, surrounded by thorny shrubs and encroaching vegetation, rose before us. Standing before the memorial it was saddening to find that letters, once riveted to a bronze plaque on the front, had been removed. From the remaining indentations it was possible to make out the original dedication:

> MUNGO PARK
> SET OUT
> ON THE 2nd DECEMBER 1795
> AND ON 4th MAY 1805
> ON HIS TRAVELS
> TO EXPLORE THE COURSE OF THE NIGER

Meanwhile, our grave faced guide was in full flow in his native tongue, while George, fulfilling the same role as his ancestors had done, obliged by translating. While the story of the explorer was not forthcoming, the ancient was claiming that British versions of his travels were untrue. Local people, he insisted, know the truth from their storytelling. The occasion reminded me of Park's own sceptical response to the oral histories of various tribes he had intercourse with, especially the *slatees* (native slave traders). Park discovered that very little dependence could be placed on the accounts they gave, 'for they contradicted each other in the most important particulars'[14] – and that was over two hundred years ago!

As the old man pocketed the reward for his services and disappeared, some villagers who spoke English had arrived on the scene. They appeared genuinely surprised when we explained that Park, who had spoken their language, kept a detailed diary of his travels, and that a book had been published from his account of his trip. It occurred to us that an information board, bearing some historical facts – such as those erected at Janjangbureh – would be helpful to locals and future visitors alike.

---

[14] Mungo Park, *Travels into the Interior of Africa*

We decided to have our picnic lunch in the shade of trees on the nearby bank of the river. Heat from the midday sun had silenced the birds, creating a sombre torpor for birders and travellers alike. It was strangely moving to be close to the spot where the explorer, with his companions and guides, had assembled in readiness for the second and fatal expedition. The thought of this lone white man travelling from such a remote place into the heart of Africa, through hostile tribal villages to reach and chart the course and exit of the Niger River, seemed both incredibly heroic and sheer madness.

On his first expedition, Park set off from this very spot, on a small but sprightly horse. For company he had a Mandingo interpreter and a local guide, each with an ass to carry the baggage and provisions, plus two local slave merchants and a native returning to his village. Some two years later, after many alarming adventures, he was to return on foot and in rags, but with his life intact. Tragically, he did not survive the second trip. While mid-stream on a boat, attempting to escape attack from a tribe, he died in the waters of the Niger. Miraculously in 1858, a British Officer recovered his journal from local people in exchange for a pocketknife.

Back at Bird Safari Camp, Mark and Richard set off in a small motorboat to deliver staff members employed at the camp to the mainland, and then, with a promise of fresh fish for the evening meal, to a good fishing spot on the river. Exhausted from the expedition, the birder collapsed in his tented camp. His bird count had peaked at two hundred and ten. Meanwhile, Mark had arranged for me to meet a direct descendant of Musa Molloh, a former king of the Empire of Fulada. Such was the importance of this powerful king that a commemorative tomb has been erected to his memory just south of the river.

The descendant, a fresh faced young man with shoulder length Rastafarian-styled hair, was proud to tell me of his nineteenth century ancestor king's reputation as a great warrior, as well as his clever dealings with both British and French colonial powers. He looked at me with wide-eyed incredulity when I intimated that the king's former wealth was built not only on gold, but on the proceeds from trading in slaves. His family's oral history, which he proudly assured me was correct, as it had been passed down from person to person, failed to include the king's slave trading activities, which records show were ongoing into the twentieth century.

Previous research into the king's life revealed that, along with the Islamist rulers Foday Sillah and Foday Kaba, the warrior king ruled over a powerful army in mid-nineteenth century Gambia. In 1850, intent on extending the Islamic faith to displace traditional faiths practiced by the Soninke-Mandinka people, the Islamic rulers led their armies in a *jihad* or holy war. Known as the Soninke-Marabout Wars, the fighting continued until 1901, when the Marabouts were finally overthrown by colonial powers.

While Foday Sillah and Foday Kaba met their deaths, Musa Molloh signed a treaty of non-aggression with the British and French and survived. His flouting of this agreement led to his exile to Sierra Leone. Finally, stripped of political powers, he was allowed to return to his village, Kesser Kunda, where the royal tomb built in his memory was declared a national monument in 1974.

The visit to Janjangbureh and my conversation with the young descendant of Musa Molloh reminded me of a passage in Ryszard Kapuscinski's *The Shadow of the Sun* – a passage which explores the difference in thinking between European and African minds. The author, Sadig Rasheed, the Sudanese director of the Economic Commission for Africa, expresses a concern as to whether African societies will be able to assume a self-critical stance enabling them to move on. He believes that, unlike the European mind with its bent for self criticism, analysis and enquiry and endless seeking to move forward, the African mind has a tendency to consider criticism to be a malevolent attack, a sign of discrimination, even racism, a tendency to lay the blame for evil on others, on other forces. 'Africa must wake up,' Sadig Rasheed concluded.

Collecting my books and maps, I made my way through growing darkness to the lamplit dining area, to find the barman on duty and a bottle of wine in place on our table.

I poured a glass and, unfolding a map, traced my finger downriver from our base on MacCarthy Island to our next riverside staging post, *Badi Mayo* (River Monkeys), the celebrated chimpanzee nature reserve. Looking up, I saw the welcome silhouettes of Mark and Richard. They were empty handed, but they were here. Freshly caught fish were not on the menu after all.

Badi Mayo, Chimpanzee Reserve

A small baboon with a melancholic expression was watching us expectantly and gripping the side of a boat with long human-like fingers. We had drawn alongside to allow a local man, who worked at the reserve, to join us. As he clambered into the stern of our vessel and the neighbouring boat drew away, the baboon started screaming pathetically.

'What on earth's wrong?' I asked.

'It's Sarjo. He's been looked after by a white woman and wants to come to you.'

It was a flattering introduction to an impressive set up. Not for baboons, but chimpanzees. Three of a cluster of five forested river islands in the heart of the River Gambia are home to rehabilitated chimps. At the last count, there were eighty five – three generations – who, thanks to the dedicated lifetime of the pioneer Stella Brewer, are living and protected on their island reserves.

It was from her book *The Forest Dwellers* that I learnt about the years of her life that Stella spent looking after rescued chimpanzees. After teaching them to fend for themselves in Abuko Nature Reserve, she attempted to reintroduce them to life in the wild at Mount Assirik, in Niokolo Koba National Park, Senegal. The rescued chimpanzees had to undergo a complete retraining course in foraging for wild food, building nests and responding to predators.

From Stella's writing, it is clear that the time she spent at Mount Assirik was so much more than a project. Her prose is charged with the emotion of someone living and breathing every action, every achievement and every failure of her charges. In the end, the biggest problem her chimps faced was violent aggression from resident troops of wild chimpanzees in the park. This came to a head after a severe drought in 1977-78, when the wild chimps began to terrorise the Abuko group. In 1979, fearing her chimps would be killed if they stayed, they were collected together and taken to begin a new life in the recently gazetted River Gambia National Park.

A stilted waterhouse reception surrounded by a verandah and screened against mosquitoes as well as the sun, marked the entrance to the Visitors' Centre at Badi Mayo. We were greeted by Michelle, who was currently acting as hostess and running the centre. Iced drinks prepared us for the climb to an isolated tented safari camp; set under a river cliff way up the forested hillside, it was our lodging for the night. Suffice to say that the winding stairway was steep and temperatures high. The recompense: like eagles in an eyrie, we had magnificent views over the treetops, down to the river and across the sky-held water to forested islands. A further reward was the shower. In true African safari style, it was open to the sky and, at the time of my ablutions, allowed uninterrupted viewing to a passing troop of baboons. Whether their barks were of approval or disapproval it was impossible to tell.

A late afternoon boat trip is the highlight of every visitor's stay at Badi Mayo. Although the forested islands provide a safe retreat for the chimps, it transpired that there are not enough fruit trees to satisfy their dietary requirements. To accommodate this, regular supplies of maize cobs, slices of pumpkin and watermelon are distributed. Just as we were preparing to set off, Michelle arrived with another guest in tow. We had been joined by Lyn Hughes, the wanderlusting editor of *Wanderlust* magazine. Lyn had been recovering in her cliff-side chalet from countless hours off-roading through heat and dust to reach the reserve. After a champagne reception at a five star hotel in Banjul, the bone shaking road journey to Badi Mayo, which included being stopped and interrogated by police, had been a potent reminder of Africa in the raw.

Once the supply boat had been laden with food for the chimps, plus cameras and recording equipment for Lyn, we joined Michelle and Bubacar – Stella's chief local guide for some ten years – in an accompanying boat, and prepared to follow in its wake.

By chance, Richard and I had witnessed the camp's evening ritual of fruit being hurled from a boat onto the islands on our way upstream to Bird Safari Camp. Then, as on this occasion, it was the noise of the engine that alerted the chimps. Within minutes a huge alpha male, balanced over the water's edge, was barking and hooting ferociously and shaking the life out of a tree. His display of dominance was not without the threat of fearsome aggression. Ironically, it also prevented him from getting to the front of the food queue. Within seconds, a succession of benign chimp faces appeared from the forested curtain of leaves. Meanwhile, struggling to maintain my balance in the wallowing boat, I was attempting to get some chimp shots while half-listening as names and histories rolled off Bubacar's tongue.

'Frankie's mother was shot leaving her terrified of cameras – she thought they were guns. Jumbo,' he continued, 'he's from Spain – he smoked cigarettes and wore trousers to amuse tourists. Those chimps born on the islands, they have no fear of humans.'

I recalled more familiar names from my reading of Stella's book – William and Cheetah, Ann and Pooh, Albert and Tina – the founding members and ultimate survivors of the horrors of illegal trafficking. Of these, only Pooh remained alive. He, along with sixteen other original inhabitants, represents the oldies among three generations of chimps.

More chimps were emerging to retrieve generous slices of watermelon from the water's edge. One youngster, hanging nonchalantly from a branch while enjoying his spoil, was watching us watching him. Frankie and her son Felix sat quietly munching amongst clusters of leaves. The most memorable moment was when a young chimp, just a few metres from me, held my gaze before loping towards a leafy screen, giving me curious sideways glances as he went. An extraordinary silent yet intimate exchange.

I was disappointed to learn that the planned screened and stilted viewing hides on the islands had not yet materialised. I had imagined a stealthy approach, slicing through the water in a dugout canoe, stealing onto the island and watching intimate family moments of grooming and play unseen – a privilege to be enjoyed by future visitors.

'That's Hexus.' Bubacar was pointing to a male sitting contemplatively to one side.

'And Pooh?' I asked, interested to hear news of the favourite from my reading.

'Pooh,' he replied, smiling. 'He's a survivor. He knew his time as an alpha male had passed and let his son Gorko take control. Gorko wasn't so clever. He was violently deposed.'

It was the propensity for violence in chimp lives that I found so disturbing; that it reflected a similar trait in humankind, their nearest relative, was truly sobering.

With food supplies gone, the last of the chimps disappeared into their forested stronghold. As the boat chugged downstream, we passed a great cloud of butterflies clothing the foliage of a tree in a glistening canopy of delicately fluttering wings. We were heading towards a small satellite island, the nesting site of thousands of birds – darters, heron, egret, cormorant, sacred ibis – like a competition for the longest and most elegant neck, they perched and preened against deepening sky.

In addition to a healthy share of the Gambia's huge variety of birds, the vicinity of the park is also home to some interesting mammals. Those most frequently spotted include baboons, callithrix and red colobus monkeys, snakes, lizards, crocodiles and hippos. Those most sought after and less frequently seen, include clawless otters and manatees. At that very moment, we rounded a sweeping bend of the river, skirting a row of watching eyes and twitching ears: a deceptively comic display belying the hidden power of the submerged tank-like forms and massive jaws of a bevy of hippos.

'Farmers frighten hippos from rice fields by banging empty bottles together,' Bubacar explained.

Michelle added that there were between forty to fifty hippos in the park, the largest population in the Gambia. Emerging at night, they wreak havoc on local farmers' crops, so much so that two hippo watchtowers have been built. Each has a watchman who has a large metal drum to bang at frequent intervals during the night to keep the hippos away from fields of rice. Rumour has it that the watchmen are more alert towards the end of the month, as pay day approaches.

Someone was passing chilled cans of beer: perfect timing to ward off increasing humidity and thirst. I focused on reed fringed shallows, hoping for a glimpse of the inquisitive, eager faces and streamlined forms of a family of otters. This evening it was not to be. As we approached the waterhouse, the descending sun melted into the fiery sky.

That night, once the solar lamp was switched off, we settled under mosquito netting, draping the bed in our isolated safari tent. I remained wakeful, listening to night cries, hoping to hear the plaintive calls and responses of manatees. Instead, the high pitched whining of a mosquito filled my head, so loud and so close I was convinced it was trapped inside the netting. Armed with my pencil torch and diminishing supplies of Deet, I searched the darkness. Each time I gave up and settled down the whining started again. Finally, tiredness took over and I succumbed to uneasy sleep.

At first light, I retreated to the verandah to examine my wounds. When Richard surfaced, he confessed to a restless but not sleepless night.

'It must be your blue blood,' he concluded, inspecting his apparently bite-free limbs.

Blue blood or not, given the choice, predatory insects definitely have a history of preferring the taste of my blood to Richard's. Distracted by loud hoots and crashing branches, binoculars and camera were focused on a troop of red colobus monkeys, leaping from tree to tree. Then, my mind focused on an outsize mug of tea, I prepared myself for the downhill trek. Recovery was aided by a breakfast of scrambled guinea fowl eggs – delicious – toast and coffee.

Legs dangling over a horse-pulled cart, Lyn was leaving in style to visit The Gambia Horse and Donkey Trust: another of Stella's successful projects. Michelle explained that eight villages around the boundary of the park all benefit from the Trust, which includes a school and a clinic as well as facilities for increasing productivity of horses and donkeys through welfare and management education. Stella's holistic approach to conservation means that local people are involved and receive tangible benefits.

For Richard and for me it was time to bid farewell to Badi Mayo and board a boat that would take us further down stream. As we passed the mysteriously silent islands, I imagined sleepy-eyed chimps, spreadeagled in self-made nests of leaves, cradled in the forested tops of trees. As the islands receded, we chugged towards Kuntaur to rejoin Mark Thompson on the *Safari Queen*, for the next stage of our expedition – exploring the reaches of the mighty Gambia River.

The Wassu Stone Circles

The stones were made at the beginning of the world by giants.
The stone circles at Wassu are the burial ground of the royal family.
The highest stone marks the burial place of the king.

Oral Traditions associated with the stone circles

Whether, or not the Wassu stone circles were built by giants or, as oral tradition suggests, they mark the burial place of royalty and kings, there is no doubt that they are related to mysticism, magic and ancient times. The largest of a complex of Senegambian standing stones, they are located on the north bank of the Gambia River and have been set into pre-dug pits arranged in circles or concentric rings. In common with stone circles in other parts of Africa and Europe, the Senegambian circles of stones, of which Wassu is a prime site, continue to intrigue and haunt modern man.

Before us stretched a relatively flat area of savannah grassland, dotted with occasional thorny trees. Scattered throughout were circles of standing laterite stones. Much of the area was overgrown with long grass. Shrubs and trees growing alongside and between some of the stones made it difficult to form an overall picture of the alignment of the circles. Wandering between this complex arrangement under a peerless blue sky, a sense of the past and of past lives throbbed in growing temperatures.

This region of the Gambia, north of the river, is reputed to have been the Wolof Kingdom of Jolof around AD 300. One theory has it that at a time when the Sahara was green, the Wolof, an agrarian tribe, migrated from the banks of the Nile and settled on the fertile northern banks of the Gambia River. It was their reputation of having a strong hierarchical caste system thought to have been necessary to facilitate the work of major construction, that gave rise to the belief that it is within the early history of the Wolof that the explanation for the origin of the Gambia's stone circles lie.

However, another fascinating theory, accounting for the difference in height of each set of stones, is connected with the animist Jola people from President Jammeh's tribe: a people known for holding onto traditional African beliefs in the sanctity of the earth and the divine energy found in certain stones and groves. A European traveller recorded watching a Jola ritual that involved group members standing in concentric circles, ranging in height from elders in the innermost circles, to children on the outermost. The analogy of sanctity or magic invoked by the circles, arranged according to height, is another explanation given for the concentric arrangements on this site.

Heat radiating from the sky and from the sandbaked earth beneath our feet, we toured the site, attempting to photograph the most complete circles. These varied both in diameter, from approximately four to seven metres, and in the number of stones forming each enclosure, ranging from between ten to twenty four. While some stones have fallen and remain where they fell, those that are standing have been topped by small stones, placed by visitors who believe it connects them with the past and brings them luck. One notable difference was between those circles, enclosing a mound, defining a communal burial chamber, and those holding individual graves, which are marked by cut laterite pillars lying on their sides.

Richard was beckoning me to join him in the welcome shade of a tree. From this spot we had an overall view of a large section of the site. He was pointing out a pattern or design. Not only did the circles appear to form a line from north to south, a common feature of each was a line of Megalith Pillars on the eastern side, suggesting a solar or lunar alignment. Whatever the intention the stones, like those at Stonehenge in England or Carnac in France, mark the landscape like huge question marks. They remain as testimony to man's fascination and belief in the transience of this life and of a life after death.

Question marks followed us as we left the site and continued the downriver stages of our journey by water and land: 4x4 from Wassu to Kerewan – boat to Bintang Bolon and then the last leg, by 4x4 across gravel plains to Footsteps Eco-Lodge. Owned and run by a British resident, the lodge was located well away from package tour hotels. With its wilderness bush surroundings and nearby unspoilt Atlantic beach location, it was a cool retreat for weary travellers. In addition to pink domed rondavel huts set around a shaded pool and bar, it boasted some impressive eco-features including solar and wind-energy, as well as composting toilets. I was surprised and impressed by the absence of unpleasant odours.

There was a family feel to the hotel with a distinctive northern England flavour among the staff, visitors and near neighbours, who had upped sticks from the UK to settle in the Gambia. It is as well to be dog lover: a variety of four-legged friends appeared to idle the hours on sun loungers and dining furniture alike. Dinner on an upstairs balcony, under a star dusted sky, was a fitting end to our river trip. An early night and a late start was our plan before a leisurely visit to one of a number of forest reserves on the following day.

Abuko Forest Reserve

Eddie Brewer (OBE), a legendary figure, whose drive and energy brought nature conservation to the fore in the Gambia, set up and established Abuko Forest Reserve in 1968: a place to safeguard both the habitat and rescued animals, including the Gambia's first rescued chimpanzee. Originally protected as a water catchment area, the enclosed land contains a pristine remnant of gallery forest along the sides of the Lamin stream.

Gallery forest, fed from groundwater as opposed to rainforest which is fed from rain, once natural throughout the River Gambia region, is now a very rare habitat and found only in a handful of forest reserves. It was to Abuko that Eddie Brewer and his daughter Stella brought and cared for varieties of wild life including William and Tina, among the first of a number of rescued chimpanzee, a scheme that was to develop into Stella's remarkable Badi Mayo project.

The planned trip to Abuko took me back to Stella Brewer's account of her first visit to the site with her father. Stella's love of the place, the fauna and wildlife so evident from her writing, began while tracing the movements of a leopard that had been killing a local farmer's pigs. Following the leopard's trail, Eddie and Stella squeezed through a hole in a fence, close to the Lamin Stream:

I compare that hole in many ways, with *Alice's Looking-Glass*, for beyond we discovered an incredible world we had not known existed. With each step, we became more enchanted by what we saw. We were walking from the familiar savannah into the cool, damp atmosphere of a tropical rain forest. The further in we went, the more mysterious everything became.

– The Forest Dwellers

Such was the discovery and beginning of the reserve we were about to explore. A footpath snaking through a canopy of trees led to just one of a number of crocodile pools. Unlike the Nile crocodiles in the President's safari park that are fed daily supplies of slaughtered domestic stock by park attendants, these crocs survive on a natural diet of fish, frogs and turtles, among other wildlife living in the reserve. At the site's impressive Darwin Centre, a field station for research and the training of local people in all aspects of biodiversity and conservation, we joined other visitors on the balcony-cum-viewing platform. Armed with awesome looking binoculars, cameras and an equally impressive array of supportive stands, they were seeking to spot some of the incredible diversity of birds native to the Gallery Forest, or searching the Lamin stream for monitor lizards, clawless otters, crocodiles and more.

Dodging further congregations of birdwatchers and their equipment, we made our way beneath the light excluding canopy. Here, many thousands of species of fungi and plants are visited by damselflies, dragonflies and butterflies, as well as being home to amphibians, reptiles and at least two hundred and fifty varieties of birds. As the forest thinned and became Guinea Savannah and the sky was visible once more, the pathway led to an animal orphanage at the near end. Apart from some spotted hyenas who have spent their entire lives in captivity, the orphanage caters for injured animals and those rescued from ill-treatment or being kept illegally as pets. Baboons, antelopes and parrots were visible in the large caged pens.

Temperatures were high and there were no facilities for visitors at this far end of the reserve, the place we had arranged for our driver to meet us. Delayed by a puncture, he then made full recompense by taking us for lunch to one of the most characterful places in the Gambia. Built on the banks of Lamin Bolon, Lamin Lodge is a favoured refreshment stop for visitors returning from a variety of river cruises ranging from: 'Birds and Breakfast' and 'Champagne and Caviar' to a 'Sunset River Cruise'.

Reminiscent of the crooked house lived in by the crooked man but on a far grander scale, the lodge has been constructed from the split trunks of trees, with the main building rising to three storeys and with each storey growing from the thatched roofing of the previous section. The first sighting of the lopsided building rising haphazardly from surrounding mangrove swamp suggested that the entire place was about to collapse like a pack of cards. A similarly constructed rickety walkway took us to the cool interior. Here the combination of comfortable seating and gourmet food provided a welcome and memorable pause in our sightseeing travels.

Makasutu Forest Reserve

'Where is your group?' we were repeatedly asked when we arrived at Makasutu Cultural Forest. Contrary to our expectations, it seemed that visits to the reserve are organised in strictly regimented groups, accompanied by a guide for a half or a full day, including talks, walks and boat trips along the bolon. As independent travellers, we had clearly upset the organised scheme of things. Finally, when it was understood that we had flouted all the rules and our visit didn't fit into the carefully timetabled routine, a guide was assigned to escort us on a walkabout rather than a tour.

Set alongside a bolon from the River Gambia, this area of forested bush swamp was rescued from complete destruction, just in time, by two Englishmen, James English and Lawrence Williams. How the project came into being makes fascinating reading. After three years of searching the Gambia, and many more searching the world, for a suitable piece of land to create a tourism project, James English discovered Makasutu on Christmas Eve 1992. Then, after a three month trip to England, he returned to find two hundred palm trees from the surrounding area had been cut down. The owners and the forestry department were contacted. On the discovery that tree felling and overgrazing were becoming prevalent throughout the forested regions of the Gambia, it was decided that the only way to protect the area was to buy an area of land and fence it. In the not so distant past, elephants and other wildlife roamed in these forests before finally meeting their demise as a result of the trade in ivory.

On his travels in the Gambia in 1795, Mungo Park asked the local people why, instead of killing the elephants, they didn't train them to work for them as the people in Asia did. They laughed and accused him of telling white man's lies. Then we learn from Stella Brewer's writings that some of the first tourists to visit Gambia came on the promise of Hemingway-style hunting trips. However, by that time, most of the big game had already been shot for ivory, skins or to satisfy the whim for wildlife pets, and so it was that sun-seeking tourism in the Gambia evolved.

There was a pleasant feel to *Makasutu* (Holy Forest). A haven for birds and visitors alike, it is blessed with a variety of open but shaded places set about with locally made bamboo furniture, places to watch and listen or simply to sit and cogitate. Such is the global reputation of the reserve that a team from Cornwall's Eden Project was filmed on a visit earlier in the year. Makasutu also boasts some upmarket 'floating' accommodation; a houseboat or a lodge on stilts, overlooking the bolon was voted best eco-hotel in the world by *The Sunday Times* (UK). We added Makasutu's Madina Lodge to our list of places to stay on a future visit to the Gambia.

Sandele Eco Retreat

A Roman-styled villa, complete with a high domed roof and through the open doorway the vision of a luxurious king-size bed, elegantly draped with swathes of net curtains. This was the scene before us when we arrived at Sandele Eco Retreat. Catering for discerning, independent travellers, Sandele was a rare find, especially in this region of West Africa. It was more dream than reality.

Not only was it real, but we had the honour of being the first visitors to spend the night in one of four recently completed Roman lodges. Cool and spacious, our lodge had the feel of what it must have been like for a wealthy Roman escaping from the heat to enjoy the cool elegance of his villa. Only the frescoes were missing. Apart from the cathedral-like space under the dome, the ultimate luxury was the surrounding quiet; nothing except bird song and the rush and shushing of waves on the great crescent beach, fringing the Atlantic Ocean. We had enjoyed waterside settings at a number of locations in the Gambia, but not this sheer indulgence to go with it.

Sandele Eco Retreat, the master plan and beachside project of an English man, Maurice Philip and his partner Geri, was still in the early stages of development. In spite of the sheer scale of the plan, Maurice looked as at ease in this other worldly setting, as if he were supervising afternoon tea in an English country garden. Teacup in hand, he explained that he had leased the land from neighbouring Kartong, and offered people from the region employment and training in both building and running the resort. However, this was no modern day building project. In order for his employees to receive the training required for building Roman-style domes, Maurice funded and sent them to learn the necessary skills at Auroville Earth Institute in India.

Founded in 1989, the institute researches, develops, promotes and transfers earth-based technologies through training courses, seminars, workshops, manuals and documents providing consultancy within and outside India. It was during the time Maurice's recruits spent at Auroville they learnt the techniques of building arches, vaults and domes for the project. These techniques have been successfully put to the test in the recently completed lodges, including the one in which we were to spend the night.

While on a tour of the site, George, our guide, explained the plan for a further six, five star domed guest lodges to be set along the ridge overlooking the bay, while a further stylish block of twenty rooms for guests attending conferences is also under construction. George had long, loose limbs and a loping stride that Richard could match, but which left me tagging along behind them like an out of breath dog. Finally, there was a pause. Before us stood the triple chamber of an environmentally friendly sewage system: standing shoulder to shoulder – to one side of the row of domed villas – like mini-pyramids, they outshone their status.

Next on the agenda was a stop to examine a machine where bricks, made from local earth, are impacted to the right size. 74, 35, 42: figures chalked on an ancient school blackboard recorded the number of bricks turned out that day, enabling the men to keep track as well as encouraging friendly competition.

Finally, we headed inland to a place currently used as a quarry. George explained that this was to be the spot for a full Roman-styled auditorium.

'For meetings,' he added. 'Responsible tourism, architecture, creative writing, hotel catering and wave-energy to fuel a generator.'

We were impressed. It was a remarkable setting within sound, if not sight, of the ocean and shaded by a forest of trees.

'Already students from some UK universities come on visits,' he explained. 'They learn from watching and from the work we are doing.'

Minutes later, we were strolling through dunes of sand that fringe the great crescent bay of Sandele, from which the centre takes its name. Held in the embrace of a perfectly sculpted semi-circle of dunes, shallow waves crept over warm sand, sinking without trace. George pointed in the direction of a hollow among the dunes where several people stood, arms stretched towards the sky – a yoga session, conducted by Geri, was in full swing.

Appetites sharpened by the tour we were more than ready for the wine list and dinner by candlelight, under a star-flecked sky. Fellow guests included two literary agents from London and a couple who, like us, had been on an up-river trip to the former slave trading port of Janjangbureh. For one person it had been a journey into the past, a journey to the place where his ancestors were sold into slavery before being transported to Jamaica where he was born and grew up. He admitted that the experience had been moving and thought provoking, something he needed to do to allow him to move on with his life.

As wine glasses were filled and the first in a series of delicacies served, I asked Maurice what had inspired him to undertake such an imaginative and demanding project.

'It started as a dream or vision. I wanted to create a centre of excellence; something different that included responsible tourism, luxury and peace – offered in a way that maximised benefit to the local community.' He paused and smiled wryly. 'In twenty five years, all of this will belong to the local people.'

Replete and drowsy, we headed for our domed lodge. At first, the sensation was one of huge space and emptiness rather than comfort, but the true nature of the place was yet to be revealed. Not only were we asleep within seconds of sliding between the sheets of the luxuriously draped bed, but neither of us stirred until past nine o'clock the following morning. The magical aura created by the womb-like domed space, coupled with the hypnotic distant shushing of waves had combined to create the most perfect night's sleep in living memory.

Bathed in the luxury and peace that Maurice desired, the 'Wow' factor of his achievement is huge. Along with the impressive number of projects we had encountered, set up by English people who have devoted their lives to preserving and promoting aspects of the Gambia's unique natural environment, Maurice Philip's wonderful legacy is there for the benefit and enjoyment of local people and future visitors alike.

Afterword

Stella Brewer Marsden, the pioneer of chimpanzee rehabilitation, and the founder of the Chimpanzee Rehabilitation Trust (CRT) was suffering from cancer at the time of our visit. Stella died, aged 56, on January the 24th 2008. Appointed OBE in the 2006 New Year's Honours List for services to wildlife conservation and development in the Gambia, she is buried alongside her good (chimpanzee) friend Zwockle in the camp, at Badi Mayo: the place which owes so much, and meant so much to her, and where her family believe her spirit keeps watch over her chimps.

Rock of Aphrodite, Pafos

Tombs of the Kings, Kato Pafos

Crusader Castle, Kolossi

Monastery of the Life-Giving Spring, Troodos Mountains

Stone Barn Church, Panagia tou Asinou: Our Lady of the Pastures

Angel of Annunciation fresco over the Engleistra (enclosure) of Agios Neophytos

Richard enjoying Ayios Andronicos wine, Panagia Chrysorrogiatissa Monastery

Stavros Stavrouni serenades us on his bouzouki

Cyprus

Laughter loving Aphrodite fled to Pafos in Cyprus, where she has her sacred precinct and an altar fragrant with incense.
Homer, *The Odyssey*

Island of Love

Pafos, March 2008

'People swim to rock to find love.' Giorgios, our driver, pulled over at a cliffside viewing-point and was pointing to the largest of a tumble of rocks, washed by luminescent waves: the celebrated Rock of Aphrodite, marking the birthplace of the goddess of love who, according to Greek mythology, was born of sea-foam and drifted to Cyprus on a shell.

The alternative name, *Petra tou Romiou* – Rock of Romios – refers to the Byzantine hero who hurled gigantic boulders into the sea to keep invading Arabs at bay. Both legends help to immortalise the mythical and historical past of the former Hellenistic and then Roman provincial capital of Pafos. It was from 1300 BC that the first waves of Achaean Greek merchants and settlers reached the island, spreading the Greek language, religion and customs. The cities of Kition, Kourion, Pafos and Salamis were established, and the cult of Aphrodite born.

Cyprus had been on our 'must visit' list for some years. A halfway house between our home base in England and former home and work-base in the Gulf, it had become a favourite place among an increasing number of expat friends to set up home in preparation for retirement in the sun. Equally, we were intrigued by its rich historical past which, in a number of ways, correlated with that of some of the countries we had explored – notably Oman and Ethiopia.

The discovery of the remains of the Neolithic beehive settlements of Khirokitia – 7000 to 6000 BC – brought to mind Neolithic settlements, as well as the eastward facing beehive tombs that we visited in Al Ayn, Oman. Furthermore, in both countries by 3000 BC, stone tools and weapons were replaced by copper. Such was the reputation of each as a source of this valued mineral, that the name Cyprus is derived from *Kupros*, the Greek word for copper, while Sumerian tablets refer to *Magan*, Oman, and its early copper mining industry. Just as camels were used to transport copper in Oman, so the Venetians used camels to transport this valuable and much sort after mineral from mines in the Troodos Mountains to Pafos. Finally, it was the additional asset of wooded slopes, necessary for the smelting of ore and shipbuilding that attracted traders, settlers, invaders and pirates to Cyprus and Oman.

Undoubtedly the strategic location of the island of Cyprus at the eastern end of the Mediterranean is what drew so many nations to its shores: Phoenicians, Persians, Hellenes and Romans; Byzantines, Lusignans and Venetians; Egyptians, Ottomans and British, to the Greek Cypriots and finally Turkish invaders, that occupy the divided island to the present day.

Roman Ruins and Crusader Castles

Our travels were to be of the self-indulgent kind. Based at the comfortable Bay View Hotel, we were within easy reach of Pafos, the adjoining coastal region with its treasure-trove of ancient remains, and within equally easy access of the Troodos Mountains, home to the island's Orthodox monastic present and past. Unlike the Lower Gulf whose ancient coastal monasteries did not survive the sweep of Islam, Christianity in Cyprus, like Christianity in Ethiopia, showed a remarkable resilience and flowers to this very day. In the eight days at our disposal, our plan was to dip into the island's deserted and living pasts. Where better to start than among the tombs of kings?

'Not to be missed,' our self-appointed guide insists as he leads us down carved, worn steps to Egyptian inspired rock-cut tombs. Explosions of poppies invade porticoed courtyards where imposing columns and entablatures uphold the land overhead and guard the entrance to the 'Tombs of the Kings'. Raided but not destroyed, the awe-inspiring City of the Dead was bathed in silence, broken only by the contented notes of nesting doves.

It was after the death of Alexander the Great that Cyprus came under the control of the Hellenistic Ptolemies of Egypt. Arches, pillars, ancient tombs and stone mosaics remain as compelling reminders of former lives and beliefs. There were no longer kings in Cyprus at this time – the 3rd century BC – but the internment of leading citizens of Pafos is reflected in their impressive atriums. Surrounded by Doric columns, burial niches have been cut and hollowed into rock walls. The sense of a hallowed place, where souls of the dead have been set free, endures. Now beyond the silence, the relentless grind of encroaching sea can be heard as it undercuts the cliff face, threatening to invade these once venerated chambers of a lost world.

The towering columns of Apollo's Temple wedged against blue sky create an imposing end to Kourion's Sacred Way. Herotodus wrote that Greek colonists from Argos founded Kourion, the most impressive of Cyprus' sites. When the Romans took control they adopted the Greek gods: Aphrodite became Venus, while Apollo Hylates, Protector of the Forests, took over from the Greek deity, Apollo of the Woods. Fine Doric columns that rise into achingly blue sky outline the sanctuary and frame a walkway leading to a shrine, where the god was worshipped. An early convert to Christianity, the city suffered from Nero's persecution of Christians and suffered again from severe earthquakes. Kourion was rebuilt and then abandoned after devastating seventh century Arab raids.

The Odeon, a second century Greek then Roman theatre, takes centre stage. Built into the side of a hill overlooking the sea, its lovely location shows off to advantage curved stone seating that once accommodated 3,500 spectators. Far better suited to Greek drama than the savagery of gladiatorial Rome, the rejuvenated theatre has revived its classical beginnings: concerts and plays, staged throughout summer, include performances of works by Greek dramatists and Shakespeare. That the Odeon's romantic setting also attracts newlyweds was clear. As we prepare to leave, one wedding party disappears, and another arrives: bride, groom and attendants distribute themselves among tiers of seats in preparation for a photo shoot.

Behind the theatre we follow a line of columns and partially rebuilt walls that outline the House of Eustolios: one of a number of excavated houses and villas belonging to wealthy Romans, each a depository for remarkable mosaic displays. After the earthquake of AD 365, Eustolios generously donated his baths and an annex of his house to the city declaring it to be a cool refuge, sheltered from winds. A further inscription, referring to the 'venerated signs of Christ' that protect the house, makes sense when, from a raised wooden walkway, we look down on delicate pink and blue fish and bird motifs: Christian symbols, carefully preserved in mosaic floors.

Further uphill we skirt the remains of a 5th century Christian basilica, a Roman Forum and so much more that I was transported to time spent wandering through the remains of Libya's magnificent Roman coastal settlements. They too suffered a similar demise from earthquakes, marauding hordes and despotic invaders. Another surprise and reminder of Libya was an earlier face to face meeting with the naked bronze form of the second century Roman Emperor, Septimius Severus – last encountered in a more dignified pose at the entrance to the city of Leptis Magna, the place of his birth. This larger than life figure of the Emperor competes for attention with the sculptured marble statue of Aphrodite in the local museum. Immortalised as the ideal of feminine beauty in Botticelli's Birth of Venus, even without her arms, the graceful figure of the naked goddess continues to draw the crowds.

A heavenward thrusting dome, seven colonnaded aisles, the swish of robes over mosaic floors, the fragrance of incense – I conjure the former glory of the fourth century Roman basilica *Chrysopolitissa* – Our Lady of the Golden City. Thought to have been the seat of the Bishop of Pafos until destroyed by Arab invaders, the basilica was replaced in 1500 by the church of Agia Kyriaki. Currently on loan from the Orthodox diocese, Agia Kyriaki is used by both Catholic and Anglican expatriates – confirmation that, despite differences that arise in dogma and ritual, a shared core of faith remains at the heart.

A truncated column, a saint and a legend: named St Paul's Pillar, the broken column standing before us – said to be the place where the evangelist was tied and scourged – was the focus of a bevy of cameras. Although no scriptural evidence supports this belief, that the apostles Paul and Barnabas were here as missionaries in AD 46 is confirmed.[15] The remarkable success of their mission is highlighted by St Paul's conversion of the island's pro-consul, Sergius Paulus to Christianity, making Cyprus the first country to have a Christian ruler.

Success on this island did not come without suffering. Appointed Bishop of Salamis, the place of his birth, Barnabas is reported to have been stoned to death by the city's Jewish community and then buried secretly by his cousin, Mark the Evangelist, on the outskirts of the city. Four hundred years later Bishop Anthemios of Constantia (Salamis) found what was believed to be the place where Barnabas was buried. A handwritten copy of Saint Matthew's Gospel, recovered from the tomb, is said to have been instrumental in persuading the Emperor Zeno to grant self-determination to the church in Cyprus. Today, *Apostolos Varnavas* Monastery replaces the original church built over the saint's tomb. The monastery, church and monks' cells house the Archaeological

---

[15] Acts of the Apostles, Chapter 3

Museum, attracting pilgrims and visitors, who come to pay homage to the island's special saint and patron of its church.

Recalling the mere outline of events so closely linked with the heart and survival of Christianity on the very soil where the Evangelists once stood was a pretty inspiring end to a first day among the ruins. It also fuelled our interest and excitement for further discoveries and encounters in the days that lay ahead.

***

The honey-coloured stone walls and turreted battlements of Kolossi Castle glow in morning sunlight. An impressive reminder of the defenders of the Christian faith, this romantic medieval citadel became a stronghold for Crusaders, driven from the Holy Land. In 1191, Richard the Lionheart, leader of the Third Crusade, took possession of Cyprus from the despotic Byzantine Emperor Isaac Comnenos, married Berengaria of Navarre and had her crowned Queen of England. A year later he sold the island to the Knights Templar. When the Templars were indicted for heresy, it was handed over to the deposed king of Jerusalem, the French nobleman Guy de Lusignan. The Frankish Hospitaller Kingdom, the knight founded, ruled Cyprus for the next three hundred years. Byzantine castles were refurbished, and cathedrals built.

As always, it is the artwork associated with those who lived and loved and died that keep the essence of what they were and believed alive. Beneath a mural of a cross on the east wall, I focus my camera on a coat-of-arms – Louis de Magnac's (Grand Master of the Knights Hospitaller) – then, carved onto a block of stone, placed against the battlement wall, the Lionheart's Crusader shield.

Meanwhile, my Lionheart has moved on to investigate a ruined fourteenth century sugar mill. I find him inspecting an abandoned giant-sized stone waterwheel that once turned in the millrace of a nearby aqueduct. We are surrounded by overgrown land that replaced fields of sugar cane, wheat, cotton and grapes, once cultivated by the Hospitallers' servants on feudal holdings.

Like Kourion, the ancient city kingdom of Amathus enjoys a lovely coastal setting and complex history. While Richard has been distracted by a circling bird of prey, I focus on a line of marble columns – the remains of a colonnaded portico that once surrounded the white stone floor of the Agora complex – currently under restoration. Less upstanding outlines of the Acropolis, an early Christian basilica and baths unfold. The remains of circular stone houses and further extensive ruins of this once vast city cover the hillside and stretch to the coastline, where the Phoenician harbour and sections of the city walls have been lost to invading sea.

'It was the Arabs,' a young attendant assures us as we prepare to leave the site. 'Arabs destroyed it.'

History declares that Amathus was once an important Phoenician stronghold that sided with the Persians against the Greeks, thereby retaining its eastern links via the gods worshipped here, Egyptian and Eastern, as well as Greek. An administrative capital in Byzantine times, it was also the birthplace of St John, the Almoner – the founder of the Order of the Knights Hospitaller. By 1191, when Richard the Lionheart arrived, Amathus was in decline. Ancient tombs were plundered and stones from beautiful edifices were taken to be used at the Crusaders' headquarters at Limassol. Then in 1869, the deserted city was plundered again. Dressed stone from the site was transported to be used in the building of the Suez Canal. Today, the Amathus Beach Hotel overlooks the sea as the city kingdom once did. Ancient tombs uncovered during preparations for the construction of the hotel continue to make for an uneasy alliance between past and present.

Brightly painted fishing boats and modern yachts crowd Kato Pafos harbour. The past emerged in the solid outline of the Ottoman fortress that overlooks the shoreline, while a line of half-submerged stones mark the breakwater that once sheltered Greek and Roman ships.

Today, the atmosphere of this former busy trading port is relaxed; pavements overflow with street tavernas and waterfront terraces. The place is so laid back that for locals and ex-pat residents alike, drinking and driving go hand in hand. John, an expat friend and recent offender, recalls the warning he received when he was stopped and tested by police: found to be 'over the limit' – he was reprimanded by a wagging finger and a reprieve, 'Take care, you don't do it again!'

We sip glasses of Commandaria wine. Thick and sweet, not unlike a liqueur and produced from grapes grown in the Troodos foothills, it takes its name from the Knights' Commandery at Kolossi Castle. Highly regarded since Roman times, the vines cultivated by the knights were so esteemed that some were transported by the King of Navarre – Count of Champagne – on his way back from the Crusade: a reminder that even French champagne can lay claim to Cypriot origins. For Portuguese traders, shoots of Commandaria transplanted in their homeland produced a wine that was to become the ancestor of Madeira.

On a fleeting visit to the nearby House of Dionysos we encounter the wine god himself; amidst sensuous mosaic displays he is in triumphal procession, riding a chariot drawn by two leopards. From a snaking walkway we gaze upon scenes of hunting, wine making and illicit love: Ganymede carried off by Zeus in the form of an eagle, Neptune falling for Amymome, and Apollo swooning for the love of Daphne.

As a second day among the ruins comes to an end, we make our way to the hotel. I plan to swim but just the touch of the pool's ice cold water on one temperature-testing limb is enough to change my mind. Unlike Oman, where an icy dip is an antidote to unrelenting heat, evening temperatures here are on the wane. I join Richard for a more relaxing option: sundowners on our balcony, overlooking the palm-fringed shoreline. We scan a horizon that has witnessed so many arrivals and departures; imagine Cyprus as a stepping stone to the Holy Land, Antioch, Constantinople and Rome; examine maps for trails to tiny

Byzantine churches, tucked into mountain folds; monasteries crowning valley heads.

Across the empty bay darkening sea merges with the great dome of sky, releasing a shower of stars.

Of Monks and Monasteries

Stopped in our tracks by an angel hovering over the entrance to a cave, we pause to admire magnificent eagle wings and silken robes. In this delightful fresco, the solemn faced Angel of the Annunciation lifts his right hand over us with an air of poise and calm. A stairway takes us to an arched verandah that supports and provides access to the cave entrance.

This once remote spot in the Troodos Hills is where the twelfth century Cypriot hermit Neophytos sought a solitary existence. A small natural cave in a cliff face was the starting point. This he proceeded to transform into his *Engleistra* – enclosure – and then, by hand, hacked a small adjoining cell to serve as his bed, office and finally, his tomb. Ordained a priest in 1170 by the Bishop of Pafos, Neophytos' saintly reputation spread; the number of monks wanting to join him and the number of visitors wanting to meet him increased. To retain his solitude, the determined monk dug further cells above the *Engleistra*, one with an adjoining overhead tunnel. Intent on keeping his seclusion, he installed a ladder which he diligently hauled up after him.

On the outer walls, fading frecoes lose their heads and taper into obscurity. Inside, it is a different story. We come face to face with a line of forbidding monks. Forward facing in the Byzantine linear-style, their soul-searching gaze penetrates the very depths of the soul. Holding crosses and parchments, inscribed with the formulae for salvation, their sombre demeanour casts a cloud of misgiving.

Further into the cave, the outlines of more elegant saintly forms take on the curves and hollows of undulating walls. This fluidity of form gives these saints a more suggestive air of salvation. Even so, scenes of supplication and terrible suffering shroud the place in solemnity. The Nativity too is denied any sense of joy. Pious figures, painted in sombre blues and browns, stand in rows; soulful eyes stare into eternity.

The monk's cell with its rock-hewn tomb bears witness to the austerity of his life, and the fervour of his belief. Then an intriguing fresco of the saint, held between two angels, emerges. Hands crossed over his chest, the sombre Neophytos has grown wings and is at prayer, supported by the angels. The angels have furrowed brows and don't look too pleased with the charge in their grasp. Once again, solemnity overpowers any sense of joy.

A need to escape from a growing feeling of despondency takes me towards a shaft of sunlight slanting through the half open door. I breathe sun-flecked air and look down on the mellow stonewalls of the working monastery, the rose-scented garden and vine-covered slopes. Here, a sense of life and peace endures. Founded by the saint's followers in 1220, the seventeenth century restored church and working monastery of Agios Neophytos stand against the hillside, overlooking the hermit's caves.

Sadly, a series of unseen dramatic events were to bring misery not only to Neophytos and his followers but to the Orthodox clergy and people. Seven years of tyranny from the self-declared ruler of Cyprus, Isaac Comnenos, were followed by the Crusader occupation. Cut from Byzantium, the Orthodox Church lost its authority and much of its property, and sought the seclusion of the Troodos hills. A prolific writer, the saint expressed his anger towards invading Crusaders:

Concerning the Misfortunes of the land of Cyprus
England is a country beyond Romania in the north, out of which a cloud of English with their sovereign ... sailed towards Jerusalem ... But the English king, the wretch, landed in Cyprus. The wicked wretch achieved nought against his fellow wretch Saladin but achieved this only, that he sold our country to the Latines.

– *Ancient Worlds LLC*

Finally in 1570, tragedy in the form of conquering Ottoman Turks arrived. While the Catholic Church faced annihilation – on the plains below churches were destroyed, glorious Gothic cathedrals turned into mosques – Orthodox monasteries including Neophytos were looted and sold, the monks forced to scatter. Ottoman cruelty and punitive taxation served to strengthen a quiet renaissance that had grown between Cypriot Orthodox and Catholic, Christians and Muslims.

Then for Agios Neophytos, what seemed an end was merely sleep. Like the attacked and looted monasteries of Ethiopia, the monastery was reborn. In 1611, the monk Leontios began the work of restoration. Before us, the Venetian-styled dome of the basilica rises above honey-coloured walls. In spite of so much looting and destruction, Agios Neophytos, monastery, church and museum, remain a treasure house of wall paintings, precious icons, sacred vessels and manuscripts, including the writings of the saint, attracting pilgrims and visitors worldwide.

Of Saints and Sinners

When the church door opens and your eyes slowly adjust to the gloom, magnificent Byzantine religious frescoes begin to emerge, like photographs coming to life in a darkroom.

George McDonald, *Cyprus/Spiral Guide*

In the twelfth century, in the secluded wilds of the Troodos Mountains, a blossoming of Orthodox monasteries and tiny churches took place. Resembling stone barns, they remained unrecognised; unrecognised they remained unsought, and survived as safe repositories of the nation's spiritual belief. This was the world we sought. A world of deep rooted Christianity, vineyards and wineries – the ultimate survivors of despotic invaders – among the forested peaks surrounding modern Pafos.

Leaving the tourist zone of sunbaked beaches, banks and bars, hotels and restaurants, we followed an artery interweaving between red roofed villas, huddles of ancient stone houses, clutters of shops and roadside tavernas that stagger through banana plantations up vine-covered slopes to hidden churches and red-roofed, sky-reaching monasteries crowning valley heads.

The peaks of Troodos rise to 6400 feet at Mount Olympus. Named after the Greek mountain home of the Olympian gods, its highest peak *Khionistra* (snow-tipped) – marked by the white geodesic dome of a British military radar installation – appears and disappears as we climb and wend our way round tree-covered spines that spread bony white fingers towards the plains below. Forming the island's mountainous backbone the hills are snow-covered from January to March, offering skiing, and in high summer a cool retreat from overheated coastal plains.

High on the slopes, north of the sulphur spring resort of Moutoullas, we sought and found the eleventh century monastery of *Agios Ioannis Lampadistis* – St John of Lampadou; beneath a complex of pitched rooftops, two small Orthodox churches and a Latin chapel huddle side by side.

From the moment we step inside, what was plain and unadorned on the outside takes on a wondrous form. As our eyes adjust to the gloom, magnificent wall paintings emerge: faded coats of arms, lions and dragons of the Crusader world, and a Latin chapel, where naturalistic murals and the Venetian love of colour combined. Saints with fluid outlines inhabit a geometric world, showing a movement between Byzantium and Renaissance. Lithesome horses carry Magi, dressed in flowing robes, to a Babylon that was at once set in stony desert and on an Umbrian hillside. Further gospel scenes merge people, action and landscape in a world where beliefs and art styles meet and yet remain juxtaposed.

We stand and gaze in silent wonder, attempting to absorb the detail of Christ's triumphal entry into Jerusalem that grows from a nearby wall. 'No flashlights' the rules declare, leaving itching fingers and cameras that would flash of their own choosing impotent. Shutters closed.

In an adjacent isolated valley, we find *Agios Nikolaos tis Stegis* – Saint Nicholas of the Roof. We stand for a while, taking in the remote hillside setting and stonebuilt walls that did indeed resemble those of a well-kept barn. The eleventh century cruciform church and monastery merits its title by the addition of a second overhanging tiled roof, affording extra protection against frost and snow to the original cross-in-square vaults with a central dome.

That the church with its treasure trove of frescoes suffered under the Turks is confirmed by the Russian monk and traveller, Basil Barsky. On a visit in 1735, he noted that it was a small monastery with two gristmills, many fields, and a forest enabling it to make enough money to cover Turkish taxation. There were no monks when Basil Barsky was here, but he was so enamoured with the place that he spent four days sketching the monastery and absorbing the beauty of the surroundings.

Today, the monastery attracts a constant stream of visitors. Each summer it becomes the spiritual centre of the lives of Christian groups who camp in the grounds. Its survival is said to be a miracle. In 1987, a fire spread through the camp, reaching the church walls. Just when hope was lost, the wind direction changed, blowing great tongues of flame away and towards the forest. The building was spared. Eye witnesses believe that Saint Nicholas himself intervened and prevented the fire from destroying the church and the extraordinary artwork within.

Inside, we pause beneath the crown of the dome. From over our heads the all-merciful eyes of Christ *Pantocrator* (Ruler of all) looks down and into our very souls. In fact, the entire hierarchy of paradise appear: glorious angels, saints and sinners, hands uplifted towards the heavens, as if the entire scene is about to unfold before us and the angelic troop burst into a magnificent 'Gloria in excelsis Deo'. More serious figures with deep staring Byzantine eyes emerge: Christ the alms giver; the handsome battle-clad haloed saints of Theodoros and Georgios, stand their ground, poised for action.

None can compare with the unique rendering of the fourteenth century Nativity scene of the Virgin mother breastfeeding the Divine child. A sense of naturalism and emotion flows from the womb-like globe encompassing the heavenly pair, who are surrounded by an angelic host, a shepherd playing a bagpipe, the Magi and earth-based souls that look this way and that as if communing, one with the other, over the miracle that has occurred.

Said to be the most lovely of Cypriot churches, *Panagia Tou Asinou* - Our Lady of the Pastures - stands on a hillock in the shade of eucalyptus trees. From the outside, the utter simplicity of pale stonewalls against pine-draped hills takes the breath away. We fumble with cameras and then proceed to the doorway where, again, we are stopped in our tracks. This time it is a fresco over the church door, which shows the founder kneeling and presenting his miniature basilica to Christ.

I Nicephorus Magistro, a pitiful supplicant, erected this church with longing, in return for which I pray that I may find thee my patron on the terrible day of Judgement.

If we were impressed by the outside, then it was the inside that overwhelms and, at times, confuses. Heavenly scenes slowly appear to reveal paradise that is at once available and yet held tantalisingly out of reach. I focus on the half-dome of the apse where Our Lady of the Pastures, flanked by two archangels, remains poised between heaven and earth. Crowding the wall, apostles and evangelists wait in anticipation. A sense of hope increases over the sanctuary, where the ascending Christ appears both majestic and stern while all about him his followers surge; their status symbolised by books or swords, they represent a strict hierarchy and dogmatic tradition in the world below. Furrowed brows and lifted hands are stern reminders of the need for penance.

Angels dressed in flowing robes hover between heaven and earth, over saints who reflect the triumph of heaven. Their straightforward gaze invites us to glimpse the spirituality within their souls. A throng of Orthodox saints we do not recognise gather about the one we do: Saint George sits astride his white horse with the boy who serves the coffee he demands before slaying the dragon, perched behind him – an idiosyncratic touch to remind us of his humanity.

If the hope sought by the onlooker is to be found, then it is from the dome of the narthex. Here, the kindly Almighty stares down from a star-filled sky; his unblinking and forgiving gaze offers salvation, while his thumb and third finger touch in the sign of an eastern blessing. Beneath him, a gathering of magnificent angels with powerful wings and golden ringleted hair unroll the heavens: an invitation we aspire to be worthy to achieve.

If there is a lesson to be learnt from the Troodos churches, it comes from the immediacy of the extraordinary artwork displayed on cloistered walls: a compelling visual representation of the church, conceived as a microcosm of the universe. From Christ Pantocrator, looking down from the star-filled heavenly dome, to angelic hosts hovering over ascending saints, to gospel narratives and scriptures linking God to man in the world below.

The following day, our journey will take us to higher ground, into the realm of legends, heavenly glows and the outward show of glory.

Miraculous Icons and Stairways to Heaven

Dramatically sited high in the Troodos Hills, Our Lady of Kykkos – Cyprus's wealthiest and most powerful monastery – encompasses all the majesty of two thousand years of Christian heritage. That the monastery survived fire and the terrible looting exacted by the Turks in 1821 is something of a miracle. After executing the island's Archbishop and remaining bishops, Ottoman invaders are said to have carried away sixteen camel loads of gold, silver and objects made with precious stones. There is little of historical importance left except the monastery's most precious object – the icon of Our Lady of Mercy – one of several on this island said to have been painted by Saint Luke.

While the Byzantine churches remained hidden and therefore safe, splendid Greek Orthodox churches and monasteries, like Kykkos, that announce their imposing and dramatic presence on hilltops and at valley heads suffered looting and attempts at annihilation, only to be reborn. The claim that supernatural power, rooted in icons of the Virgin Mary, is responsible for the birth and revival of at least three of the most magnificent of the Troodos monasteries continues to capture the imagination and intrigue.

A lovely and fluid wall painting shows the Kykkos icon, held aloft by two monks while two altar servers walk backwards before it, swaying frankincense burners in its path. Following in their footsteps, the twelfth century Byzantine Emperor Alexius I Comnenos, trailed by a column of helmeted soldiers, raises his hand in a gesture of giving. The icon was a gift to Kykkos from the Emperor, in gratitude to a Cypriot monk who healed his dying daughter.

Like the constant stream of visitors and pilgrims, we make a tour of the arcaded and imposing premises, capturing images of the lavish and, at times, heart-stopping modern mosaics. Set in a blaze of gold, a serious Virgin, unfolding the formula to salvation, stands guard to one side of the entrance. Domed ceilings hold painted scenes of the Virgin and child. Flowing lines and floral designs encompass angels above while below, journeying Magi and shepherds point to the overhead star.

Renowned throughout the Orthodox world, Kykkos has been instrumental in maintaining Cyprus' Hellenism throughout centuries of foreign domination. That Archbishop Makarios entered the monastery as a novice at the age of twelve and rose to become its abbot before becoming the republic's first president, has added considerably to its prestige. Both the icon, known for its efficacy in answering prayers, and the Archbishop's tomb in a cave on Throni Hill, behind the monastery, continue to make Kykkos the premier pilgrimage place in Cyprus.

Sharing a dramatic origin, stemming from the discovery of a glowing icon of the Virgin, Machairas Monastery also shares magnificent views over the eastern foothills of the Troodos Hills. On this occasion bathed in an aura of light, the legendary icon was said to have been detected inside a cave by two hermits from Palestine in 1148. The Byzantine Emperor, Manuel 1 Comnenos, ordered a monastery to be built on the spot. Following two fires – in 1530 and 1892 – the monastery had to be rebuilt.The venerated icon survived and, protected by a silver shell, is now kept in the iconostasis of the church. We made a fleeting visit, adding some impressive angel portraits to a growing catalogue of heavenly scenes.

If we came away from Agios Neophytos Monastery with a sense of foreboding, we left both Kykkos and Machairas Monasteries with a sense of the wealth and formality of much visited religious sites. Then a metaphorical stairway took us to a breathtaking heaven. Our destination was the restored *Panagia Chrysorrogiatissa* Monastery.

Its very name – Our Lady of the Golden Pomegranate – is steeped in an alluring combination of legend and history. The pomegranate fruit, being symbolic and the slang for breast, creates a fascinating and, on this island, not unusual link with the golden breasted goddess Aphrodite. In common with both Kykkos and Machairas, the monastery's foundation is attributed to a miraculous icon of the Virgin. Like the goddess, this icon is said to have floated over the sea and alighted on the shores of Pafos.

The story told is that in 1182, a number of hermits lived in the vicinity of Kremasti. One night, during the feast of the Assumption, one of the hermits, named Ignatius, saw a light in the distance. Intrigued, he went to investigate and came upon a glowing icon of the Virgin. On his return, he stopped to rest and had a vision of an angel, who instructed him to build a monastery in that very location. Ignatius told his fellow hermits; together they built a monastery, dedicated it to the Virgin and by common consent, decreed that Ignatius was abbot.

From the start, we fell in love with the monastery's rustic appearance; the way the building follows the curve of the land, now fronted by a similarly accommodating tarmac road. It survived both the Franks' attempts to convert Orthodox Christians to Catholic, and then the terrible oppression and pillaging of the Turks. Restored but not overly modernised, its appeal is reflected in a naturalness provided by its very lack of symmetry: overhanging wooden balconies, shaded walkways, lined with potted plants and, best of all, a sense of welcoming informality from portly black-robed monks. Its artwork – icons and wall paintings, gold and silver engraved vessels and embroidered vestments – is there for those seeking to indulge further into the heritage from its monastic past.

Our self-indulgent visit was to photograph the monastery's outer rustic form and stunning mountain views, before sampling its famous wines. Then, just to let us know that things do not always go according to plan, we are halted in our tracks. On an archway over a porch, a wall painting of the Dormition of the Virgin grows before us.

Portrayed in sombre browns and greens, a faded and thoughtprovoking scene of haloed saints, sad eyes fixed on the Virgin's lifeless form, unfold. With memories still in mind of a modern rendering of the eastern Byzantine form of the Dormition at Kykkos, we are confronted by a different story. In the Kykkos rendition, the figure of Christ holds a child in his arms – a metaphor for the Virgin's resurrected body and soul – over her lifeless adult form. This Orthodox artist shows the adult Virgin, a smaller version of her lifeless form, hands lifted towards heaven, in the very act of ascending to the waiting figure of Christ. Meanwhile below, an angel is brandishing a sword over a lurking satanic figure. This artist appeared intent on making clear that Satan never gave up hope of collecting even the purest of souls – a reminder that art, like oral history, can tell different versions of the same event.

Having captured the scene on film for later contemplation, we gravitate to the monastery's vine-covered trellis and prepare to sample the celebrated Monte Royia wines.

'*Kopiaste,*' invites a kindly monk, with an impressive silver beard and smiling bespectacled eyes, as he hands us glasses of the selected dry white Ayios Andronikos wine.

We learn that the monastery's abbot, Brother Dionysos, was appropriately named. After a lapse of forty four years, he was responsible for putting the Monte Royia Winery back on its feet. We drink to his health and to heavenly views across sun-drenched, vine-covered slopes that unfold to a panorama of skyward reaching peaks.

When the melting sun slides below the treed horizon, we head once more for the beating heart of Pafos, the sun blessed golden city – on this occasion to meet up with friends from Dubai at Kompoloi Taverna & Restaurant.

'Eat once and you will want to come again,' promised Stavros Stavrinou, proprietor and chef de cuisine.

There is no doubt it that *Meze* that is King. All we have to do is sit back and enjoy: grilled *halloumi* (goat's milk cheese), *kolokithakia* (courgettes), *tahine* (sesame dip), *koupepia* (stuffed vine leaves) and *lountza* (smoked pork marinated in red wine). As wine glasses are emptied and refilled, with none other than Aphrodite, the Goddess of Cypriot wines, dishes keep appearing. Our host grows merry and serenades us on his small bouzouki.

'Stavros,' he croons. 'S for star. F for flower. L for love.'

It was Greek to me, but who needs sense on the Island of Love?

***

Legends, traditions and stories concerning miraculous Theotokos icons said to have been painted by Saint Luke continued to intrigue. It is known that Saint Luke was a gentile, a native of Antioch in Syria and that he was a physician, enlightened in the Greek medical arts. It is also evident that he had a special connection with women in the gospel, especially the Virgin, and that he had keen narrative skills. It is in Saint Luke's Gospel that we hear of the Annunciation, Mary's visit to Elizabeth and the Magnificat – surely, the most memorable and lovely of prayers – as well as the Presentation in the Temple and the story of Jesus' disappearance, in Jerusalem.

For three hundred years of Byzantine rule in Palestine, Jerusalem had been a Christian city. Then, with the adoption of Christianity as the official religion of the Roman Empire, it became the centre of the Christian world. A direct result of the ensuing development and lavish spending was a flourishing of religious tourism and a trade in relics, including everything from the chains of Saint Peter, nails that fastened Christ to the cross, the cross itself, as well as paintings of the Virgin. This trade enabled the relics to reach Constantinople; very often they were transported via Cyprus, the closest stopping-off place or port of call en route to Europe, India, Russia, Syria and beyond – to places where miracles attributed to the icons are said to have occurred.

There is no hard and fast evidence that Luke was, or indeed that he was not, an artist. That he was an artist with words is self evident. His descriptions of the events in the life of Christ have become inspiring and favourite themes of Christian painters throughout the world. That icons of the Virgin associated with Luke may or may not be his artwork does not detract from the miraculous events witnessed and ascribed to them. These vary from dramatic accounts of the delivery of Russian monks and monasteries from the plundering raids of Mongol hordes, attributed to the icon of 'Our Lady of Vladimir', to quiet discoveries of glowing icons by saintly monks in Cypriot caves, once inhabited by hermits.

To this day, the monks in Cyprus continue the tradition of icon painting. In Stavrovouni Monastery, perched at 2,257 feet in the Troodos Range, icons painted by Brother Kallinikos are sought by collectors worldwide. From his studies in Athos in Greece, he has inherited the genuine Byzantine way of painting using tempera on linen over wood, liquid wax and oil, mixed with gold leaf, and he even makes varnish with turpentine from his own pistachio trees. A small Madonna and child will set you back three hundred Euros. Whether or not you can expect a miracle is not part of the bargain.

Reaching the Horizon

In a very real sense this world is a wilderness through which we are passing – because this world is not our home. It is merely a land through which we are temporary and short-term travellers. So like any traveller, we must see the journey itself, interesting though it may be, as simply a means to a much more important end. While we travel through this life, our eyes should be set firmly on the horizon stretching out in front of us, searching for our true home.

– Father Michael Wheaton

On our return from Cyprus, we held an extended family lunch party to celebrate the launch of *Kiss The Hand You Cannot Sever*, a memoir of my earlier travels through Libya. One week later, celebrations were overshadowed by consternation: Richard had been diagnosed with bladder cancer. Within five months, the cancer that we had been assured was treatable and curable was out of control. Disillusioned with the failed treatment Richard was receiving at the local hospital, I spent the last weeks of his life seeking help and advice from top cancer specialists nationwide. Finally, as organ after organ was taken over by the cancer, even I had to accept that it was too late. We were facing the untimely end of his 57 years of life. My pleading with Richard to 'rage against the dying of the light'[16] was over. We held hands and shed tears and promised each other that we would continue our travels in the world to come.

Now that the terrible reality of our forthcoming parting had sunk in, I realised that preparations had to be made for Richard's last earthly journey. I was Catholic. Richard was not. As if it were meant, the last years of our travels had taken us from landscape and people and wildlife, on a pilgrimage of sorts. In Ethiopia and finally Cyprus, we had come face to face with the Orthodox Christian church, whose deep-rooted faith and survival, in spite of powerful and devastating Islamic attempts to destroy it, touched the very core of our being and strengthened our belief.

With an aching heart, I asked Richard if he would agree to a requiem mass at the Holy Cross Catholic Church at Topsham, a place that we had come to love. His assent was immediate. Now I needed the consent of Father Michael Wheaton, the priest in charge. Both Father Michael and I were relative newcomers to the parish and strangers to each other. Since all my time was spent at the hospital, we arranged to meet at the in-house and aptly named Oasis Restaurant. Living up to the tall, dark and handsome cliché, Father Michael stood out from the crowd. There was no identifiable dog-collar, and I had forgotten the red scarf I had told him I would wear so that he could identify me. It was the aura and an air of

---

[16] Dylan Thomas, Do *Not Go Gentle Into That Good Night* (poem to his dying father)

expectancy that drew me to him. From the first moments of our meeting, he became my Angel of the Lord.

I took Father Michael to meet and talk with Richard. With his mother, Kathy, bearing her grief at his side, we said the 'Lord's Prayer' together. Eyes closed, hands pointed towards his chin, Richard's calm acceptance and readiness 'to go gentle into that good night'[17] was testimony to his belief and tremendous courage. As Father Michael blessed him and left, a sense of finality and helplessness flooded over me.

Just days later, when Richard lay heavily sedated with morphine, I held his hand and repeated my promise that I was with him, would always be with him and that we would continue our travels in the world to come. Though he no longer had the strength to open his eyes, attempts to do so and faint muscle movements in his hollow cheeks assured me that he could hear my words.

***

If there was any comfort to be had in the days that followed Richard's death, it came from an unexpected quarter. 'Funeral Director, Painter & Decorator' read the sign over the Topsham family home and work premises of Mr Turl. Inside, there was no formal funeral parlour, and the man in charge was no formal funeral director. Casually dressed in a large navy sweater, he resembled a portly fisherman. My daughter Catriona and I were invited to be seated at a large wooden table in the family kitchen. In the centre, on a tumble of files and papers, a black and white cat sat nonchalantly grooming. Meanwhile, pausing in her task of cutting up vegetables at the kitchen sink, Mrs Turl set about making coffee. Believing the scene would have amused Richard and met with his approval transformed an occasion that the very thought of had filled me with dread. Equally in pall-bearing roll, Mr Turl's adaptable workforce, dressed in well-worn mourning apparel and with long hair neatly combed and tied back, would have earned a wry smile.

In some respects, possibly wishful thinking, the Holy Cross Church reminded me of the tiny Byzantine churches in the Troodos Mountains of Cyprus. For a start, it is small, and set on the side of a small hill. There is no hidden cupola under the pitched roof, with the all-forgiving figure of Christ Pantocrator looking down from a star-studded sky; no glorious ringleted angels unrolling the heavens; no amazing frescoes of saints and sinners crowding the walls. Nevertheless, the somewhat idiosyncratic décor is distinctive.

Apart from various statues and a *Theotokos* icon – a definite throwback to Cyprus – the interior artwork, of the main body of the church centres on a large red hand-carved form of a cross that hangs from the beamed roof above and before the altar. In similar red-orange tones, arresting paintings of the Stations of the Cross based on designs by Benedictine nuns, line the walls. Décor apart, the

---

[17] Dylan Thomas, *Do Not Go Gentle Into That Good Night* (poem to his dying father)

church was in Topsham and the right size for a two family orientated service in preparation for Richard's last earthly journey.

Father Michael conducted the dignified and moving requiem mass of belief, forgiveness, trust and love. Themes echoed in his chosen gospel reading adding both comfort and reassurance.

Gospel: John, 14, 1-4
Do not let your hearts be troubled.
Trust in God still, and trust in me.
There are many rooms in my Father's house;
If there were not, I should have told you,
and, after I have gone and prepared you a place,
I shall return to take you with me;
so that where I am
you may be too.

As we left the church, and followed in the wake of the coffin, I knew that this was both an end and a beginning. An unbearable sadness, the sadness of separation and loss, was taking hold. Something made me look back. As I did so, I caught a glimpse of the black cross on the church spire etched against blue. The entire building and a nearby pine tree, with arms uplifted towards 'God's sky' – Richard's words – were haloed by a splendid rainbow.

Afterword

There were so many moving tributes and messages of condolence and support from former colleagues of Richard's, as well as from friends and family members worldwide – we were international people. Among these, the one that made me deeply sad and yet filled with gratitude was from my long-distance son Mark, from his home in Nelson, New Zealand. In retrospect, Mark's flying visit to England and stay with us in our Exeter home just weeks before Richard's cancer was diagnosed seems intended.

We want you to know that although there is nothing we can do, we think of you often and I thought I would write a few lines to let you know. I did not know Richard very well, but can sense that he was a great companion for you and a great supporter of you.

You will always have memories of those amazing travels and adventures, and the landscape and wildlife that you enthused about during our walks together. Of course, so much more too – the simple act of closeness, togetherness and sharing and even, sometimes, (in vain) struggle to get out on the Exe – so unlike sailing in Dubai!

Everything that surrounds you must seem like pointed reminders of what you had, yet none of this would have happened if you had not been together for that time. But you must live in this time and grief is like emptiness isn't it? Like waves of it too. But the waves will steady eventually, and there are new experiences waiting for you.

Everyone who comes into our lives brings us something: a gift, a lesson and maybe the end of that friendship or relationship is for us to know ourselves a little better to ' know the place for the first time'. Seeing the amazing tapestry of our lives for the huge challenge and many opportunities it offers us, not always easy and sometimes impossibly hard.

Think of all the doors you have walked through and the opportunities that opened up to you. It takes courage to love and to be loved is a real blessing. Pablo Neruda said that, 'it will rain all night and all of the day. My feet will march to where you are sleeping, but I shall go on living' – which you will do, if not now then tomorrow, and if not then the day after, because of who you are and because simply you are still loved. And that, in whatever language, and religion and culture, is the only thing that matters.

Bibliography

The Gulf
John Bullock, *The Gulf* (Century Publishing, London, 1984)
Dariush Zandi, *Off-Road In The Emirates* (Motivate Publishing, 1991)
Asha Bhatia, *The U.A.E. Formative Years 1965-1975* (Motivate Publishing, 1995)
Adrian Murdoch, *Bread and Circuses/ Nestorian Church in the UAE* (The National, 2008)

Oman
P.S. Allfree, *Warlords of Oman* (Robert Hale, London, 1967)
Ian Skeet, *Muscat and Oman* (Faber & Faber, 1974)
Philip Ward, *Travels in Oman: Arabia Past and Present* (Oleander Press, 1986)
Sir Donald Hawley, *Oman & its Renaissance* (Stacey International, 1987)
Heiner Klein and Rebecca Brickson, *Off-Road in Oman* (Motivate Publishing, 1992)
Ronald Codrai, *Oman, An Arabian Album* (Motivate Publishing, 1994)
Andrew Taylor, *Travelling the Sands* (Motivate Publishing, 1997)
David Roberts, *On the Frankincense Trail* (Smithsonian Magazine, 1998)
P M Costa, *The Great Mosque of Qalhat* (Journal of Oman Studies, Volume 12, 2003)
Sean Mooney, *Oman Today* (Apex Publishing, November, 2000)

Africa
Ryszard Kapuscinski, *The Shadow of the Sun* (Penguin Books, 1998)
Aidan Hartley, *The Zanzibar Chest* (Harper Perennial, 2003)

Namibia & Botswana
Laurens van der Post, *The Lost World of the Kalahari* (Penguin Books, 1958)
Veronica Roodt, *The Shell Tourist Guide to Botswana* (Shell Oil, Botswana, 1998)
Deanna Swaney, *Zimbabwe, Botswana & Namibia* (Lonely Planet, 1999)

Ethiopia
John Graham, *Ethiopia, Off The Beaten Trail* (Shama Books, 2001)
Tim Lapage, *An Expedition to Southern Ethiopia* (Independent Safari, 2001)
Frances Gordon & Jean-Bernard Carillet, *Ethiopia & Eritrea* (Lonely Planet Publications Pty Ltd, 2003)
David Turton, *Lip-plates and the people who take photographs* (Anthropology Today, Vol. 20, Issue 3, 2004)
Philip Briggs, *Ethiopia* (Bradt Travel Guide, 2005)

The Gambia
Mungo Park, *Travels into the Interior of Africa* (Eland, 2003)
Lyn Hughes, *Wanderlust Travel Magazine* (September 2005)
Craig Emms/Linda Barnett, *The Gambia* (Bradt Travel Guides, 2006)
Cees Noteboom, *Nomad's Hotel* (Vintage, 2007)
Stella Brewer, *The Forest Dwellers* (The Chimpanzee Rehabilitation Trust, 2001)

Cyprus
Lawrence Durrell, *Bitter Lemons of Cyprus* (Faber, 1957)
Colin Thubron, *The Hills of Adonis: A Journey in Lebanon*
 (Heinemann, London, 1968)
Colin Thubron, *Journey Into Cyprus* (Penguin, 1986)
Paul Harcourt Davis, *Cyprus, Globetrotter* (New Holland, 2000)
Vassos Karageorghis, *Ecclesiastical Treasury, Chrysorrogiatissa Monastery*
 (G. Leventis, Anastasios, 2003)
A. Papgeorgio, *The Monastery of Agios Neophytos* (Nicosia, 2005)
Giorgos Kakkouras, *Saint Nicholas Of The Roof* (Trans. Dr. Andreas Vitti, 2005)
George McDonald, *Cyprus, Spiral Guide* (AA Publishing, 2006)

UK
Peter Sager, *The West Country* (Pallas Guides, 1996)
Dylan Thomas, *The Poems of Dylan Thomas* (New Directions, USA, 1971)

Recommended for independent minded travellers

Ethiopia plus, plus
Tim Lapage: Safari Experts LLC
P.O. Box 680098
Park City, UT 84086
435-649-4655 (phone/fax)
safari@safari experts.com

The Gambia
Mark Thompson
Hidden Gambia Holidays Ltd.
Skype name: hiddengambia
Skype tel. +44 (0)121 288 4100
Gambian mobile: +220 7336570
www.hiddengambia.com

Botswana: The Okavango Delta
Gametrackers
Orient-Express Safaris, Maun, Botswana:
safaris@orient-express.com
Tel: (267) 660 302 Fax: (267) 660 153

Discovery Adventures
Explore
www.explore.co.uk
Tel: 0844 875 1892